Touch of Silence

A healing from the heart

Jan Kennedy, Ph.D.

Cosmoenergetics Publications
San Diego, California

COSMOENERGETICS PUBLICATIONS
P.O. Box 86353
San Diego, California 92138

First printing: Publication date, February 16, 1989

6/93

Library of Congress Cataloging-in-Publication Data

Kennedy, Jan.
    Touch of silence.

    Bibliography: p.
    Includes index.
    1. Touch--Therapeutic use. 2. Healing. 3. Abused
women. 4. Women--Health and hygiene.   I. Title.
RZ999.K46   1989   616.85'82'0088042   88-35349
ISBN 0-938954-08-3

Cover design: Nancy Norall
Photographer: Victor Avila
Interior artwork: Cher Threinen and Rick Blanchard

To

The Way Of The Female Warrior
(In honor of women who are courageous and kind)

Accepting responsibility, caring for all we create,
Teaching through example the oneness of our fate,

Maintaining the connections, healing of the wounds,
These are our objectives, we mirrors of the moon.

We are the female warriors, loyal to our fight
For love and truth and kindness on our journey to the light.

Rodijah, A Female Warrior, October 1, 1988

Contents

Acknowledgments

I want to acknowledge Mary Burmeister for teaching me the art of Jin Shin Jyutsu. Her gift of love and wisdom brought me joy, and taught me how to live in the light.

Many thanks to my readers, students, clients, and friends, who encouraged me to write this book. I never dreamed it would take this long. Thank you for keeping after me, and for still being there even when the home stretch turned elastic and the finish line disappeared.

I'm ever so grateful to Jo Rudolf for her superb editing. Thank you for your careful scrutiny. I appreciated your many valuable suggestions.

Finally, thank you to all the *Female Warriors* who have touched me so deeply. It has been such a privilege for me to be with all of you. Each one of you has contributed something to this book, and being with you has helped me to heal.

Introduction

The Door

Children flirting with the door until it chanced to open.
Bounding through with disregard, the silence soon was broken.

Willful trundlers on the path playing "kick the can."
Led by the game, they lost the path and purpose of the plan.

Until they went the way that all containers go,
And wound up in a crowd with those who may not know

'Tis time to stand in line again and call out to The Door
To open gently one more time and with its light restore

Courage mixed with love in little children growing wise —
Children filled with holiness and kindness in their eyes.

I chose to write this book for women as part of my own courage to heal, and to help me step lightly, as I walk along the path. Healing and walking the path are one and the same. Healing is an awakening to wholeness, and the path is a sacred ritual.

When women have been hurt, what they both want the most and avoid the most is touch. What they want is a touch that reaches them softly and moves them from the inside out, and what they avoid is the kind of touch that pokes and probes at them from the outside in. Inner touch moves within us when we feel safe and express kindness toward ourselves and others. This touch within enables us to feel sensual and to relate intimately with others.

When we've been hurt, we often stop feeling, which hurts us more because the absence of feeling leaves us empty and dead inside. As a result, we seek outer stimulation to awaken our senses so we can feel alive. Ironically, the greater our emptiness within, the more we're apt to seek extreme sensory stimulation through overwork, danger, drugs, and the emotional drama of addictive relationships.

Sharing sexually with another is dependent upon being touched within. It's one of the few rituals left in which sharing with another person has almost nothing to do with performance and everything to do with safety, kindness, and wholeness.

Competition is often like the outer touch of sensory stimulation and sexual relating that leaves one feeling empty afterwards. Ritual on the other hand, is generally like the inner touch of feeling and sexual relating that moves one spiritually within. When we compete, someone wins and someone loses. One person is "more than," "right" or "better," and the other person is "less than," "wrong" or "not worth as much." Ritual is a cooperative performance between everyone who is participating in the ritual. If the purpose of the ritual is sane and healthy, the only way anyone can lose is if everyone loses because everyone's success depends upon every person who is part of the ritual. Competition encourages spectators; ritual encourages participants.

Each time we interact with others, the moment can be either a ritual or a competitive event. Healthy rituals like celebrating graduation, taking office, Thanksgiving, birthdays, and wedding anniversaries are intended to be safe, kind and spiritually fulfilling. On the other hand, even healthy competition instills an element of danger, violence and spiritual separation. Rituals are generally formal because informally we're usually rewarded for being competitive. Intimate relationships only work when performance is cooperatively shared like a ritual, and yet, paradoxically, we've all but lost the spiritual essence of the wedding ceremony as ritual. The wedding ceremony was originally a formal statement of this spiritual truth about sharing, not what it has become— about the burden of duty and obligation, and the right to legally batter one another monetarily.

Intimate relating depends upon wholeness within each person. Some people agree to *feel* inside but refuse to *cooperate* with others in the physical world. Others agree to cooperate in the physical world but refuse to acknowledge what they really feel. This kind of relating becomes competitive, codependent and addictive.

Very often the feeling person who refuses to cooperate in the physical world, refuses because it's difficult to feel while experiencing fear and anxiety about performance. Likewise, the unfeeling person who seems so agreeably helpful, may refuse to feel because it's difficult to be obedient and compliant while honoring your feelings about the need for self-expression and self-respect. This kind of inner division paves the way for addictive-codependent relationships.

Sexual relating may be the only time some women allow themselves to feel. This may be the only "time-out" from the empty search for sensory stimulation. Living in a world that's competitive, often violently so, leaves few opportunities to embrace the cooperative safety of ritual. Many of our social and religious rituals have lost their spiritual essence.

It's hard to be kind and loving toward one another if we compete for position by arguing that one sex is superior to the other. Men have been taught competition — physical, financial and sexual — from their cradles. Women in the latter part of the twentieth century have been moving into the business world and learning how to compete. Now, as we move closer to the twenty-first century, an issue that at first appears to be one between men and women is looking more and more like a human issue.

It's difficult to feel safe being human if we must continually demonstrate our excellence comparatively in order to regard ourselves with worth and respect, and it's almost impossible to be kind to others when we regard them as potential threats to our position. As women, even though we can only address our half of the whole ritual between men and women, we can still heal our wholeness as ritual within. We can become whole human beings through our willingness to get safe, be kind to ourselves and others, feel whatever we really feel, and trust a Higher Power to spiritually enlighten our feelings so we can be peacefully sensual and courageous within.

As I searched for inner resolution, there were periods when the wholeness of the circle moved illusively like a wave that waxed and waned. What had become of the Tao (the Way)? When would the rhythmic ritual be restored? During one of those times, I put my plight to rhyme and brought forth the following poem.

CYCLES

As Saturn turned to see himself reflected in the mirror,
Two axes spun in place to join each other on the sphere.

Flames lept forth to blend themselves in passion — then in blame,
And the Muses of antiquity conspired to split the flame

To separate the fires and lift the god from up above
While the goddess struggled vainly to restore the light of love.

But whispers fanned the god like bursts of wind that blew
The words "you must control the taming of this shrew."

And tame he did until one day his mastery was complete
When he straightened up to overlook small embers at his feet

And turned his back upon the glow bereft of any flame —
Nothing left of interest, nothing left to blame.

The embers dimmed in mute despair; the goddess felt her fear,
And Saturn turned to see himself reflected in the mirror.

**This is a book about kindness and about a healing ritual that
will reveal the power of love hidden in the wisdom of the heart.**

Touch softly and listen for the silence.

1

The Way Of
The Female Warrior

Are you a survivor of rape, physical battering, sexual molestation, or mental-emotional abuse? If you're a woman, the answer is almost always, "yes".

Women have suffered a peculiar kind of cruelty and abuse just because they aren't men. Females, regardless of age, race, nationality or creed, have all been identified as weak or inferior by various standards. These standards were derived from assumptions about females with regard to physical, mental, emotional, and ultimateley moral weakness as well. Most females are not as physically strong as most males. Based upon physical weakness relative to males, the rest became a set of circular self-perpetuating assumptions (i.e., females need to be protected by males and sheltered from the ravages of the world; and once they've been sufficiently "protected," they're no longer capable of functioning in the world; and since they're not capable of taking care of themselves, they have no right to think or act independently and are expected to obey male authority).

Eventually these assumptions became standards so interwoven with definitions of feminity itself that they were ultimately used to evaluate which women were "ladies" and which ones weren't. Females who

7

acted like women were granted the privilege of being loved and protected by men. Women who acted like "ladies" were treated with kindness and respect. Poor women or low class women were rarely considered ladies. Females who refused to "know their place" as weak, inferior human beings were generally punished in some way.

Most of the doorways to being feminine or ladylike were exits from the soul and pathways toward bondage. Some of us balked and were treated unkindly. We deserved what we got, we were often told. No matter where we turned, the path turned in upon itself. Many of us felt cruelly abused if we had to give up our human rights in order to be accepted and loved by others. And yet, the pain from being socially shunned and shut out from normal mating, marriage, and family was almost unbearable, because then we had no social identity at all.

We became property or possessions if we did act "like a woman should" — and if we didn't, we became worthless objects to be trashed, or bad people who needed to be punished until we learned how to behave properly. Although the laws are slowly being changed to create *legal* equality between men and women, destructive sexual biases still exist. These biases get passed down from one generation to the other and result in violence, sexual abuse and cruelty toward women.

Men batter, rape, and molest women, and women become mothers who batter and abuse their children who in turn grow up to continue the insanity and violence between human beings. When destruction of this magnitude extends to the majority of families across the nation, our human rights and integrity are questionable, and our ability to survive as a prosperous country is at stake.

Two false myths seem to be perpetuating dysfunctional relating — individually, in couples, and ultimately in families. The first myth demeans females and declares them inferior to males, and as an assumption believed to be true, it paves the way for the second myth. The second myth validates male superiority by legally and professionally supporting the first myth to prove that it's true, and in the "proving," it paves the way for human rights and needs to be assessed within the boundaries of the myth. This *sexual* bias interferes with and distorts normal sexual behavior, and it prevents kindness and intimacy between men and women.

Challenging Myth #1

So...you were lucky enough to be born under the star of "Sugar and spice and everything nice"—and wimpy and cute and hopefully mute so you'll be abused by a machismo brute who'll hook you in bondage like Pan with his flute.

It's difficult to talk about female sexuality and what it is without first discussing what it isn't. It's not a privilege bestowed upon you by the Equal Rights Amendment, and—you can put your hand down—it's not like getting a hall pass so you can take care of personal needs. Female sexuality comes with the territory when you're born.

Little female babies would probably surprise everyone who is culturally encrusted with myth, denial, and a masculine one-for-all-and-all-for-one gender in the world if these babies were observed a little more and defined a lot less. Encouraged and empowered as wonderful human beings who have rights, feelings, and intelligence, these little babies would probably grow and mature into strong, sensitive, passionate women.

It's extraordinarily difficult to experience your sexuality when you must first agree that you're not worth much, and that you'll obey the man in your life and earn your keep by doing what you're told. And this may come as a complete surprise to some people in dysfunctional relationships, but punching a woman's lights out and treating her cruelly is your greatest insurance against having to relate with a genuinely sexual woman. Women who "make love" after being abused are frightened, degraded animals seeking safety, survival and love through the closest thing they have to touch and intimacy.

Healthy women are comfortable with their sexuality. They don't have to wear sexy clothing and act dim-witted and compliant around men. Sexual women are powerful, creative individuals. Unfortunately, individualism, strength and intelligence have been attributed primarily to men for so long that when women express these traits they're either cited as exceptions to the rule or labeled masculine.

Healthy sexuality is inevitably accompanied by healthy self-esteem, a by-product of being valued and respected for more than your ability to cheerfully clean up after everyone and never "rock the boat." Sexual women rock the boat and the bed and the school systems and the world. Sexual women reach out and touch others with their minds as well as their bodies. They aren't objects and appendages to be used solely as support for masculine needs.

Women think, feel and express themselves differently than men. And yet, when we're sexually aroused and excitingly passionate, we sometimes stifle ourselves like good little codependents and not only ruin it for ourselves but men as well. We perpetuate the myth by acting as if it might be true and we'd better play it safe, and in the end, we make it more difficult for ourselves to shift from self-abuse to healthy behavior.

Female sexuality has been mythically denied, distorted and fantasized for centuries — the story of Adam and Eve may have been the precursor of codependency and addiction. Adam got the credit for the first human act of procreation rather than Eve, and Eve got billed for causing Adam to get involved with substance abuse and carnal knowledge.

Nuts. As we all contact our Higher Power, let's ask not only for the serenity to accept the things we cannot change, the courage to change the things we can, and the wisdom to know the difference, but also for love and cooperation and respect between men and women everywhere.

Challenging Myth #2

Current attitudes about sex, pleasure and power extend into history with dark roots that have been especially devastating for women. These twisted roots reach back to the Han Dynasty when men were taught that women were subservient tools for men's pleasure, and that a woman's role was to enhance the superior position of the man. Other gnarly threads emerge from the trials for witches when jurors and others in attendance gang-raped the women as a regular pre-trial event.

Rape, battering and abuse are all crimes of power and rage. Men who violate women in this way often feel powerless, and they need the arousal of anger and the ability to control or destroy women to feel powerful. Women who are self-abusive become subservient to men so men can use them for their pleasure. Such women act as if it's fitting for men to measure their power and virility by denying women safety, self-respect or kindness.

Women who deny themselves pleasure or power compromise themselves sexually. Sexuality, pleasure and power are so interwoven, that invariably when any *one* is repressed or denied, all *three* are fundamentally unavailable or become perverse and distorted in their expression. With respect to women, I daresay it might be difficult to experience your sexuality, pleasure or power if you were forced to serve men's pleasure and vanity, denied your ability to work, and tortured, brutalized and raped simply because you were a woman, not a man.

We're moving into an age when women have begun to demand respect and equality. However, as females begin making the transition from subservience to self-assertion, they often emulate a masculine image of what power and authority look like. Not surprising at all when you consider that the attributes of feminine power — nurturing, gentleness, receptivity, and feeling — were the very ones that got us defined by comparison to males as weak and ineffectual, and resulted in our being tortured and burned at the stake. So, some liberated women have developed the same insensitivities, aggressions and violence that we women griped about in men when we were subjugated. Impotence is powerlessness, and aggression results in tension, not pleasure. Emulating behaviors that destroy another's sense of power and pleasure is not conducive to sexual intimacy, whether this behavior is perpetrated by male or female.

Although all of us have both masculine and feminine principles within, we as women are an embodiment of the feminine principle. This inner, receptive, reproductive principle is expressed in many ways. For example, protecting and nurturing are expressed as gentleness and kindness, which help human beings feel safe within; discipline and care are expressed as listening and encouraging, which enable human beings to act in accordance with their word; healing is imparted with a presence that is "willing and allowing," which communicates respect for the spiritual essence of another and acknowledges the wisdom of a Higher Power.

As women recover their courage and self-respect, healthy families will emerge to heal the roots of darkness with progeny of light. In many ways, the "female dark ages" seem to be ending. Feminine power is beginning to be recognized and acknowledged as contemporary woman learns more about the Goddess, and a whole lot less about being a man in drag.

Healing Ourselves From the
Trauma of Cruelty and Abuse

There's an ancient mythology about what certain tribes of Mongolian warriors did to release fear. According to the story, these warriors practiced an art called "Chua K'a" each time they returned from battle. To do this, they sat down and went over every inch of their bodies by pinching and kneading tiny areas at a time. In doing this, they relieved fear from their bodies so they could return to battle fresh and courageous. They knew that the body held memories of the fears and anguishes they had experienced on the battlefield, and that if these emotions remained within them, they would interfere with their performance and ability to survive. The practice of Chua K'a helped release the fear from their bodies and restored their courage.

Just living through the ups and downs of stress and anxiety is a little like going out to battle each day of our lives. We hope it won't be this way and we do the best we can to live courageously, but disappointments and worries are as much a part of life as fun and success. As disappointments and worries continue year after year, they attach themselves to past experiences and old memories. Eventually, little incidents become big ones, and people become fearful and have less tolerance for things they used to handle with ease.

As people grow older, they're often more cautious because they've learned to expect the unexpected. However, some people also become bitter and begin to distrust life. Others become defensive, angry, depressed and sad. People who are bitter and depressed tend to age prematurely or become ill. These people need a fresh infusion of life in their body-minds to restore their courage.

Sometimes we accept debility and illness in older people as a natural process of aging. But do we need to live our lives insufficiently satisfied and unwell just because we're getting older? There's increasing evidence to support the notion that age and longevity don't necessarily equal debility and illness, and more importantly, that people can survive serious traumas and tragedies and still live happy, healthy, satisfying lives.

As much as we try to avoid stress and disappointment, all of us know that sometimes we can and sometimes we can't — and sometimes when we can't, unbeknown to us at the time, disappointment may be an opportunity to heal spiritually in ways we never dreamed possible. We know that jobs are lost, homes burn down, loved ones leave or die, and accidents happen. However, there is another kind of tragedy that almost no one accepts or understands when it happens to them and that is the tragedy of cruelty and abuse.

CRUELTY AND ABUSE

Cruelty and abuse include all behaviors which are destructive to ourselves or others. Abusive behavior hurts or harms human beings, but doesn't necessarily imply that the abuser is intentionally indifferent to the suffering of others or gets satisfaction from seeing others suffer. Cruelty implies just that. Cruel people are disposed to inflict pain and suffering on others, and they derive satisfaction from doing so. Sadistic people intentionally inflict pain and hardship on others to derive sexual gratification through cruelty.

Masochism, a form of sadistic self-abuse, is an abnormal condition in which sexual excitement and satisfaction depend largely on being subjected to abuse or physical pain whether by oneself or by another. Masochistic people derive pleasure from being offended, dominated or mistreated in some way. They have a tendency to seek such mistreatment, and they tend to turn any sort of destructive tendencies inward or upon themselves. It's the polar opposite of sadism and both are the end result of having been cruelly abused by others.

The more obvious forms of cruelty and abuse are rape and battering, child molestation, vicious verbal attacks, neglect, and deprivations. Less obvious are the ones often referred to as the "mind fuck." These are the ones in which the tormentor deliberately teases, seduces, lies, distorts, denies and in general sets up the other person to go crazy. The term "mind fuck" is apropos because the peculiar kind of torture inflicted is cruelly calculated to destroy the victim's sanity, and the tormentor generally derives great delight and a displaced sexual satisfaction in doing this.

Everyone who abuses is not necessarily cruel even though they do hurt other people. Men who rape are not necessarily sadistic but some are. People can be abusive as a reaction to their inability to cope with physical and emotional stress or as a reaction to their feelings of powerlessness. Cruelty and sadism are also reactions but not necessarily to anything current. Instead, the tormentor seems intent upon getting a disintegrative reaction from the victim while he or she remains cool, detached, indifferent and in control.

People who have been the recipients of cruelty and abuse are generally traumatized differently than people who become ill, get injured in accidents, lose their jobs, or suffer the loss of loved ones. Even so, recovery from any trauma involves the following: awareness of what happened, acceptance that it did happen, letting go (grieving), and healing (restoration of the physical body, sanity, courage, self-esteem and the willingness to go on living).

When people have been abused or treated cruelly, the following things are generally true

1. Survivors of abuse are generally recovering from repeated trauma rather than a one-time incident.

2. Survivors of abuse tend to feel punished and often suffer from guilt for having made the other person abuse them.

3. Survivors of abuse try to avoid any more punishment by altering their behavior to conform with the abuser's demands.

4. Survivors of abuse behave as if their abuser has control over them even if they're adults.

5. Survivors of abuse often suffer from an agonizing awareness that they didn't try to stop the abusers or tell someone who could, and thus, they feel as if they cooperated with their abuser and agreed to being abused.

6. Survivors of abuse tend to be attracted to their abusers and will return again and again to the same person or to people who behave toward them in the same way.

7. Survivors of abuse begin to apologize for normal behaviors that most people take for granted.

8. Survivors of abuse have a low sense of self-esteem and lack courage.

9. Survivors of abuse almost never have a normal sexual life, their sexuality has almost always been undermined, and their sexual expression tends to be absent, distorted, or perverted in some way.

10. Survivors of abuse become highly suggestible to their abuser's reality about them, and strongly conditioned toward behaving self-destructively whether their abuser is around or not.

Except when there's guilt, healthy people tend to recover from trauma in such a way that they don't become self-destructive. Whereas people who have been abused generally find it very difficult to feel good about themselves for long periods of time — sometimes for life. Well-meaning friends may not understand a victim's seemingly strange self-destructive behavior, especially if the victim is an adult. It seems inconceivable to them when a victim refuses to leave a situation that is obviously painful and demeaning, and usually danger-ous as well. To them, it's as if the victim has no will-power or sense of self-respect — which is very often the case.

Friends may eventually turn away in disgust or just sheer fatigue from the hopelessness of it all. They don't understand that they're asking the victim to do what he or she wants most to be able to do but often truly cannot. "How can this be?" you might ask.

"How can this be?"

Cruelty and abuse dehumanize people and they become less conscious of reality. When people are terrified, they tend to dissociate, distort reality and deny what actually happened, and begin to fantasize safe realities. They become conditioned to alter their behavior to try to avoid punishment and to gain some control and predictability for their safety. These altered states of consciousness, and feelings of fear and unpredictability make them highly suggestible and open to being controlled by the abuser. Eventually, the victim behaves like a person who has no will of her own.

In this highly altered state, victims hear the abuser's highly distorted expressions of love, caring and concern, or threats, criticisms, and degrading remarks, and the victims store these words in memory as if they were their own. As a result, they come to believe that they must behave in certain ways in order to be loved. They begin to have new images of themselves as people who are worthless, bad, and deserving of punishment. Eventually, they lose all spirit and thus, the will to live. Most importantly, they lose their ability to create their own reality or have any control over their own destiny, and instead, they feel dependent upon the abuser for their safety, reality, and self-worth.

The last point above is the most insidiously destructive component of being abused. Victims recognize that the abuser apparently has the power and the right to dictate their reality and to deliver the punishing blows of abuse. As a result, the abuser also becomes the only one who has the power and the right to restore their sense of self-worth, good feelings and safety, and to say when they have been good enough so the punishment will end. Because of the tendency to dissociate (a kind of mental escape from danger) during fear, victims tend to black-out during terrifying moments and may have little or no recollection about what actually happened. As a result, their reality flip-flops and they begin to believe and to behave as if the abuser were actually kind and loving and they were worthless and bad.

This is the most frustrating part for friends and others who try to assist victims in getting free. Logically, everyone knows that the victim is in danger of dying, whether it's a slow death from depression and self-destructiveness or a quick death from violence. But the situation is not logical — far from it. It's much more analogous to someone being hypnotized and told that she is a chicken and will behave like one for five minutes every time she hears the word "no." Logically, everyone including the person who is hypnotized will know and agree that she is not a chicken, but illogically, everytime the hypnotized person hears the word "no," she will behave like a chicken for five minutes.

Because the hypnotized person cannot account for her behavior due to amnesia (no memory) for the moment in which she was told that this was her reality, this person will make up reasons for why she behaves this way. She will blame someone or something for having caused her behavior, and will vow never to let it happen again. She will try to take control so it won't happen again, and may begin to behave superstitiously (i.e., if I always wear green, I won't act like a chicken because chickens aren't green, or if I chew gum, I won't be able to cluck).

Eventually, friends may suggest that the person needs help because she is acting nuts. This can lead to the person running around wearing green, chewing gum, acting like a chicken — and *denying* that she is doing any of it. In other words, the last point of control may be denial..."it's not happening." Or the rationale could get real elaborate. The "chicken" may tell others that she has muscle spasms in her shoulders and tics in her throat to account for her flapping and clucking. This is denial with an explanation for the behavior.

Some chickens who fear being *wrong* more than they fear being a chicken may tell all their friends, "This is just the way I am. You'll just have to learn to accept me for who I really am." In other words, the chicken is just fine, with a few flappy, clucky quirks that *really* good, kind folks will accept and understand. This puts the responsibility in the hands of others by letting them know that something's

wrong with *them* for criticizing and trying to change the chick
After all folks, you'd act the same way if you had muscle spasms in
your shoulders and tics in your throat.

As time passes, the chicken may develop new relationships with
people who like to fix and feed chickens, or with people who get
satisfaction out of looking great in the presence of people who act like
chickens. Since we now have a match, these people will agree with
any rationale the chicken offers for her behavior, and will do their best
to keep her a chicken forever.

People who have been battered and raped or have suffered long-
term abuse often become dehumanized and act like "chickens." They
tend to feel guilty, dirty or ashamed at some deep level of self. They
cannot accept that they have or had no control over the behavior of
their abuser. It's too frightening for victims to acknowledge that other
human beings, often ones they love and depend upon, will arbitrarily
without provocation at any unsuspected moment turn into monsters of
rage and violence and batter them until they wimper and grovel into
submission. And what's more, submission itself may be a powerful
trigger for getting violated again, possibly killed.

Every human being needs to be able to predict the consequences of
her actions or she will become increasingly immobilized until she is
paralyzed and dies. This is such a basic human need that we take it for
granted until someone deliberately assaults our right to have it.
Imagine for a moment that you lived in a world where people drove
on whichever side of the street they chose to drive and only stopped
at red lights if they were in the mood. Imagine that shopkeepers and
clerks could take your money and refuse to give you what you
purchased if they didn't like the way you looked at them or the outfit
you were wearing that day. Imagine that anyone who became sexually
aroused could throw you down on the street and relieve themselves on
you if you happened to appeal to them. Imagine that anyone who
became enraged had the right to beat you or kill you if you happened
to be nearby when their mood struck.

...ne that whenever any of this happened and you ..., all your closest friends and family would gather ...t it was all for your own good because so many p...... ...ou.

What would you do to stay alive in this kind of world? This is the world of the victim who loses all ability to control or predict her safety. This is the life of the victim who becomes a "chicken" and loses all sense of self-respect and courage, and instead, settles for living in chicken shit until someone wrings her neck. We all know that we *can't* live in a world without the rules and the order that enable us to take responsibility for our safety and our actions toward others. We know this so instinctively that each and every one of us will fantasize, distort, deny and rationalize frightening, confused realities to try and organize ourselves so we can predict our safety and be free to move and live.

When we're arbitrarily violated and abused just because some people need to dominate and control other people to satisfy perverted needs or to vent their rage, we generally have no place to put this information within our normal organization of reality. Generally this gets organized within the reality of what we know about punishment. We learn as children that our behavior produces consequences and results. We learn that when we do something wrong or bad we may be punished by being spanked, deprived of our normal freedom, chastised or restrained in some way. As a result, we learn to behave differently so we can receive rewards such as love, freedom, approval and fun instead of punishment. However, when the punishment is arbitrary (abuse), altering one's behavior in accord with the concept of punishment as a discipline to correct irresponsible behavior will not stop the abuse. When people are predisposed to be cruel, they will behave that way no matter how "nice" you are.

Abusers need to have people to abuse to relieve the emotional tensions of fear and rage that live within them. When victims alter their behavior, abusers will find new reasons for why the "good" behavior sent them into a rage and they will essentially make a mockery out of anything the victims try to do until the victim's behavior is again all "bad" (another way of saying that the victims are inherently bad or worthless). Once this atmosphere is established, abusers, by contrast, become the ones who are all "good" and have all the rights and power to decide reality.

The abusers are the ones who are hanging on to a thin thread of control by finding victims they can turn into simpering, whimpering flesh to be used over and over again to reassert their need for power and control. While the process is not identical, it's similar to deliberate brainwashing which has been used to reduce strong, sane human beings into crazy, dysfunctional animals. To do this, abusers have to insure that they have someone captive and dependent upon them in some way.

People can become captive without the use of force just by virtue of losing their will. This is a spiritual loss. If abusers can break someone's spirit or take over her mind through suggestion or sadistic mesmerism, they can break her will. When we're brutally attacked, our sanity is assaulted, and in the midst of it all we panic, become confused and highly suggestible. We record everything and store it in our minds and bodies irrationally and it lives there like a post-hypnotic suggestion waiting for various triggers to release it.

Victims are often amazed at their irrational behavior when someone points it out to them. But the difference between them and people who have not been victimized is that the victim's awareness is generally an intellectual understanding that they're behaving strangely rather than the deep conviction and inherent aversion others might feel. In fact, victims often seem strangely fascinated and attracted to their abusers — a clue to the hypnotic process that has taken place.

To maintain some sense of sanity, even if it's a false one, victims tend to store information about their abuse the same way they store information about being punished. To the amazement of others, victims begin to feel guilty about what happened as if they caused it to happen. If it happens more than once, they begin to feel shame. In long-term abuse, victims very often begin to apologize to their abusers.

Eventually victims begin to rationalize what happened by making excuses for the person who is hurting them, and by making up reasons why they deserved to be hurt. It's not uncommon to hear victims say things like, "I knew I shouldn't have held my face that way, she hates that expression;" "I should have known he'd be home early and had dinner ready on time;" "I should have asked him before I changed the color of my lipstick;" or "I should have known she was tired."

Victims begin to apologize for normal behaviors that most of us take for granted. They begin to believe that they should magically know whatever their abuser needs or thinks without being told. Victims have to either fantasize that this is true or admit that they have no control over being arbitrarily hurt by their abuser. Thus, fantasy and denial become methods for control and predictability to maintain some semblance of a sane reality. Because fantasy may be all a victim has to keep her sane, she may turn vehemently upon anyone who tries to point out the facts without first providing safety, nurturance and new alternatives for her.

Other ways victims take control of their reality so they can reduce their anxiety about unpredictable abuse is by "telling" on themselves first, by demeaning themselves in advance, and other irrational self-destructive behaviors like substance abuse, or cutting and burning themselves. Two important things get satisfied here. First, the victim takes control of her own abuse which gives her a paradoxical sense of power and predictability. Second, the victim gets the punishment over with in her own way so she can get right to the nurturing, caretaking and healing which generally follows. It's an irrational way to get a needed time-out from being arbitrarily violated and from the sheer weariness of trying to be "good" enough for permission to live safely and sanely.

When victims have moved into the phase of apologizing and trying to make amends with their aggressor, they're out of touch with reality, highly suggestible, and hooked into a nightmare of self-destruction and possibly death. They become like little children who try to be good so they won't be punished anymore. But the abuser escalates in his or her abuse because it's *not* punishment, and the victim *can't* do anything better because she never did anything wrong to begin with.

Abusers *need* to control their victims. They *need* to vent rage. Abusers will keep changing the rules so they can keep getting angry. When victims become so good that no one could possibly hurt them, abusers will use anything to justify their rage so they can keep up the brutality. Abusers are out of touch with reality. They were out of touch *before* they began brutalizing and molesting people, not *afterwards*. Abusers don't know why they behave the way they do anymore than the victim does.

What Can Victims Do?

The first step for victims is to acknowledge that they're out of control. The situation is out of their control. The abuser is out of control. Victims are powerless and have no control over being continually abused if they remain in the situation, and they cannot do anything to control what has already happened to them.

Here's the hitch. Victims who are out of control rarely have enough sense of self to leave on their own volition. In fact, they're usually so beaten down that they seem to have lost their will to live. Their spirit is broken and they've become discouraged, disheartened and dejected. However, with or without intervention, *victims are the only ones who have the power to leave and at least be willing to have their life be different and to allow change to happen.* I cannot emphasize this last sentence strongly enough.

The above paragraph appears to be a catch-22. It appears to say you can't do it but you must do it. What it really says is that you are powerless to do anything if you stay, and that the only power you do have is to admit that you're powerless and to leave and be willing to put yourself in the hands of others who will protect you and guide you until you can do it for yourself. It also says that once you are protected both from the abuser and yourself, you must at least be *willing* to have your life be different and you must at least be willing to *allow* change to happen. In the initial stages before you or anyone else can expect you to *do* anything, you must first be *willing* and *allowing*.

But — "Am I Really Powerless?"

Usually, when victims have been battered, the first thing they may want to do is go back to the abusers to set their reality straight. If you've ever done this, you're not weird nor are you necessarily someone who enjoys pain. Your behavior's weird because you're going to get hurt again, maybe even killed — but *you're* not weird. I say this because *you're* not even awake, your brain is in gear but its circuits are jammed. You're doing the best you can to unjam them but you really need to be in the repair shop instead of playing bumper cars.

Your brain thinks you've been punished. It thinks, "Since abuser hurt me, I must have done something wrong. Since abuser punished me, abuser must have the power or right to do that. Since abuser inflicted the pain, abuser has the power to take it away and soothe me and make it all better. Since abuser has the power to evaluate me and judge me and say when I'm wrong, abuser also has the power to re-evaluate me and say I'm good." Then it thinks, "I'll just run right back to abuser and say I'm sorry and do something nice for abuser...and then your brain begins to dream...'and then abuser will put his arms around me and hold me and wonder why he ever did that and suddenly realize how much we love each other and we'll make love and it will be different and we'll both look back on this someday and laugh and'..."

Caught up in fantasy, which by the way is the only thing that *feels* good right now, your brain encourages you to run home to abuser, get squashed into oblivion, and begin round number nine hundred and ninety-nine. *You,* or what's left of *you* knows better—your brain, the "chicken," doesn't...and the longer you stay, the less of *you* there'll be and the harder it'll be to get out. The same thing applies to rape victims. Rape victims rarely go back looking for their rapist so they can work things out between them. Rape victims may not know the rapist and so they don't necessarily have a "but he's really wonderful when" fantasy reference point to cling to when everything else is too horrible to register and admit. But rape victims also have memories of guilt and shame that encourage them to alter their behavior with others, so they often become very, very good to *superstitiously* ward off anything very, very bad ever happening to them again. They may run back to the rapist symbolically through their attitudes and behaviors even though they don't physically return to that person.

When abuse and battering happen between adults, it usually involves sex—the forced act of sex, sexual implications and innuendos, sexual perversions, or two consenting adults who have a sexual relationship. The sexual aspect of abuse makes it more deadly. It has greater impact, the pain lasts longer, the addictive hook is stronger, and the debilitating effects are worse. When sex is involved, whether the abuser is your lover, a parent or a rapist, the impact of the pain and degradation registers in your genitals and pelvis and gets stored there as a body memory to interfere with future sexual interactions, creativity, and vital life energy.

Sexual energy is hypnotic. It's the foundation for magnetically attracting, arousing, charming and often bewitching others. When this energy is highly aroused and intense, it has a mesmeric effect upon the person it's directed towards. Surprise and confusion pave the way for suggestion and are also hypnotic. The person who has been surprised and is momentarily confused will be open to whatever suggestions an abuser directs at them. Fear is a condition of surprise, confusion, and suggestibility, and also leaves a victim vulnerable to an abuser's distortions of reality or their angry, degrading words and behavior.

You are powerless if you stay because abuse registers in your brain *the way it is perceived in the abuser's brain,* and thus, you will side with the abuser in strange ways afterwards by emerging from the abuse with a *new self-image defined and projected by the abuser.* You are powerless because you have no self-image or identity that excludes being abused.

If you've been the victim of any kind of abuse or cruelty, the first step you must take is to acknowledge that you are powerless and out of control if you're still in the environment of abuse. The next step you must take is to remove yourself from this environment by seeking immediate assistance through hot lines, social service agencies, and trusted friends and family. The next step is to get yourself supported in all ways through recovery groups, counseling, work, and health care. *Do not try to do it alone.*

I've Admitted That I'm Powerless and I've Left — Now What?

In the initial stages of recovery, you must be "willing and allowing" as you receive support and begin to change. Let others who are kind and nurturing and professionally knowledgeable take control for awhile and guide you toward a new, healthier reality of yourself. Take a break and let yourself follow and learn for awhile in an atmosphere that is not based on right-wrong, good-bad, or reward-punishment. Let your self-discovery and receipt of kindness be a reward that demands nothing more from you than your willingness to participate in self-discovery and kindness.

You may need to learn how to relate to people all over again — or for the first time in your life. You may need to accept work that is less challenging or stressful for awhile. In other words, you may need to simplify your life greatly so you can focus upon your actual needs to heal and to recover your spiritually conscious self who is willing to live joyously.

Recovering the Spiritually Conscious Self

Once you've removed yourself from an abusive environment,

established a network of support, and become "willing and allowing" for healthy change to happen, you're ready to begin some other methods to facilitate the release of trauma so your spiritually conscious self can emerge to restore your courage and self-respect.

Your recovery process began when you accepted your powerlessness and acknowledged that you were out of control. The next steps to take are: to become aware of what happened, to accept that it did happen, to let go (grieving), and to heal (restoration of the physical body, sanity, courage, self-respect, and the willingness to go on living).

Become aware of what happened: Strive for the actual facts rather than interpretations about why it happened. Keep in mind that there are lots of ways to communicate with people besides viciousness, humiliation, shouting, kicking and punching. There are also a multitude of ways to discipline people and encourage them to behave in healthy ways without lying, degrading, threatening, or violating.

Learn about the many different ways in which human beings express love, caring and concern for themselves and one another. Hurting someone is not the way any of us express love. Sexually molesting someone is wrong and the person doing it is ill even if he or she seems sane in other ways. Viciousness and violence are acts of destruction, not acts of caring and concern. People can become angry and upset and express their anger without becoming vicious or violent. Anger is not an abnormal human emotion, but the way in which it gets expressed may be abnormal, extreme or abusive.

Remember to list acts of omission as well as those of commission. Acts of omission are passive, suggestive behaviors that generally fall into the "mind-fuck" category; whereas acts of commission are usually easily observed as deliberate acts of aggression and abuse. Extreme cruelty can occur from acts of omission which generally involve not doing things which would normally be expected. For example, cruel people may refuse to speak to or touch the person who loves them but readily respond to others in the presence of the one they've shut out. They may "forget" or ignore birthdays, special occasions, or basic human kindness with someone who loves them, but give gifts to or demonstrate kindness and interest in others in comparable situations. They may deliberately omit necessary information in order to cause an employee to fail on the job, or a lover to be late for an event, or a spouse to be dressed inappropriately for an occasion.

All of these are acts of omission. In other words, the abuser didn't actually *do* anything. Thus, all of these instances may be dismissed as "accidents," forgetfulness, or "just your imagination" — or with, "you should already know how I feel about you, I shouldn't have to prove it." Acts of omission tend to have their greatest impact on the cruel person's child, spouse, lover, close friend, or employee. The cruel person will either suggestively set up expectations in the victim or use cultural or basic human expectations to twist the knife of cruelty and wound.

This kind of behavior is cruel and abusive. It isn't normal and it isn't kind. I don't care what *you've* done in the past. Unless you were the perpetrator of long-term abuse on the person who is now behaving this way toward you, the only part you play in your own abuse is the willingness to have anything whatsoever to do with your abuser so long as he or she behaves this way toward you. There is no excuse for being deliberately cruel to other human beings. It doesn't support the health and well-being of either parties, and both participants need help sobering up.

Accept that it did happen: This means exactly what it says. Your're safe now and it's time to begin lifting the protective covers of fantasy, denial and distortion. Begin with whatever you can and the rest will come in time. Some realities will be obvious, others may seem confusing, and still others will be unavailable because you've stored these incidents safely away in your memory and can't recall them at will.

The first step in acceptance may be the hardest — it actually did happen. "It" may be years of being beaten and molested by your father, or one incident of being brutally attacked and raped. It may be years of being shut out of your husband's arms while he made love with anyone but you, or years of verbal viciousness from your mother about what a worthless person you are. Whatever "it" is in your life, it must be identified and accepted before you can let it go and heal. If it didn't happen exactly as you say it did deep within yourself, then you can't go any further in your healing — and you will, unless restrained in some way, probably go blindly out into the world and find someone who will do "it" to you all over again.

Awareness of what happened is not the same as acceptance about what really happened. We can be aware of what happened and still deny that it was in fact cruel and abusive. In other words, if I recall accidental tripping and breaking my leg, I will store this information differently than if I recall that you deliberately stuck your foot out and when I tripped and broke my leg, you said it was an accident and I agreed with you because you were my father and I was only six years old.

The first incident doesn't necessarily involve issues of self-esteem, love or violence, but the second one involves all three. If I put this incident on my first list to show that I'm aware that my father stuck his foot out and tripped me, and then I deny that it was deliberate and subsequently omit it from my second list which calls for acceptance of the abuse I received, I'm still fantasizing a loving father and refusing to accept that he did something mean and hateful to me.

Awareness of what happened can be primarily an intellectual process; whereas, acceptance moves all of us into feelings and emotions. At the level of acceptance, our brain-bodies get rearranged with about as much finesse as an earthquake in charge of renovation. Remember, people who've been terrified and tormented by someone they love cannot fully accept what is actually happening to them while it's happening. To accept what actually happened is to recall the truth and the horror of that truth which has been so successfully denied until you were safe and could know it and accept it. *Don't do this process alone — get professionally supported and join a recovery group as well.*

Acceptance will be one of the most powerful experiences you'll have in your process of recovery and will prepare you for the *most* powerful and transformative of all — letting go. As you accept, your first realizations will probably be painful. Until now, you've protected yourself from pain by fantasizing something different. This was the best you could do or you would have done something else. A big part of acceptance is accepting yourself and what you did to feel safe. You did it well, you were successful, and you survived. Now it's time to ever so gently tell yourself the truth.

You may have to face many unpleasant things. Perhaps the hardest one of all is that someone you loved and depended upon didn't give a hoot about you except to use and abuse you. You as a self, a human being who hurt from physical and emotional pain, mental confusion, terror and loneliness, were insignificant, or worse — you were just contemptible, snivelling flesh who deserved to be laughed at, mocked and degraded. It's at this stage of acceptance that people will say, "But I know that underneath it all, he really loved me," or, "I know she really cared, she just didn't know how to express it."

Perhaps. Perhaps they did love you. But I think assessments about what they actually felt toward you can be made more consciously after you've healed and not during your phase of acceptance. Don't second-guess what they did or didn't feel, and don't confuse being loved with being hurt. If you accept that someone can secretly love you and yet openly and continuously abuse you, you may never have the opportunity to experience being loved by anyone. Part of you will want to prove your fantasy and magical second-guessing to keep your reality intact, and you'll probably find another person who will secretly love you while they coop you up in a prison of chicken shit.

Let go: Letting go is analogous to grieving. Letting go will occur during all phases of your recovery—it's fundamental to healing. As you let go, you'll experience an enormous sadness and grief like a loss too terrible to bear. Your first response may be to instinctively hold in or hold your breath or escape in some way through denial. You may want to take drugs, drink alcohol, go to the movies, fall asleep, or just daydream and fantasize.

People wonder why they feel such a horrible loss about giving up pain and abuse, and why they feel so sad when they're getting well. That's not what you're grieving about. You're grieving the loss of your fantasies and all the lost years and moments of yourself that you can't do anything about. For example, what if your lover viciously humiliated and degraded you for ten years, and during that time you fantasized that he really loved you and you daydreamed about your future together once you were married. When you accept and let go, you'll grieve the loss of ten years of your life and all the moonlit nights of love and tenderness that never existed except in your fantasies. You may wake up to the fact that he never reached out to you with warmth and love even once during those ten years, and now you're all alone and actually have been for a long time. If you don't experience grief and loss over that one, you've probably gone to the movies stoned on something.

You can't achieve grieving by going for surgery or taking megavitamins. You achieve grieving by noticing that god-awful pain in your gut and by moving your awareness right down into it so you can *really* feel it. You can facilitate grieving by being willing to let your tears flow, but you can't actually grieve if you just cry and refuse to remain aware of what you *feel* as well. Consciously feeling whatever you feel is a *must* during letting go and grieving.

Why? What for? What happens? Well...are you ready for this?? How about rejuvenation, transformation and enlightenment. Nah, I didn't think you'd buy that. Everyone knows that someone as downtrodden, depressed and miserable as you, will be lucky to get a job, a place to rent, and food on the table. Besides that your body's bloated, your head is fuzzy, and you're threatened by daisies because they remind you of sunrise. Well, I'm here to tell you that grieving may make diuretics obsolete, seriously challenge the market for "uppers," and create a perpetual sunrise of life within your body.

Remember the chicken who flapped and clucked whenever she heard the word "no?" Grieving is a process of awakening from all those post-hypnotic suggestions you've maintained through fantasy and denial. Your body won't have to flap and cluck anymore, you get to become a real human being, and you'll know a lot more than chickens do. Now if that isn't rejuvenation, transformation and enlightenment, I'll chop down my daisies. It's a process of letting the light into all those dark areas of pain and confusion, and that light heals your body, shifts the way you look and act, and brings new knowledge and awareness.

Heal: When people really heal, their wounds disappear. It's not enough to heal the cut and broken parts of the physical body — sanity, courage, self-esteem and the spirit of life must be restored as well. There are many, many ways to encourage healing and sustain health. Whichever ways you choose, you need to include a human network of support to sustain you physically, mentally, emotionally and spiritually, and you need to support yourself physically, mentally, emotionally and spiritually on a regular and consistent basis.

You can participate in recovery groups, change your diet, get more sleep, play volleyball, meditate, get massaged, go to church, walk, get counseling, lose some weight, change jobs or whatever you need to do to insure that your behavior is self-supportive and healthy on all four levels rather than self-destructive on any level. Also, you must not accept abuse from anyone. This doesn't mean you should confront everyone who is rude and insulting to you. It just means that you don't have to agree with it or participate in it in any way. Not accepting abuse is both an inner and outer process. Walking away is not enough if you still find yourself with doubts about your right to be treated with kindness and respect.

Support groups and counseling will be your strongest reference points for reality for awhile until you're strong enough to do it for yourself. But a lot of the rest will be entirely up to you. If you don't eat well or clean your environment or treat yourself with love and respect, no one else can or will do it for you. And if you'd rather be a chicken for the rest of your life than genuinely feel the terrible pain you do feel, it's ultimately your choice on some level. There are people who do truly understand how helpless you may feel, but their love and understanding won't get you to the other side — you have to jump over the line and never look back as you leap into an unfamiliar world of thoughts and feelings and a very different you.

Touch Of Silence

One of the ways you can facilitate the release of trauma is through the methods of touch presented in this book. This art of touching is a silent communication of light between you and the person touching you, or you and the light within yourself. All of the flows will help but I'll suggest some that are especially relevant if you've been abused.

You need to restore your central core of self so the Main Central Flow will always be important to your healing. You'll also need to be able to receive and circulate the vital energy of light throughout your body-mind in a balanced manner, and the Major Vertical and Minor Diagonal Flows will help you do this. Because you've experienced so much fear, include the Kidney and Bladder Flows in your program as well. Last of all, do the Thirteen Release to help you release grief and sadness, and restore your sexuality and creativity.

As you learn more about the rhythms and interactions of all the paths of energy in your body, you'll begin to include other Flows that support your healing process. Sometimes in the beginning, it's best to get started right where it will help the most and to experience the powerful effects of this gentle art before you try to understand it intellectually. Eventually you'll probably want to learn more but in the end, it's fairly simple—you need light within your body-mind and this light must move continuously in a harmonious manner to create and maintain a healthy, integrated self. When this happens, the physical body heals and you'll feel happy, peaceful and satisfied.

When you begin to practice these Flows on yourself or with your partner, you may feel more uncomfortable before you feel better as painful memories surface, and body tissues begin to heal. But once you start to feel better, you'll feel better than you ever have. Your physical appearance will begin to change and you'll look more youthful and rested. You'll begin to take care of yourself by resting more, eating well, and organizing your environment and appearance in a more pleasant way. It will be easier for to think more clearly, and you'll be able to feel all of your feelings once again. Don't hurt yourself by being critical and condemning of the ways in which you progress or the speed at which you heal. Never deny what you feel, and always tell yourself the truth the best you can.

It's Never Too Late

Several years ago I was mugged by two men as I walked up the steps to my home one night. I fought my attackers and screamed loudly enough for people to hear me all around my block but no one came out and after almost ten minutes, one of the men pulled a knife and cut my handbag from my shoulder before he ran down the street to join the other man who had gone to get their truck.

When I was mugged, I elbowed my attacker, jumped over an embankment down into the mud, and wrapped myself around a Yucca tree where I remained. I didn't know it was a mugging. I thought I was going to be hauled off in their truck and raped and possibly killed. I had been severely beaten, raped and threatened with death once in my life. I vowed it would never happen again.

After the mugging, I remained fearful and began to have difficulty continuing my work. I couldn't seem to recover and seven months later, I was drinking scotch with an unquenchable thirst for something I couldn't seem to satisfy. I quit my work, sold my home and moved to a smaller house in a quiet neighborhood where I hoped to heal from the irrational fears that haunted me day and night. Instead, I was seriously injured in an accident (unrelated to drinking) just two weeks after I moved.

The accident was a godsend in many ways, but I didn't know that until much later. My injuries were worse than anyone initially recognized, and I was in constant pain for just over a year. Initially, I drank even more because I was in such physical and emotional pain that I just wanted to escape. Drinking became a way of life for the next eight months until one day I suddenly realized that I was slowly and methodically killing myself when what I really wanted to do was live. I called AA for support, stopped drinking at once, and never drank again.

When I stopped drinking, I was faced with the most excruciating physical and emotional pain I had ever experienced in my life. I called a friend of mine who also practices this art of touch healing and together we set to work to untangle the mystery of my dilemma. We met three times a week and within two months I was pain free for the first time in a year. One day while she was working with me, my body doubled up so intensely that my head came up off the cot as I stammered out the words, "my father was a cruel and angry man." It was the first time in my life that I could *speak* about being abused and *feel* how I really felt when I was abused *both at the same time.*

Once my data memories and feeling memories integrated, I began healing very quickly. Within rapid succession much more began to be released as we eroded the intense complex of memories and emotions. The mugging had triggered a dark well of feeling memories safely barricaded from my consciousness. It had ripped the rape scene loose and left it floating like a disconnected wire that burned and sizzled.

When I was beaten and raped, I had just turned seventeen years old. My father blamed me for what happened, and he told me that no man would behave that way toward a woman unless she encouraged him to do it. Then he cut me out of his life completely, except for periodic vicious attacks, for the next 21 years. Before he died, he wrote a note and attached it to his will. In it, he mentioned me and said, "Give her a dollar, that's all she deserves." When he died, I wasn't told because my stepmother didn't want me to be present at his funeral.

When I was mugged, several things happened to contribute to my uncontrollable fear. First, it simulated the rape of years ago and released all my feelings associated with that time including my father's irrational behavior toward me. Second, it aroused intense feelings of helplessness both from the attack itself and from the fact that no one came to my assistance, even though approximately thirty neighbors came out after the mugger's truck pulled away and they all told me that they did hear me screaming. These feelings of helplessness were the same ones I'd felt as a child when no one came to my rescue as I screamed out for help the best I could.

As soon as I became more integrated and realized what had happened, and the depth of healing I was actually experiencing, I called the Rape and Battered Women's Hotline and became part of a women's group for two and a half months. Although this was thirty-three years after I'd been raped, it may as well have been the day after, because I released emotions as intense as if it had just happened. The next thing I did was to work with spiritual guidance and healing imagery with a female counselor while I simultaneously continued to receive Flows from my friend. Little by little, we were able to recover and release memories and feelings.

During the final stages of this book, I experienced a powerful healing between myself and my parents one afternoon during prayer. I began my prayer by genuinely thanking both of them for everything they had done or tried to do for me. Suddenly, their faces appeared before me and each one had a look I'd never seen them have before. Their eyes twinkled with kindness and understanding, and at once a deep love and wisdom passed between us.

Even if you don't consciously recover all of your memories, you can still know that the destructive ones are losing their power and that healing is taking place by the way you feel and look, and the people you attract. When we haven't recovered, we vibrate like victims. We can go right out there into the world and find the only abuser in the bunch, no matter where we go. Our vibrations say "kick me" and abusers get all excited and jump right into an instant relationship with us.

It's actually less like a relationship than an entanglement. It seems very exciting and stimulating because it pokes all our "off" buttons of shutdown and denial into an "on" position of *remembering* like a wake-up call at camp when some joker sticks her head into the tent and yells "fire." Boy does that adrenalin start to flow and the heart acts like a tom-tom at a rain dance — and we immediately call it love. Hell, what do we know?

But the Touch of Silence heals and changes our vibration and the images we have about ourselves. This alters who we'll attract and who we'll be attracted to, and ultimately how we'll handle things if an abuser happens to trip over us during a party. All of a sudden, abusers don't sniff us out like chicken farmers at the market. And wonder of wonders, we seem to quit clucking over their feed sacks.

You don't need to remember that your mother thought you were a changeling and boxed you up for the Salvation Army, if all of a sudden it just doesn't matter anymore. It probably won't occur to you to ponder over whether or not you were secretly loved by someone who hurt you, when you begin experiencing the real thing. It takes time but not as long as you might imagine. A new vibration brings new people and experiences into your life, and if you've been diligent about accepting and letting go, your grieving will cleanse those dark areas and enable the light to enter. New memories of love, courage and self-respect will get tucked away in your body-mind to remind you daily that you're loved and you matter — your presence here on earth does make a wonderful difference.

2

Brain-Body: Mind-Body

What happens to people after they've been abused? The word for what happens is "conditioning," which occurs in the brain-body. The way out of conditioned attitudes and behaviors is dissolution and renewal in the light, and creative action which takes place in the mind-body.

The classic example of conditioning is the story about Pavlov and his dog. Pavlov rang a bell everytime he fed his dog until the dog began to associate the sound of the bell with being fed. Eventually, Pavlov was able to ring the bell and the dog began to salivate for food. It's not natural for a dog to salivate when it hears a bell. This isn't a natural physiological response. The dog learned to do this by being "conditioned" to associate a natural response (salivation) to the smell of food with a neutral stimulus (sound of the bell).

There are other forms of conditioning as well. For example, if you put a pigeon in a cage with a food hopper (dispenser) on one end, and you release food periodically, the pigeon will learn where the food is. Then, take a natural pigeon behavior like turning to the left, and everytime you see the pigeon turn to the left, release food. Pretty soon the pigeon will superstitiously turn to the left when it wants food, and it will think that's what it needs to do to get fed.

Abused people *learn* to act nice or compliant or apologetic when they see, hear, or feel abuse. This is an unnatural response to being abused. Running away or fighting back are natural physiological responses to being hurt or attacked. It's physiologically natural to feel angry or afraid. It's physiologically unnatural to feel kind and safe.

Some of this unnatural behavior results when abusers rationalize their violence and cruelty, and act as if it's punishment. "Rationalizing" means that the abuser treats you unkindly and then tells you that it's for your own good, or it's because you were "bad" or "wrong" for not having dinner ready at 5:00 p.m. In other words, they blame you for their unkind behavior or violent disposition.

When you're under attack, you're highly suggestible. You'll hear the abuser's words as if those words were logical, and you'll begin to believe, for example, "If I was a better person, they wouldn't hurt me." In this way, you *learn* to act "nice" so you won't be hurt anymore. It's a little like hearing that, "Men won't hurt women who act like ladies," therefore if you get hurt by a man you must have been behaving in an "unladylike" manner. Then you read in Emily Post that a "lady" never sits with her legs uncrossed, never raises her voice, is always sweet and polite, never farts, burps, sweats or snores, and you decide that all you have to do is act like a Stepford Wife for the rest of your life and men won't hurt you.

Homework for this section is to discover one thing you do automatically everytime you hear a Pavlovian bell. For example, if your name is Elizabeth and someone calls you Betsy, do you automatically regress to age five and begin to act like daddy's little girl?

Don't do anything with what you discover except to write it down in your notebook or journal. These are the kinds of things that disappear as you begin to heal, and six months from now, you'll be able to go through your journal and check off everything that's disappeared. This builds inner confidence and courage.

What Happens In The Brain-Body?

When we believe that abuse is logical and we learn to act nice so we won't be hurt anymore, we confuse our bodies and open ourselves to craziness and illness. Natural, normal feelings of anger, fear, sadness, grief or worry become associated with acting as if nothing's wrong, or by behaving obediently and lovingly. Behavior (action) sets up a pattern of learning in the body and becomes incorporated in our bodies in such a way that this eventually becomes our identity or what we call our "self."

Acting nicely and lovingly becomes associated with physiological changes normal to states of fear, anger, sadness, grief or worry. These physiological changes alter your metabolism, hormones, blood pressure, breathing patterns and muscular tensions, just to name a few. This in turn alters your entire cellular chemistry and your brain. Your brain in turn alters your body, behavior, feelings, etc., and tells you what you must do to get out of the horrible predicament you're in because if you don't, you'll get sick, or go crazy or die — or all three. No wonder some people *feel* better when they act mean or irresponsible — their wires are crossed.

Survivors are people who listen attentively to what abusers say or seem to say so they'll know what to do or not do. Abusers are cruel and abusive so what they *say* makes no sense at all — but it's all we've got so we use it. We're highly suggestible to what abusers say to us and we wind up subconsciously absorbing their commands, their viciousness, and their distortions of reality.

Eventually, we form a self-image congruent with surviving abuse and we do the best we can to fulfill this image, because through the power of fantasy and denial, we can at least keep our bodies from freaking out and making us ill. When we fantasize, we use the mind to create an imagined reality that's safe, and this safe reality gets communicated to the brain which signals the body that we're okay. For example, in the middle of being terrified, we fantasize that all we have to do is "be nice" and everything will be wonderful, and this fantasy goes to the brain. The brain says, "Oh, okay if you say so," and it stops making us shake, faint and throw-up, and instead, switches us into la-la land and we start smiling sweetly while we're getting smashed.

Did you know that there's a low incidence of many serious life-threatening diseases such as cancer among populations of crazy people or people who are intellectually retarded? Up until now, your weird behavior, that has baffled all your friends and possibly you, has been saner than you might think. It enabled you to live. It helped you survive. Ironically, you didn't survive because you were weak, you survived because you were strong. Many women didn't make it. What you've done rarely works for a lifetime unless you join the ranks of crazy people, but it wasn't all that bad in a pinch.

Homework for this section is to notice one emotion you feel, and to notice if what you feel is congruent with what you do and say. Go easy with this one. Do not — I repeat, do not — try to change your behavior or tell anyone else what you're doing. Just notice. For example, when I *feel angry,* my neck gets tight, and I *smile* and do what I'm told to do. When I *feel scared,* my butt tightens, and I *laugh* and make jokes. When I *feel sad,* my shoulders tighten, and I dominate everyone and *brag* about myself. Note: none of these behaviors is congruent with the emotions.

Behaviors And Attitudes That Result From Abuse

1. Someone approaches you sexually in a normal healthy way and you feel you have no right to say "no," or you can't say "no." You have feelings of frustration and guilt for not having better control over your behavior and you feel as if you should.

2. Whenever someone comes to you with a hard luck story, you do your best to make things better for them. Regardless of the situation,

you may feel ultra-responsible as if it's all your fault. You have continuous feelings that you're to blame when bad things happen.

3. You have feelings of guilt whenever you put yourself first. It's as if you owe other people for your right to exist. You feel obligated to comply with what others say you should or shouldn't do.

4. You have feelings of low self-worth as if everyone else is better, more important, smarter, stronger, or has more authority than you do. You never feel able to trust your inner guidance about what's best for you.

5. You are insignificant trash, feeling ugly, lazy, stupid, fat, inarticulate, and downright nasty. Not only are you not worth much as a person, you're not even a useful or attractive object. You feel shame, embarrassment, rage and depression.

6. If I make it up and stick with it, then it'll be real. You trust your fantasies and dreams more than what seems to be real. Magical thinking, mind-brain separation, can lead to dissociative states, blackouts, and totally weird behavior.

7. I'll teach others how to behave just like me and be nice like I am. You work to get agreement for your behavior so you won't feel so isolated and alone — and if others act like you, it must be okay. This sets up urges for control, gang-up, and us against them. You have feelings of aggression and defense.

8. I'm less than, therefore I deserve X (i.e., to be treated the way people treat me, to be poor, to always obey and never think for myself). You have feelings of defeat. You adjust your behavior and attitudes to accomodate what others have said about you. You experience loss of your will power, spirit, will to live, creativity,

willingness to risk, and are basically just marking time until you die
— and surviving the best you can.

We learn that we don't have rights and that we're responsible for
what's wrong. We learn that we're insignificant trash or that we owe
our life to others so they can be comfortable and feel better about
themselves. Interestingly enough, two simple things will move you
in the direction of courage and self-respect—kindness and pleasure.

It's very difficult to hurt yourself or anyone else when you're aware
of being kind to yourself and them. Kindness is gentle and compassionate and has nothing to do with acting "nice." Kindness is
magically healing and always socially acceptable.

When you discover what gives you pleasure, and you seek to fulfill
that in all of your life, all eight points disappear from the list. It's very
difficult to feel pleasure in your work, home, relationships, play, and
in meeting your personal needs and still feel violent, "less than," or
obligated to others. Pleasure is not superficial diversion, excitement
or amusement. It's a deep inner quality that is experienced when
we're spiritually satisfied. Pleasure comes from wholeness and sanity
and the ability to complete creative action generated from the inside
out.

Homework for this section is to discover one person in your life
who is kind.

How Does The Body Tell Us We've Been Abused?
Keep in mind that abuse can be self-inflicted or imposed by others.
The body doesn't know the difference. It especially doesn't know the
difference when we deny doing it to ourselves and project the blame
onto others.

1. Body posture. We hold a multitude of postures as expressions of

fear, anger, worry, sadness, and grief. When we try to hold them all all at once, we get downright ugly.

2. Muscle tension. We get lock-jaw, eye-fixation, hump-backed, curled lips, knock-kneed, and gnarly — and then we buy the best make-up and the latest fashions and wonder why we don't look like the ads.

3. Extreme emotional reactions. We get hysterical when Lassie dies, remain nonchalant when mother is buried, and swing at the waiter who touches our shoulder as he leans down and softly asks if we're ready to order. Eventually we do things like burst out laughing when our friend tells us that she's dying of cancer, or we go into a rage in the middle of an orgasm.

4. The usual. Stomach aches, vomiting, incontinence, PMS, asthma, allergies, headaches, high blood pressure, constipation, diarrhea, cancer, heart attacks...

5. Feeling empty and dead. This is probably something like a corpse would feel if a corpse could feel. Tissues, bones, organs and fluids all revert to simple matter when a person is dead. The body regresses to simpler states unless life energy moves through it. This movement of energy is what gives us feeling, life, animation and consciousness. It also counteracts gravity and gives us a sense of buoyancy and joy. As the life in us begins to wane, we feel heavy, empty, tired and dead.

The body signals us about abuse by becoming ugly, fat, lumpy, twisted, and rigid with tension. The body can't rest well or work efficiently and tells us that everything's an effort or basically no fun at all. The body begins to struggle to breathe, digest food, or learn anything new.

One of the simplest ways to bring your body back to life is to begin to *feel* whatever you actually feel and to notice where you feel it in your body. Feeling comes from the life-energy moving through your body. It's impossible to have a "dead" body when you have feeling in it.

Emotional reactions are signals that we have feelings (inner guidance) we're refusing to acknowledge because we're lying, denying, distorting, and/or dissociating. You won't have emotional *reactions* like anger, fear, worry, sadness and grief when you're *willing* to feel and *allow* those feelings to be there. Feelings tell us about our current state of being and let us know when we're on the right track and when we need to change.

Change requires *creative* action (action that's not obligatory). During creative action, we create (see, imagine, visualize) from something unknown (nothing) and act upon it, which moves us away from what *is* known even though it often seems better than *nothing*. When we're afraid to come from nothing into something new, we refuse to act upon our feelings, and then we get emotional in the hope that our circumstances will change or the other person will change — so we don't have to. This makes about as much sense as wanting a raise, being afraid to tell your boss that you want a raise, and then getting upset and smashing the coffee machine in the hope that now your boss will not only know that you want a raise, she'll give you one.

Homework for this section is to do one kind thing for your body this week. For example, give it more rest, take it for a massage, take it on a picnic, feed it wonderful things, or give it a break from the abuse you've been putting up with.

What Happens If You Continue Living Your Life Like A Chicken?

1. You'll continue being destructive to yourself and others, and you won't have a healthy relationship with yourself or anyone else.

2. You'll be addicted to codependent bonds of abuser and abused.

3. You'll be addicted to denial, fantasy, sado-masochistic excitement, and/or alcohol and drugs.

4. You'll repeat behaviors and posturings in an obsessive-compulsive way until your body will begin to distort from tension and you'll look and feel awful.

5. You'll have difficulty taking care of yourself in the world or finding anyone else who wants to do it for you.

6. You'll eventually get physically, mentally and emotionally ill.

7. You'll kill yourself and possibly others as well.

What Are We Doing When We Heal Ourselves From Abuse?

When we heal ourselves from abuse, we're basically dissolving the old conditioned patterns of behavior, attitude, feeling, and identity of self, and we're simultaneously creating new patterns of behavior, attitude, feeling and identity of self. This must be a simultaneous process or we'd dissolve old identities of self and have no boundaries or identity left.

The dissolving part takes place when we practice the Touch of Silence on ourselves and with others. This is a way to touch ourselves and reach ourselves from the inside out. Other methods such as meditation, Trager, Reiki, bioenergetics, massage, yoga, prayer, imagery, hypnosis, being kind, taking creative action, and experiencing genuine pleasure also help us dissolve destructive brain-body patterns

The creative part takes place when we use our mind. This is the part all of us used to survive. We used our minds to fantasize, deny, distort, project, dream, escape and dissociate. To begin to use our minds creatively for life instead of just for survival, we'll learn to do the following things: We'll become observers so we can witness ourselves and others. We'll also discover what gives us pleasure so we can begin to learn what it is we *actually* feel when we do feel. We'll also build the mind field both within and without our bodies by using the Touch of Silence. And we'll learn how to listen to our inner guides and trust our Higher Power so we can take action.

The integrative part takes place when we learn how to be simultaneously in the mind as an observer and in the body by being able to feel. First, this requires the willingness to observe and feel and secondly, the willingness to allow integration to happen. It also requires action so that the creative integration of thought and feeling becomes incorporated in the body to form a new healthy identity of self.

To begin the path of sanity and genuine living, let's look at some steps toward restoring power, courage, and self-respect. These steps involve identity, action, feeling and observation.

Identity
Have you ever reached the point where health care and counseling became your only avenue for social contact? — or — Where your state of despair and pain became your major focus for social conversation? This is a brain-body obsessive-compulsive behavior. Obsessive is when you can't get something off your mind (actually off your brain). Compulsive is when you can't control what you say and do — you behave mechanically (which is brain-body machinery).

Almost all the women in my workshops have totally or partially completed some college education, or they have been or are in business for themselves, or they have been or are professionals, or they have special talents or skills. Acting as if the whole world should behave therapeutically toward you twenty-four hours a day everyday has nothing to do with intelligence, it has to do with a basic human need for kindness that you don't expect to find outside a therapeutic situation.

I once saw an extraordinarily pitiful situation in which two people were desperately clinging to one another the best they could, just to survive, because they didn't know any other way. These two people were man and wife. She had cancer and he took care of her. She had recovered and the two of them wrote a book, but she kept having setbacks and he kept caring for her. He spoke for her. He drove her everywhere. She couldn't get well and stay well because he would have been out of a job, so to speak. But she had to get *sort of well* now and then to encourage them to go on. Their bond of nurturing and being nurtured was a substitute for real living.

Homework for this section is to observe how and when you're kind to yourself, and how and when you abuse yourself. Don't do anything about it. Don't try to change your behavior. Don't judge yourself or apologize for what you discover. Easy does it — no effort — just observe. Softly, softly, ever so gently, just notice yourself. Just being "willing and allowing" will take care of the rest. There may be some tears — just let it go.

How To Begin To Form A New Identity and Socialization

One of the first steps in forming a new identity is to identify what gives you pleasure (right now, not in the past). The next step is imagery, and the last step is action. When we take action, we complete ourselves and we're fulfilled. We form a new definition of ourselves and a new identity of self from the inside out. Definition and identity give us an idea of limits and boundaries — so we can *form* new limits and boundaries. These become values and give meaning to our lives and purpose to our existence. We gain new knowledge from the inside out (like wisdom) rather than learning from data and theorizing which come from the outside in and have no substance. We incorporate (into our bodies) new behaviors. We achieve new successes. And with it all, we experience genuine courage and self-respect.

Before you can image anew or take action anew, you must first begin to dissove old boundaries and limits of the self that you formed for survival and still hold within your brain-body — but — you must simultaneously create new boundaries and limits of the courageous mind-body self. It's a simultaneous process that erodes old conditioned patterns while you form new healthy ones. You can't do one without the other.

For example, if you break down boundaries of self formed for survival without creating a new identity, you'll disintegrate. Conversely, if you force a new identity over the top of unconscious conditioned responses, you'll have a foundation (core of being) that will sabotage you when you least expect it. Something will "trigger" you and you'll react like a chicken — at the peak of your career or in the middle of a wonderful relationship. You could lose everything and give up.

Many people try to release old memories and patterns of behavior through experiences like rebirthing. Rebirthing dissolves your boundaries by taking you back to a time when you were infantile, helpless and without limits and boundaries of self. As an infant, you were still malleable and in the process of being formed. Be very careful — you need a skilled person to provide reintegration and to help you establish new boundaries of self that are positive, courageous and self-respectful.

When people overflow because they don't have boundaries of identity or set limits for themselves, they become abusive. They invade the limits and boundaries of others because others have no rights around this person. For example, people without boundaries may go on overflow by talking non-stop in a purposeless, wandering manner, or they may imagine that you love them and begin calling you anytime of the day or night. Also, people without boundaries can't take creative action because all purposeful action requires the ability to set limits.

Homework for this section is to list ten things that give you pleasure. Pleasure is not the same as amusement, diversion, or excitement. Pleasure is a feeling state that comes from the inside out and occurs when we're being true to ourselves. Do flowers bring you pleasure? Or maybe it's having your hair brushed, or watching a weaver's hands, or feeling clean sheets on your naked body. You'll only know as much as you can feel.

Action

All action is a process of creation and destruction. You *destroy* the action of going to the movies at 8:00 p.m. when you *create* the action of going to dinner at 8:00 p.m.. You also destroy the action of eating dinner at 7:00 p.m. when you create the action of eating dinner at 6:00 p.m.. To act at all, you must know what you're going to do, when you're going to do it, and how to do it, and then you must actually do it.

Thinking about it and fantasizing it, talking about it and rationalizing it, getting emotional about it or sick over it — do not lead to action...but they do lead to internal commands of "start-stop," "yes-no," repetitive creation-destruction physiological processes in your body. This eventually leads you into confusion, nervousness, craziness, frustration, emotional explosions, violence, illness, or death.

Action leads to wisdom. It leads to knowledge deeply based within the cells of your body and gives you courage and self-respect. You can't take action congruent with health, courage and self-respect until you actually become courageous and do respect yourself. This is part of the wisdom in the Twelve-Step programs — you must take action because only by your actions will you actually know how deeply courageous and wonderfully healthy you've become.

In other words, you won't need someone else to vote on you or to evaluate you and tell you you're right or wrong once you learn how to take creative, conscious action. It's an inner process that shows up in action and then becomes incorporated within every cell of your body to guide you like a teacher within so you can keep going forward in life.

For example, if you decide to paint the fence, you need to know what color, which paint, brush or roller, when, what day, what time and how to do it. If you don't do it, notice what got in your way or what you said got in your way. Action involves commitment, values, creativity, intent, independence of self-expression, skill, and so on. Not a bad way to start the process of courage and self-esteem.

Homework for this section is to choose one job you've been meaning to do and complete it. While you're planning what you're going to do and how you're going to do it, notice all the commitments you're making. While you're doing the job, notice that you're the one doing it. When the job is complete, put everything away and then notice how you feel and write down three times when you've felt like this before. Put down the first things that come to mind — what you feel now and when you felt that way before won't necessarily be logical.

Regression And The "I Can Do It" Process

Whenever any of us is ill or out of sorts, we tend to regress. Regression is a process of moving from the complex toward the simple so we can feel safe. When people are seriously ill, they often behave like little children or tiny infants. When we become overwhelmed with pain and confusion, the simplest tasks seem like too much for us and we instinctively regress by doing what we can to escape from responsibility. Sometimes we become dependent upon others for our safety and welfare. Sometimes we just refuse to get up out of bed or we sit around and daydream or we go get stoned on something.

Regression is a signal that we need to follow the "KISS" method generally known as "Keep It Simple Stupid." "Stupid" is abusive and misleading so I'll suggest an alternative called "Three Magical Kisses." As you discover yourself moving into regressive behavior "Keep It Soft And Simple" — in other words, be kind and gentle with yourself. When you think of kindness remember, "Kindness Is Safety and Serenity." And as you begin to move forward into creative action, remember also that "Kindness Is Sane and Sober."

Remember the little engine that thought she could. She began with "I think I can, I think I can" and she did it and then moved into "I thought I could, I thought I could." "I think I can" never worked very well for me because it always left me with a thread of doubt and never moved me into action. Instead, I use a little process called "I can do it" that moves me right through overwhelm and confusion into creative action.

Here's how to do it. Start with small tasks and say, "I can do it" and then do it. If it requires effort, you're going too far, too fast for you. Don't let anyone tell you that you're not going fast enough — they can't possibly know — they don't walk in your moccasins or have the body, brain, chemistry or experiences that are all unique to you. Go back to simpler tasks (action) that can be completed when you say "I can do it."

For example: If you're going to write a letter, what usually stops you or prevents you from writing the letter is the thought, "I *should* write Mom," which is an attitude of resistance based on the implication that you wouldn't do it if you didn't have to, and that you have to because she's making you do it. In other words, you have nothing to say about the whole activity — you only do what you're told. This is not creative action and it's abusive to yourself because it destroys your identity of courage and self-respect.

Taking creative action and writing a letter to mom involves taking charge of yourself and the action you use to express that self — and it starts real simple. Since it's a letter, you look and see whether or not you can do the following things: Can you find a piece of paper? Can you find a pen? Can you find an envelope? Can you find a stamp? Can you put these things on a table? Can you write the date and Dear Mom on the piece of paper? Can you say a few kind things about yourself one line at a time? Can you ask her a few kind questions about herself one line at a time? Can you say something kind and gentle at the end and sign your name? Can you fold the letter and put it in the envelope? Can you lick the envelope and seal it? Can you write her name and address on the envelope? Can you write your name and address in the upper left-hand corner of the envelope? Can you lick a stamp and put it in the upper right-hand corner of the envelope? Can you find a mailbox and drop the letter in?

Homework: For one whole day, do the "I can do it" process. Each step of the way, ask the simple question about the task, look and see if you can do it, and then say, "I can do it," and then do it. In the beginning, you might need to say, "I can do it," a thousand times a day followed by the action of doing it just to get you through the whole task or the whole day. Focus on each little thing you actually can do and then do it, and the first thing you know, the whole thing will be done. Each time you do this, it keeps you focused, keeps you in your body, and keeps you aware of what you *can* do — just keep it simple.

Simple has nothing to do with a feeble brain. Simple has to do with healing from the terror and anxiety you've been dealing with all your life. When people are filled with terror and anxiety, they go into shock and paralysis and can't move or speak at all. People who are anxious and terrified can't fry an egg, drive a car, get to an appointment on time, or locate their keys. Terror and anxiety make everything seem complex and overwhelming. Action erodes both the experience and the conditioning of terror and anxiety.

Action brings you courage and self-respect — so only do what you can successfully do. Get a "win" on any level, no matter how small, and I promise you, you'll become a strong woman of excellence in everything you do. Keep in mind that you won't be "right" or perfect or okay by anyone else's standards of excellence. But you will have an inner strength and an outer expression of excellence totally unique to you. The ways in which you express this excellence will evolve as you evolve in your courage and self-respect.

When you focus on where you're able to act, and actually do act, you build strength, identity, courage and self-respect. It will look as if you're just getting lots of work done when in fact you'll be dissolving the old you while you're creating the new you (transformation); and you'll be dissolving stuck places of tension and confusion while you're creating movement and life (rejuvenation); and you'll be dissolving unconscious, mechanical, Pavlovian brain 'thinking' while you're creating conscious, creative, spiritual mind thought (enlightenment).

In other words, you can stay in the world and get your work done, and actually use all your problems and your work to become creatively whole, youthful and aware. It goes without saying that you must become safe first. Again, keep it simple. Don't sell your soul just to get safe. You need food, shelter, clothing, human contact and a gentle, simple place to work until you become stronger. Don't worry about the three-story house, your professional complexity, or your status as an important, responsible person — get safe first and fast. Nothing else matters if you lose your will to live — and you may if you don't recover your courage and self-respect.

Get Safe

Theoretically, we often believe that we can stay in an abusive relationship while we heal because we believe in the power of prayer or the power of the mind to heal those around us as well. There's both truth and fallacy in this belief. It's true that the mind as a spiritual dimension of ourselves has the power to heal the brain as a physical dimension of ourselves. It's fallacy to believe that *our* minds are the *only* minds influencing us or the people who are abusing us. It's true that our minds influence the way we are and the way other people experience us. It's fallacy to believe in our omnipotence (all powerful), omnipresence (all presence) or omniscience (all knowing) when we've just begun to heal.

Some people learn about the power of the mind and then act as if someone handed them a magical formula that guaranteed happiness, peace and goodwill between all human beings and told them how to begin using the formula — and so they took it, read the first line, accepted what it said, and assumed a position of power and control over all evil in the world simply because they held the formula in their hand. The power of prayer or the power of the mind lies with each individual who is interconnected with like minds in a group. A group begins with two or more people and grows invisibly around the world.

We are physically separate human beings, but we are spiritually connected. Paradoxically, we act as if we're physically dependent and spiritually independent. It appears to be that way sometimes. Physical cooperation emerges from spiritual cooperation, not the other way around. When people aren't spiritually cooperative, they use control, manipulation and violence to achieve physical cooperation through obedience and subjugation.

No one can act for us. No one can digest our food for us. No one can meet all our physical needs without giving up their life for us. Sometimes it takes ten people to physically take care of one person who has quit taking care of him or herself. Sometimes one person can destructively impact hundreds of other people by not caring responsibly for his or her own physical needs.

Spiritually, it is Thy will not mine be done. Our spiritual sustenance comes from the body of God or the mind of the Higher Power or Divine Intelligence or Cosmic Consciousness — or whatever you happen to call this Power. We are servants of the Divine and as human beings, we're all like little cells in the body of God. Spiritual power is a group power that can heal. Spiritual independence, when it's petty and willful, can separate people and destroy physical cooperation.

When we're in our minds, we're in the universal Mind field. The thoughts we get are more like thinking at the level of real truth and fundamental principle rather than at the level of transient truths like what's current in the daily news. Transient truths come from the outside in — fundamental truth comes from the inside out. When we're in our minds, in touch with our spiritual essence, whatever we receive or come to know has already been received or known for centuries by all human beings when they were in touch with their Higher Power.

The difference, the uniqueness or identity of self, doesn't come with the fundamental thoughts and ideas we get from the Mind field, it comes with the unique ways in which we *express* these truths. It comes with action. We are physically independent and unique, and we have a unique spiritual identity or pattern of self that enables us to listen to fundamental truths which are the same for everyone and then *express* these truths uniquely in some way because no one is exactly like anyone else.

To maintain your spiritual connectedness and sense of support, remember the power of the group. Whenever you feel miserable and don't think you can make it or you seem to have difficulty connecting with your Higher Power — link into the power of the group and you'll link into powerful women everywhere who love and respect themselves. It's true, you could link into miserable women everywhere as well, but not if you're focused upon the positive healing power that's there. With each group of us that forms and goes forward, the group energy will become stronger and stronger, and we as individuals will become stronger as well. It's a spiritual link and it's magical.

Just remember that none of us are out there alone with a magical one-liner that's going to keep us safe and suddenly transform everyone around us, no matter how drugged up or violent they may be, just because we pray to a Higher Power. That Higher Power works through us, it doesn't act for us.

Thirty years ago, someone gave me a little book called *The Circle of Faith.* It was a simple little book like the ones you buy for children — lots of pictures and very few words. It began with an act of kindness from one person to another and showed how the person who received turned around and gave to another, and that person in turn gave to someone else until the gift of kindness spread from one country to another and went all around the world. At the end of the story, the author suggested that the reader give the little book to someone else so that it might be passed from one person to another. So when I finished reading it, I gave it to someone else.

Gifts are like that. When someone gives to you, turn around and give to others. Don't necessarily try to give back to the person who gave to you. Let it spread around the world and keep it going. Just give, and release what you give, and know that it will keep going in some way. When someone gives to you, acknowledge their gift — that's the greatest gift you have to offer them for having given to you. Then turn around and as you overflow from having been given to, give to others and keep the fountain going. Kindness is a gift of love that heals both the giver and the receiver.

Homework we do in the workshop, *The Way of the Female Warrior:* Something very fundamental to the workshop is the giving and receiving of kindness and love. One of the things each woman does is to bring a simple gift like a bouquet of wildflowers, a plant from the garden, a favorite recipe, a small trinket, or something handmade, and she puts a note or card with the gift that has a message that she has wished deep within her heart that someone would say to her. No one signs her name to the note or card. Everyone returns to the group and puts her anonymous gift on a table to be received by exactly the right person who will read and witness her message. Thirty minutes before the meeting ends, everyone picks a gift and some of the messages are read aloud.

During the following week, each person is asked just to remember kindness — not sacrifice or goodness or niceness — just kindness to herself and everyone she meets. Abused women are like the woman who lived by the railroad tracks. Every night the train went by at 2:00 a.m., and every night the woman slept right through the noise. One night the train didn't go by and at 2:00 a.m., she sat right up in bed and hollered, "What's that?" "That" was like kindness—it was the Touch of Silence. We're so accustomed to the noise of abuse that we're often startled and alarmed by kindness.

Feeling

Feeling is an integrative mid-point between brain and mind. Feeling is intricately linked with the energetic systems of light and thus, imagery and imagination. The feelings from positive imagery lead us toward mind-body shifts in behavior, attitudes and states of being. On the other hand, the feelings from destructive fantasies can lead to full-blown emotional reactions. Emotional reactions are signals from the brain-body system to let us know that we've slipped into unconscious, Pavlovian behavior.

When we can't feel, we're able to make up whatever picture we need to so the brain-body can survive regardless of the actual reality. But the cost is craziness and cruelty toward others, behavior that is ineffectual except for ensuring survival of the brain-body, and no shift in awareness or behavior beyond the well-integrated mechanical system of survival which we learned.

In other words, without feelings, you can't go any further than you are right now, and whatever you learned about yourself and others is all you can ever know. Without feeling, you can't know about anxiety, guilt, apprehension, passion or — peace, satisfaction, joy, and pleasure. You can't know about human values related to trust, commitment, kindness, care and compassion.

You'll also have great difficulty taking conscious, creative action since you have no inner reference point for values or identity. All action will be based upon what you should or shouldn't do according to someone else — and upon what you will or won't do because you think you're getting back at "them" for shoving you around.

Emotions are not the same as feeling and have very little to do with deep inner values and a deep conviction of self. People who are freaked out and dissociated don't feel, they react emotionally, which obliterates awareness of feeling. Machines don't have creative options — they can't perform beyond the system of their machinery. Emotions result when the physically mechanical part of ourselves tries to prevent a breakdown in its habitual system of survival.

Psychopaths don't feel. Psychopaths can do or say anything to you and it never moves them in any human way. They can talk lovingly to you while they're cutting you up just as easily as they can agree to meet you for dinner and never show up or call — it's all the same, there's no meaning or value because there's no feeling. They may have a good mind and a good body but no feeling to connect the two together so there's no *reality* between their ideas, intellect and what they say...and what they actually do.

Cruel people don't feel when they're being cruel. They get physical satisfaction out of being cruel the same way you may get physical satisfaction in the form of relief from having passed an exam successfully — the tension's over and you survived the ordeal. A cruel person wants *you* to feel what they refuse to feel because it hurts so much — so they project all the anger onto you for some unknown wrong so they can hurt you, and in the hurting, they get to see you feel for them. It's vicarious — just like going to the movies and getting a thrill out of seeing other people do something you have wondered or fantasized about but don't actually want to do.

People who dissociate or black-out don't feel while they're in that state because they're not "in" their bodies. However, none of us can exist without feeling because feelings come from the movement of life in our bodies. So, when people refuse to feel their own feelings, they project those feelings onto others and then they can feel vicariously — by pretending that the feelings they have are derived from the other person's pain and misery...just like going to the movies. It's a way to trick the brain into believing everything's safe with you — but that other gal's sure having a rough time. It's a way to get some distance and escape. For example, if you've learned how to escape into beautiful fantasies and daydreams that keep you feeling safe during hard times or terrifying moments, you can at least stay alive and survive until you get stronger or can get away from a destructive environment.

What if you're a little kid who can't escape into soothing fantasies, and so you try to handle it all through logic by using your brain. When you grow up, you're the one most likely to be separated from your own feelings because you learned not to have them when you were small. They were so bad that you would have become very ill and possibly died.

As an adult, you probably have a very good brain intellectually and you probably know all the social rules by heart and can mimic them very well. However, you're going to need someone else around you to break down and feel, so you can feel those feelings while pretending that those feelings are theirs rather than yours because after all they are the ones who are screaming, crying, and falling apart. You're the person who is going to need to hurt others just so you can stay alive. Or you're the person who'll get a job taking care of people who get real emotional and freak out around you...and you'll need for them to stay that way because what you need is much more than just a job.

As adults, those of us who survive through beautiful fantasies (the mind) disconnected from feelings will most likely become the victims of those who survive through logic (the brain) disconnected from feelings. The fantasizers will pretend it didn't happen or it's all going to get better, and the logicians will know it happened but be able to blame the victim for making it happen. Since human beings can all play either role, or be very centered and integrated sometimes, and freaked out and dissociated at other times, it's not as cut and dried as I've made it appear. But generally, abused people learn to survive successfully by one method or the other, and part of their success in surviving has been their ability to discover what works consistently for them so they can feel safe.

Get Safe

Since safety and survival are the bottomline issues here, these needs must be met first before healing can take place. Safety and survival depend upon something far greater than food, shelter and work — they depend most fundamentally upon kindness and trust. Kindness and trust occur when the people who are nurturing and supportive begin by setting simple limits that can and will be followed, and by encouraging simple action that can and will be taken by the person who is healing. The person who needs to heal must be willing to heal and allow it to happen.

Supporting Ourselves and Others

If a person is an adult who is free to come and go in the world, he or she must seek support for healing, and must be "willing and allowing." If a person needs to heal and they're not willing or allowing, you can do nothing for them. The only thing we can do for others is to awaken the spirit (will to live) within them through kindness, inspiration, love, witnessing, feeling, and silence — not caretaking, niceness, self-abuse, sacrifice, words, money and code-pendence. Be kind, but don't *reward* someone for being ill and ineffectual or you contribute to their destruction. This is abusive.

This doesn't mean that you don't lend a hand when someone needs your help. There's a difference between those who need to be supported so they can live and in turn support others, and those who have become accustomed to a lifestyle of habitual dysfunction, crisis and breakdown. The latter ones are those who must be willing to get support and to use that support so they can in turn support themselves and others.

How will you know the difference? Well, give a habitually

dysfunctional person, who is still destructively willful, something simple to do for themselves or someone else, and — a) they probably won't do it, or they'll do it late, or they'll do it differently than you asked; or b) they'll get snarly because you gave them a janitor's position rather than president of the company, or you didn't pay them what they were *really* worth. Or do something kind for a person like this and they'll either act like they just did you a favor, or they'll diminish you or what you did in some way. These are just a few clues to what may occur when people aren't willing to get supported and heal, or aren't willing to allow change to happen. In this case, forget the job or your extended hand and awaken their spirit instead. One of the best referrals you can make is a Twelve-Step program.

Homework for this section is to notice what supports you in becoming physically functional and strong so you can take care of yourself, and what supports you in becoming spiritually functional and strong so you can feel and have the will to really live. Separate your lists so you can meet your needs, and in turn know when you're meeting the needs of others in a healthy way.

For example, you may have a good job, nutritious food, and a spacious place to live — but your place is so messy, dirty and ugly that you can't find anything in it, and when you do find something, it's too disgusting to touch. Disorder affects your ability to function physically, and ugliness affects your spirit. Your spiritual needs are different from your physical ones but they both affect one another and must both be satisfied for mind-body integration.

Observation

If you've been hurt, you can't undo what happened. All of us want to undo the pain. We even recreate situations that are in some way similar to what originally happened to us so we can have the opportunity to do it all differently and ease the pain. This can be dangerous. We instinctively know that handling it in new and healthy ways will release our pain and heal us (like conscious action does). But we often don't realize that we can't do this until we're safe, supported and healed. The need for undoing is in your brain-body. You'll be undoing when you begin your work with the Touch of Silence. You'll be dissolving the pain and the old identity associated with that pain.

To begin, get safe and supported. If you're drinking or drugging, you'll be in your brain-body, or dissociated in fantasy and denial — get clean and sober first. Throughout your process, you'll only be handling yourself which means you'll be able to take action on all of it without waiting for anyone else to get better or change. During this phase of moving into courage and self-respect, if you try to handle others instead of just taking care of yourself, you'll pit yourself and your behavior against them. For example, you may give yourself messages like, "I only act this way when... or because of ..." which gives your brain-body permission to keep doing it if and when it happens again.

Homework for this section is to observe how you act and what you say, and to notice what you do with your face and body around others. Don't make excuses for it or try to correct it — just observe. If you can observe yourself, you won't do it again if you notice that you're abusing yourself. Observing it makes it conscious. Only the mind can observe — it witnesses the brain — the brain will run on without you.

Detachment = Mind-Brain Integration

Dissociation = Mind-Brain Separation

Observation is a way to detach from your machinery in a *non-judgmental* way which will allow your mind and brain to integrate. Observe yourself and be kind to yourself. Don't reach out to handle others. People who've been treated unkindly (abused) tend to do for others what they won't do for themselves.

3

The Healing
Process

Did you ever cut yourself and notice what the body does to heal itself? The area swells up a little and gets all red and tender around it. It probably has some pus along the cut area until a scab forms. Then the scab drops away and the wound closes. When you begin to heal inside, something similar happens. Tissues may become swollen and tender and you may feel some pain and discomfort for a few days.

When you start to heal, muscles that have been tense will begin to relax and fresh blood and body fluids will move into the organs and cells of your body. These fresh fluids will bring nutrients to your tissues to heal and repair your body, and they will carry off dead cells and toxic material so it can be eliminated from your system and you won't be poisoned by it.

Did your foot ever go to sleep because you sat on it too long and cut off the circulation? The first thing you may have noticed is numbness or no feeling in your foot. As the foot woke up, you probably felt some pins and needles, some pain, and eventually normal feelings in your foot. In other words, when you released the tension (pressure on your foot), you felt uncomfortable first before you felt comfortable.

Did you ever leave your garden hose lying on the lawn for several weeks without turning on the faucet? The grass dies whether the hose is there or not. This is similar to what happens when we hold tension and shut off feeling. Talking about getting better but procrastinating until the right hour or day or year is like leaving the hose on the grass but refusing to turn the water on. If we wait too long, the grass becomes dry and brittle on the top, and if we continue to wait, the roots become withered and dry, and the grass dies.

When you begin to heal, vital energy moves through your body to bring life to your organs and cells. This is like getting off your foot or turning on the water so your grass can grow. As your tissues heal, you may feel pain and tenderness or notice some swelling, redness or heat. You may even get fever and chills or be sleepier than usual. You might smell funny as toxins leave your body. You might notice pus or mucus coming from your eyes, ears, nose, throat, vagina, urethra or bowels. This is just like what happens when a cut begins to heal. It's a natural healing process.

You'll notice a difference between healing, often called, "a healing crisis," and being ill. During healing, the symptoms of discomfort come and go much faster, and you'll have a sense of well-being even though you may appear to be ill. When this happens, keep your diet simple, well-balanced, and free of chemicals. Do very simple exercise like walking. Rest more than usual. Breathe fresh air and drink clean water. Keep yourself clean so your skin won't reabsorb the poisons it's eliminating. Stay in life and on the job in the safest, simplest way possible.

Healing Practice #1: Write down three or four things the human body does when it wants to heal.

What are some of the wonderful things it does so we can be well? For example, does it make you sleepy, or does it give you fever and chills?

What do you do to give your body permission to heal? For example, do you let it sleep, cover it when it needs to be covered, and bathe it after it has perspired?

How do you get out of the way so you won't make it more difficult for your body to do its job? For example, pretend that your body is your child and that your child is ill. If your child was feverish and sleepy, would you force that child to get up and clean the house, and then tell that child to go outside and be nice to a playmate who showed up in the yard? Would you put appearances and social obligations first, and your child's needs last?

Mind: Our Body Of Light

Human beings seem to have something called the mind which appears to be different from the brain. Although we can't see the mind, we can observe results and human behaviors which aren't possible for the brain to produce. Some people believe that the brain holds the key to behaviors ascribed to the mind. Since scientists, theologians and philosophers have pondered this issue for centuries, I'll describe what I believe to be true and leave it up to you as a reader to decide your own reality about the mind.

The human mind appears to be a pattern of energy linked with the Cosmic Mind. This human pattern links with an infinite wisdom that has been called God, the Creator of all. This Wisdom seems to communicate in a language of probabilities and possibilities and it appears to reach our brains both mathematically and pictorially to engage either the left (math) or right (picture) hemispheres of the brain. This Cosmic Language has been captured and described by various forms such as mathematics, astrology, physics, acupuncture, music, tarot, color, and homeopathy.

It's my intent to keep this book both kind and simple. Many women have never learned any of the cosmic language systems which are fundamental to the arts and sciences. Those of you who have, will recognize relationships that others don't. For the purpose of this book, fundamental knowledge is like a Divine Wisdom that's available to everyone via the spiritual essence of the mind. Variations of this fundamental wisdom are derived through individual expression, and this depends upon what a person has learned. Learning is a brain-body phenomena that requires education and action. You don't need to be a scientist to express fundamental wisdom. If you practice safety, kindness, feeling, "I can do it," and prayer, you will become an expression of this Wisdom and know all you need to know to live a full and satisfying life.

Complexity, as in information that can't be grasped, is abusive and tends to regress people into emotional survival responses. When people become safe, they're able to move from the simple to the complex until the complex is also simple. During healing, people move away from brain-body reactions which make things seem complex, and move toward mind-body action which reveals how much they already know and how simple it really is. If I stay simple, you'll learn how to emerge from the wisdom that moves within your being.

Sometimes people ask, "If Wisdom is so simple, why can't someone just tell me what it is in simple terms so I can understand it?" Then you tell them something like, "Just practice being kind to yourself and others," and they feel ripped off, like you're keeping the good stuff secret. No one's trying to keep something wonderful from you, you just can't explain it because Wisdom comes from the inside out, not the outside in. The only thing anyone can do is to point the way and to provide you with simple rituals so you can learn how to awaken something that's already available to you. When it awakens within you, you'll be in the same predicament as everyone else — you'll know how simple it is, but when you try to tell someone else about it, you'll probably become very complex and make a mess of it.

In this book, I'm going to describe a healing ritual and provide you with enough information to practice it. The simple stuff is: get safe, be kind to yourself and others, feel whatever you really feel, stay in the world and practice "I can do it," and pray to your Higher Power. The ritual which at first may seem complex, is a sacred ritual. It will reveal your inner Wisdom, which is safe, kind, feeling, practical, and your infinite connection with the Divine Father-Mother.

We all have a pattern of energy that both surrounds our bodies and moves like a rhythmic dance within. This pattern of energy seems to be directed by a Cosmic artist who weaves the tapestry of life continuously. In acupuncture, these paths of energy are called meridians, and ancient healers touched them into balance. These healers knew the rhythmic patterns and sought to restore balance to their continuous movement. They knew that harmony brought peace and joy and wholeness, and that people healed from ailments brought about from tension, discord and strife.

They also knew the secrets of kindness, compassion, benevolence and happiness. They knew the power of "easy does it" and "no effort." They knew how to get out of the way and be "willing and allowing." They knew absolutely that there is a Power greater than any human being, and they turned to this Higher Power for wisdom and guidance and listened from within.

These meridians are our body of light. They enable us to feel alive. When we genuinely feel alive, we also feel peaceful, satisfied, whole and courageous. We don't feel empty, abandoned and afraid. These meridians are the energy of the mind, and they link us into life and the Wisdom and Love of the Divine. We can use this energy to image and create and feel. The mind is a spiritual essence that has the power to heal when we recognize our infinite spiritual connection with all that is mind be it human or Divine.

When the meridians aren't moving in a balanced manner, people become emotional, tense, and uncomfortable. If they don't bring these systems of energy into balance, they'll become ill. If their physical body deteriorates too extensively from illness, they can die.

Some people become ill by staying in the machinery of their brain-body and refusing to acknowledge a Power higher than their brain. These are the people who become emotional, tense and destructive.

Other people avoid physical illness by escaping into their minds with fantasy, denial and distortions that make them feel safe because their fantasies fool their brain and trick it into acting as if reality is different than it really is. These are the people who become crazy, drug abusers and destructive. Either way, it's a mind-brain split that's dissociative. Dissociation = Mind-Brain separation.

When the meridians move through the body harmoniously, you can be in your mind-body as an observer witnessing your brain-body in a coordinated way. All you have to do is be kind to yourself and others, be willing to feel whatever you feel, observe yourself in a non-judgmental way, trust your Higher Power, keep your word as you go forward in your action, and keep it soft and simple ("I can do it"). In this way, you're detached because you haven't engaged your brain-body in emotion and judgment, and you've become willing and allowing. Detachment = Mind-Brain integration.

When the energy within moves harmoniously, you'll have clues to let you know this is so. You'll be able to be detached which will enable you to have integrity. You'll also become aware of what gives you pleasure. If you can't feel, you won't know what gives you pleasure. Conversely, as you become aware of what's pleasurable, you'll know you can feel. Feelings come from being alive and well. Emotions evolve from feelings that remind us of pain and imbalance.

Mind-Brain-Body

If what happens was a picture, it might look something like the diagram in figure one, page 71. The large circle is the Mind-Body which surrounds the smaller circle of the Brain-Body. The vertical line down the center is part of the continuous line of Mind-Body which brings life energy into the Brain-Body as feelings of being alive. These feelings enable us to know that we exist and have an identity of self. The life energy passes through the right and left hemispheres of the brain to bring us knowledge about life and ourselves through pictures or logic.

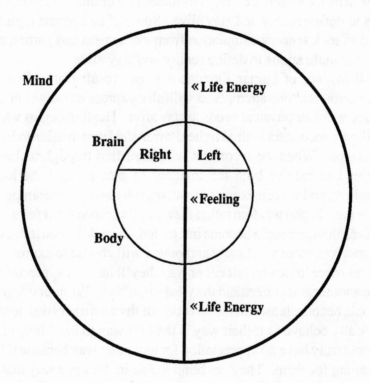

Figure 1: Mind-Brain-Body

Mind-Brain Separation

When we refuse to listen to this knowledge, we separate from the input of the mind and begin to rely upon feedback from the Brain-Body. When we do this, some of us become emotional and tend to seek sensory stimulation from romance and drama, and to use fantasies to define reality and stay alive. Some of us become logical and tend to seek sensory stimulation from excitement and games, and to use rationalizations to define reality and stay alive.

All manner of human dysfunction can result from Mind-Brain separation and our attempts to willfully express ourselves in accordance with our physical needs to stay alive. Healing begins when we willingly reconnect with a Higher Power and learn to listen to Its inner guidance. When we reconnect with the Mind through feeling, our brains can receive both the imagery of pictures and the logic of numbers, and we can express ourselves fully and give meaning to our lives based upon wisdom rather than what's transient but fashionable.

Even though people become integrated, some will choose to express themselves more artistically and others will choose to express themselves more logically, but either way they'll have an appreciation for one another and understand the wisdom in both. Without integration, people become biased in the direction of their own survival needs and willfully behave as if their way is the best way to be. Many of these people truly have no appreciation for any other way because it has no meaning for them. They are blind inside in the same way that all of us are blind to love and truth and wisdom until we awaken and see.

When blindness leads to extreme personal willfulness, we label these people crazy, cruel, psychotic, ruthless, psychopathic, addictive, controlling, and abusive. If we break these words down to a simpler way of looking, we discover something interesting. When people are crazy or psychotic, what they say and do is consistently inconsistent with physical reality. They regularly see things that aren't there or don't see things that are. They regularly say and do things that are irrelevant, destructive, or purposeless. As a result, they have total control over everyone around them unless you lock them up or drug them into oblivion.

What if their reality was so painful that they became *unwilling* to be sane and sober which ultimately led to their *inability* to do so? If this began with a breakdown in their spiritual will, it's quite possible that kindness toward them could have prevented further destruction.

Cruel people derive such satisfaction out of hurting others that they actually look for opportunities to do so. These people may physically cooperate with other people to enable them to get close enough to destroy the spiritual will in others. Ruthless people will do or say anything to get what they want no matter who else suffers.

Psychopaths will do or say anything to achieve total control like a *crazy* person, torment and hurt others like a *cruel* person, and to get what they want no matter who else suffers like a *ruthless* person. And they will only allow themselves one *feeling* (no resistance to the energy moving within) and one *emotion* (resistance to the energy moving within).

When a psychopath *feels,* the feeling is one of total worth and innocence, and when this feeling becomes challenged or unavailable, a psychopath has one *emotion* — anger — which tends to move rapidly from irritation to frustration to anger to rage, and which is always directed outwards onto other people. In other words, psychopaths are crazy, cruel, and ruthless — they *look* and *feel* innocent, and *act* angry because they are *never* to blame, and others are *always* to blame for whatever happens.

Most people who are addictive, controlling or abusive are people who aren't as committed to being consistently uncooperative and totally in control like crazy, ruthless, psychopathic people are. But if you look closely, the dynamics are the same, and the "question" is the same — "How can I meet my needs and prevent others from interfering with me?"

When we take away the label (i.e., crazy, cruel, addictive, codependent), and examine the dynamics, all the behaviors imply that other people must be controlled so one can feel safe and meet ones needs. The unspoken words appear to be, "If I cooperate with others, they will eventually hurt me," or "Other people are my enemies, not my friends."

Destructive personal willfulness results from fear. Mind-Brain separation prevents wholeness of self and leads to fear. When people have been abused, the thoughts and behaviors they used to survive can eventually cripple them if they continue to think and behave as if all people were their enemies. And tragically, we who have been abused perpetuate cruelty and abuse until more and more people behave like enemies with one another.

Healing Practice #2: Write down three experiences you've had that let you know you have something called "the mind."

For example, have you ever dreamed about something happening and then learned that it did happen just as you dreamed?

Have you ever had thoughts of a long-lost friend just seconds before that friend called you on the phone?

Have you ever prayed for forgiveness between yourself and another and then received a letter from that person in acknowledgment of the healing that has taken place between you?

Have you ever known someone who was destructive and irresponsible for years, who seemed to suddenly shift, following an act of kindness?

Have you ever been critically ill and prayed for support from your Higher Power — and awakened the next morning totally healed?

The Meridians And Emotions

There are fourteen main meridians in the body. Vital energy flows continuously along these paths twenty-four hours a day. Two of the meridians are central; the other twelve move peripherally into the organs and limbs on both sides of the body. The central meridians regulate the peripheral ones. The twelve main meridians function in yin-yang pairs to repair and maintain our physical bodies. One of the pairs (yang) removes waste and debris so toxins can be eliminated from our bodies; the other one (yin) forms new healthy tissue so we don't just waste away. Ten of the paired meridians are related to the five basic emotions, which are fear, grief, sadness, anger and worry. Two of the paired meridians are not associated with emotion. Their job is to generate vital energy in the body and circulate it throughout.

The five pairs of meridians associated with emotions are as follows: Lung-Large Intestine Meridians (grief); Stomach-Spleen Meridians (worry); Liver-Gall Bladder Meridians (anger); Heart-Small Intestine Meridians (sadness); and Kidney-Bladder Meridians (fear).

Traditionally, the words "feeling" and "emotion" have been used interchangeably. This synonomous exchange of words is similar to the traditional exchange between the words "mind" and "brain." I'm making an analogous distinction as follows: Both the mind and feelings are derived from a spiritual essence that both surrounds and moves within our physical bodies. When this spiritual essence, life energy, comes into contact with physical tissue, we're aware of ourselves and our environment via our brains. When we become aware, we make decisions and judgments that become the basis for our attitudes. These attitudes either support our willingness to feel whatever we're feeling, or they interfere with our willingness to feel.

When we're willing to feel what we're feeling, we have non-reactive states of being which are feeling states rather than emotional ones. When we become unwilling to feel what we're feeling because of our interpretation of those feelings (attitude), we react (alarm, danger, denial, "it needs to be another way"), and we either *behave* emotionally (lots of spontaneous drama and no awareness of being in the body and feeling) or we *do not behave* emotionally even though we are reacting emotionally inside (we shut off our feelings, turn cold, and become calculating and methodical).

Grief, loss and depression are *emotions* of attachment when we won't let go, and we feel as if we don't want to live without the person or thing we've lost. Healthy grieving is a process of acceptance and letting go. A healthy *feeling* state that may accompany these same meridians and the organs and tissues they serve is "serenity".

Worry and anxiety are *emotions* of anticipation that we'll fail or be less than perfect in our performance. Healthy concern, as opposed to anxiously worrying, encourages us to be careful and discriminating. A healthy *feeling* state that may accompany these same meridians and the organs and tissues they serve is "composure."

Anger, rage and frustration are *emotions* that arise when we feel stopped or blocked from doing what we want to do. Healthy indignation lets us know that we've set limits and boundaries for ourselves, and enables us to recognize that we're being abused. A healthy *feeling* state that may accompany these same meridians and the organs and tissues they serve is "gentleness."

Deep sadness, sometimes expressed as excessive jolliness, is an *emotion* that results from inauthenticity when we pretentiously play a role in life to express ourselves as "someone who's important." Healthy sadness occurs when we realize how phony we've been and begin to become real. This process is similar to grieving and requires acceptance and letting go. A healthy *feeling* state that may accompany these same meridians and the organs and tissues they serve is "dignity."

Fear, panic and terror are *emotions* of paralysis and escape when we feel powerless to protect ourselves or our right to exist. Healthy alarm lets us know we're not safe. A healthy *feeling* state that may accompany these same meridians and the organs and tissues they serve is "courage."

Our first clues to imbalance will be tension, pain and emotion. Our first clues in healing will be relaxation, well-being and healthy feelings and states of being. The twelve meridians circulate continuously on a twenty-four hour rhythm. Every two hours, one of the meridians has more energy than the other eleven so it can repair and maintain all the muscles, organs and tissues related to its system. When it's finished, it keeps enough energy to continue flowing through the body and passes the rest to the next meridian in the twenty-four hour cycle.

This is a natural healing process that goes on everyday to give us life and keep our mind-brain-bodies healthy and sound. The meridians are in yin-yang pairs of creation and destruction. Their purpose is to restore nutrients and build-up where we need it, and to eliminate waste from the body so we won't become toxic and ill.

There is another more fundamental system of energy in the body which we can use to reach the meridians and bring them into balance. Based upon Jin Shin Jyutsu (see Notes), there are three paths of energy in this system called the Main Central, Major Vertical, and Minor Diagonal. The Main Central flows from the tailbone up the center back, over the head and down the center front in a continuous circle of energy (see figure 3, page 87). The Major Vertical flows up the back and down the front of both sides of the body (see figure 4, page 88). The Minor Diagonal connects the right and left sides of the body (see figure 5, page 89).

There are points along the Main Central called chakras, and there are twenty-six points on both sides of the body along the Major Vertical (see figures 2 and 4, pp. 85, 88). These are the points we'll touch to bring harmony to the mind-brain-body. An acupuncturist uses needles and moxibustion to stimulate or sedate hundreds of points on the body along the fourteen meridians. We don't need to do that when we touch the twenty-six points ever so gently with kindness and compassion.

One chakra affects several of the twenty-six points, and one of the twenty-six points affects many acupuncture points. We can reach and balance every other system in the body through the points along these three fundamental paths.

Healing Practice #3: First, get centered, detached, relaxed and able to feel throughout your whole body. To do this, sit quietly with your spine straight and breathe very, very gently straight up to the center top of your head. Do this three times while you place your thumbs over the following fingers on the same hand in succession, one at a time with each breath: First breath — index finger; second breath — middle finger; and third breath — ring finger.

Now put your palms together like you're going to pray, and bring your hands in against your chest between your breasts and take one more breath. As you do this, ask for contact with your Higher Power, and when you sense that you've made contact, get up and stretch out flat on your back and ask that Power to move through you. Just feel whatever you feel for the next five minutes. Then thank your Higher Power for its kindness and protection, and get up.

Afterwards, spend the next hour interacting with a few people in various ways and notice if you're able to feel whatever you feel without getting emotional. Do your hard luck stories and self-pity still seem important? Do you have any interest in being defensive, bitchy or snotty and cute with other people?

How To Touch

Look at figure 2 and locate the points on the inner knees which are numbered "1." Sit in a comfortable position and gently place your right hand on your right knee and your left hand on your left knee. Become still, close your eyes and very, very softly breathe straight up to the crown of your head. Hold this breath briefly and gently exhale. Do this once or twice and then notice what you feel at points number one on your inner knees.

Most people will feel a gentle pulsing sensation under their fingertips. If you don't feel anything, remain still and relax your arms and hands until you're barely touching. Be "willing and allowing" as you listen and wait. Keep your attention on both points simultaneously and allow the pulsing to become synchronous so the pulsing feels the same in both points. As you keep your attention on the fingers of both hands at once, this will keep you centered and focused in a state of mind-body integration.

When the pulses in both points become synchronous, keep touching them gently until they become quiet and gentle as well. When this happens, you may notice a flow of energy and a kind of magnetic pull upon your fingers as the points form a pocket under your fingertips. If you keep holding these two points, you may feel squiggles of energy move in different places in your body or a sensation like warm water down your inner thighs. Or you may feel some of these things awhile later after you've stopped holding the points.

Shift your mental attitude and recall different emotions while you hold these points and notice what happens. I've done this as an experiment in my classes to demonstrate that everything you think and feel gets communicated to yourself or to other people you touch (when you're working with a partner). Likewise, everything your partner is thinking and feeling gets communicated to you in patterns you can feel under your fingertips. The difference between the two is that your partner may become restless and uncomfortable from *your* moods and attitudes if you're doing the touching, because she's relaxed and receiving; whereas, when you do the touching, you'll be detached and focused and able to observe her attitudes and emotions as they pass by your fingers and release.

When there's pain in someone's body, whether it's current physical pain, an old injury, or emotional pain, it will all feel similar and cause sharp pain at your fingertips. Toxins whether they're from infection, detoxification from cleansing, or drugs will all feel like tiny, fragmented, bits of scattered stuff that interfere with the smooth, clean feelings you normally get when pulsations are clear and healthy. Tiny rapid pulsations like a baby bird's heart generally indicate digestive problems, especially in the stomach. Deep, loose, bounding pulses generally indicate an imbalance in the Triple Warmer Meridian, and may mean more serious problems that need immediate attention.

Touch softly, pull back and listen. Be willing and allowing, and remain centered, detached, and non-judgmental (which means being aware of what you observe and feel simultaneously). Remember to be kind and compassionate. This isn't a "doing," it's a way of being. You don't need to huff and puff, exert effort and perform in order to be. Most of us have pleaded for or demanded our simple human right to exist safely and freely in the presence of kind, loving human beings. Here's your chance to feel what that feels like, and to notice the powerful impact it has on others as well as yourself.

Forcing, controlling or belittling is abusive. These attitudes don't heal, they cause people to become tense and fearful, and ultimately to regress even further. Keep it simple. When people are ill, afraid, and in pain, they are grateful for that which is simple and kind.

Healing Practice #4: Practice touching people without using your hands.

First, get centered and detached, and become kind and gentle. (see Healing Practice #3)

Then, during the next hour, go out and interact with several people in a variety of ways and as you do, keep getting softer and softer inside as you gently pull back and release and listen.

Be non-judgmental (no one's right or wrong, or better or worse) and be willing and allowing (no forcing, manipulating or controlling) as you let them be safe around you. Notice that you don't have to be aggressive to be assertive. Notice your field expand as you softly pull back and release, and feel it contract as you aggress, defend, force and expend effort.

Touch Of Silence: How To Prepare — Before And After

Before you begin, get still and breathe ever so softly straight up to the crown of your head as if the breath is going out the top of your head. Notice that your eyes may become stimulated at the outer edges and that you have peripheral vision when you open your eyes. Notice also that when you breathe straight up, the breath automatically moves down the center of your body all the way through your lungs, diaphragm, abdomen, and pelvis to reach your perineum (the skin between your anal and vaginal openings).

You'll be in a "psychic" state, and may also become aware of a point or ball of light approximately eighteen inches above the crown of your head. Imagery and feelings may be similar to those you may have had in the past when you contacted your Higher Power. Find a place to lie down comfortably on your back. Take a gentle inventory of your body and notice all the areas you can feel. When you find areas where you can't feel, be willing and allowing so you can have feelings in those areas as well.

Stay in contact with your point of light. Notice how safe and gentle and kind you feel. Afterwards you'll be able to begin touching yourself or another ever so gently with the Touch of Silence. Easy does it — just touch and move and be in this gentle state of kindness and compassion.

After you've received a "flow" (the term most commonly used for a session of touch to balance the energy flows within the body), you'll feel very relaxed and possibly sleepy. If you can rest or sleep afterwards, do so. If you can't, keep your work gentle and simple. Within twenty-four to forty-eight hours after receiving a flow, you may feel some physical discomfort, increased emotional sensitivity or nervousness and agitation. Old memories may release into your awareness in the form of flashback imagery or dreams.

You may get bitchy and easily overwhelmed. You may act regressive (i.e., childish, dependent, withdrawing) from old feelings of fear when you needed to get safe and supported. You may feel an aversion to rich food right now. You may smell funny and need to bathe a little more. You may need more than eight hours sleep for the next few days or longer.

If any or all of this happens, stay in the world the best you can but in a simpler fashion. Use the "I can do it" process and keep going forward. Just remember that you're healing so — be kind, let it happen, and be willing and allowing. Take a few moments to stop and breathe up through the crown of your head and contact your Higher Power. Stretch out a couple times a day and let feelings move into every part of your body. Use the Serenity Prayer to remind yourself that you aren't going through any of this alone.

God grant me the
serenity to accept the things I cannot change,
courage to change the things I can,
and wisdom to know the difference.

Thy Will not mine be done.

After several days, you may notice that you look softer and more beautiful. The pain will be gone and your appetite and moods will have improved. The most pressing problems just before the flow may have become history almost overnight. You may be aware of new problems. Old complex issues will seem simpler now, but you may develop new complexities. Old pains may have disappeared and you may have new ones, especially "new" pain from old injuries where you repressed the pain through drugs or by shutting off your feelings.

When this happens, you may be tempted to feel discouraged because you believe that everything's just as bad as it always was. Not so. Trauma and illness very often release in layers. This is a safety mechanism and should be respected. If you released everything all at once, you wouldn't have any identity of self. Just keep taking action ("I can do it") and gently move forward to build a new identity of courage and self-respect.

Healing is a lot like dieting. In the beginning, you may lose a few pounds and then plateau, and then, horror of horrors, actually gain several pounds. But if you stick with it, you suddenly begin to lose weight quickly and regularly — and you still look wonderful. However, if you force your weight loss on a crash diet, you usually look like the pits, and gain it all right back again once you start to eat like a human being instead of a cross between a dainty cow and a voracious hummingbird. Healthy dieting allows time for rebuilding along with weight loss and the release of toxins.

Healing Practice #5: Read the Fourth Step in *Twelve Steps And Twelve Traditions* (see Notes). All healing is the recovery of the spiritual self within, and this recovery depends upon telling the truth, accepting what is, making amends, letting go, and going forward with integrity.

If you're in a Twelve-Step program, you will either be working toward this step or have completed it in some manner. If you're unfamiliar with the Twelve-Step programs but interested, I strongly suggest beginning with Step One to prepare you for the Fourth Step.

The Twenty-Six Points

Before you begin giving yourself a flow, locate and memorize the twenty-six points (see figures 2 and 4, pp. 85, 88). As you locate them on yourself, you'll notice some that are tight and hard, and some that are sore and tender. These points need to be touched and released from tension. Other points may seem free and open and you'll notice healthy pulsations as you touch them. Some points will have too much energy flowing through them because other points are tense and blocked. These points may be bounding loosely in heavy pulsations. They'll become quieter when you release the ones that are blocked.

If you can't reach all the points on yourself, do this with a friend.

This will give you the opportunity to touch and be touched. Whenever you touch another with kindness and gentleness, you automatically touch yourself in the same way. This is a magical phenomena in the sense that whatever you give, you also receive because in order to actually give it, you must *be* it. You can't be a phony and still touch another with kindness — and so you become more and more real each time you genuinely serve another in this way.

The more you serve others, the faster your "diet" will go. This is the Twelfth Step in the Twelve-Step programs. It's really all that's left once you turn your life over to a Higher Power, accept, let go, make amends, forgive, heal and go forward. Service is a state of being and a way of behaving that emerges from this state — it's not codependent "do-gooding" so people will say you're "nice." Brain-Body people might think this sounds pretty dull because all the excitement from the games of problems and upset will be gone, and the emotional storms from the romance of fantasy and high drama will also disappear.

Instead, you'll have sanity, sobriety, health, wholeness and serenity. You'll look and feel younger and more beautiful than you ever have. You'll enjoy being alive. You'll be able to do the things you've always wanted to do. You'll have courage and self-respect. You'll realize how important your job really is, whatever your work may be. You'll be able to play genuinely and be intimate with other people. You'll experience genuine pleasure, and you'll become more fundamentally powerful and sexual than you may have ever dreamed possible.

Healing Practice #6: Find a partner and take turns locating all the points on one another. Notice what you feel when you're touching, and when you're being touched. Tell one another what you noticed and felt.

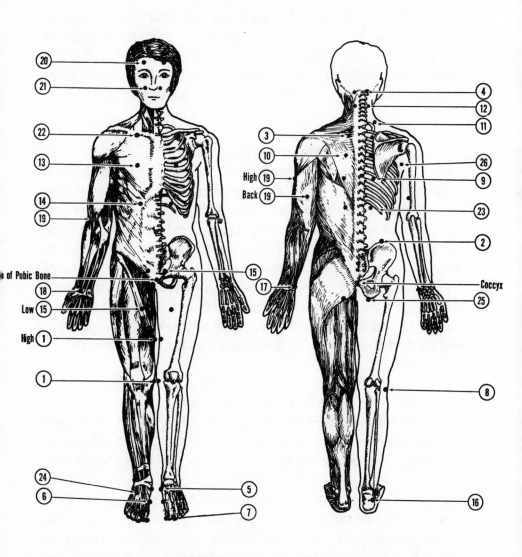

Figure 2: The Twenty-Six Points

Main Central Flow

The Main Central Flow (see figure 3 and charts, pp. 87, 90, 91) affects all the other energy flows in your body. This path must be open with freely flowing energy before any of the other flows can move rhythmically in balance. This is a good flow to do for yourself or anyone else. It will help you feel centered, peaceful, detached and in touch with your Higher Power. Each of the points along its path helps to heal parts of your total self. See appendices for further details.

Major Vertical Flow

The Major Vertical Flow (see figure 4 and charts, pp. 88, 92, 93) is a naturally occurring flow of energy that is present when you're harmoniously balanced within. All of the twenty-six points (see figures 2 and 4) are located along its path. When you touch these points into balance, you can assist all the other energy paths in the body. This is a good flow to practice to become familiar with most of the points on the body. Do the right flow if most of the tension seems to be in the right upper back and shoulders, and do the left flow if it appears to be the opposite. Each of the points along its path helps to heal parts of your total self. See appendices for further details.

Minor Diagonal Flow

The Minor Diagonal Flow (see figure 5 and charts, pp. 89, 94, 95) is a naturally occurring flow of energy when the right and left sides of your body are communicating harmoniously. This is a good flow to do to bring both sides of your Brain-Body into coordination. Do the right flow if most of the tension seems to be in the right upper back and shoulders, and do the left flow if it appears to be the opposite. Even though you may have pain on your left side, the tension may be on your right side. Choose the side with the most tension rather than the one with the most pain if these sides are different.

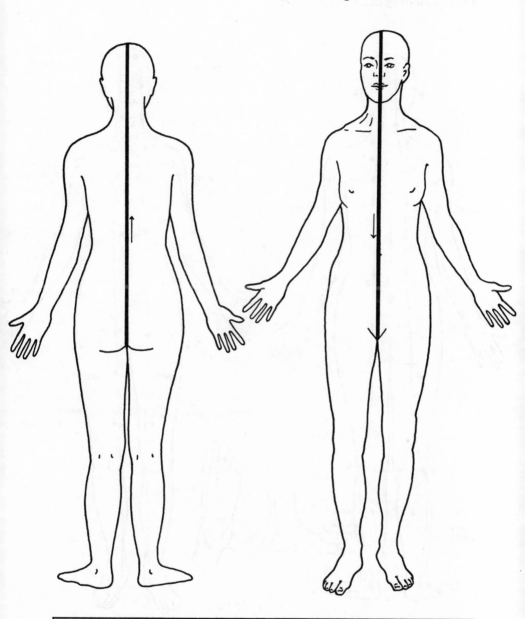

Figure 3: Main Central Flow

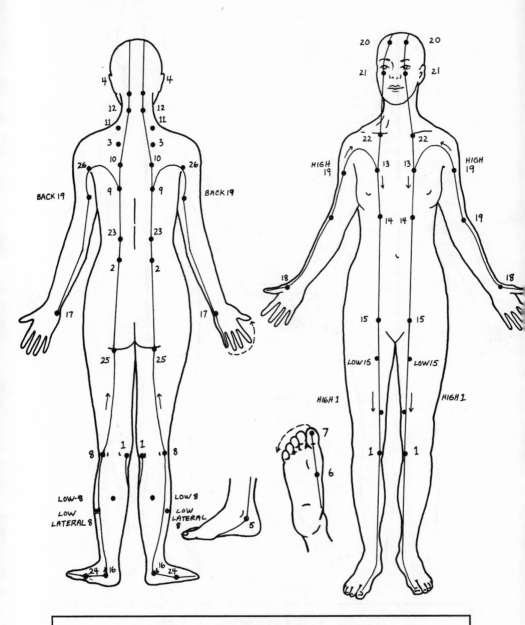

Figure 4: Major Vertical Flow

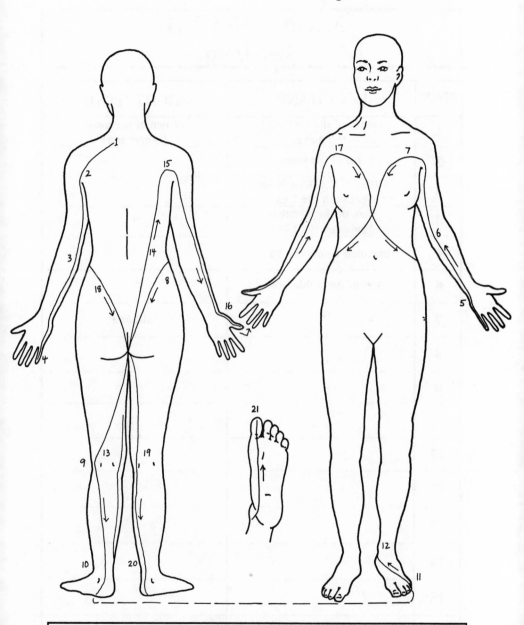

Figure 5: Minor Diagonal Flow

MAIN CENTRAL
Self-Help

STEPS	LEFT HAND	RIGHT HAND
1	center of the forehead (third eye)	crown of the head (center top)
2	tip of the nose	"
3	center of the breastbone (between the 13's)	"
4	base of the sternum (between the 14's)	"
5	one inch below the navel	"
6	top of the pubic bone	"
7	"	tailbone
8		
9		
10		
11		
12		
13		
14		
15		
16		

MAIN CENTRAL
Sit Right

STEPS	LEFT HAND	RIGHT HAND
1	on the spine between the 9's (seventh thoracic)	at the base of the sternum (between the 14's)
2	on the spine between the 10's (fifth thoracic)	"
3	on the spine between the 3's (third thoracic)	"
4	on the spine between the 11's (first thoracic)	"
5	on the spine between the 12's (third cervical)	"
6	"	the tailbone
7	on the spine between the 23's (twelfth thoracic)	"
8	on the spine between the 4's (at the base of the skull)	"
9	on the forehead between the brows (third eye)	"
10	on the breastbone between the 13's	"
11	one inch below the navel	"
12	top of the pubic bone	"
13		
14		
15		
16		

MAJOR VERTICAL
Left Flow - Sit Left

STEPS	LEFT HAND	RIGHT HAND
1	right 20	left 12
2	right 21	"
3	right 22	"
4	right 13	"
5	right 14	"
6	right 15	"
7	left 1	"
8	left 5	"
9	left 6	"
10	left 7	"
11	left 25	left 2
12	"	left 23
13	"	left 9
14	"	left 10
15	"	left high 19
16	right 14	left middle finger

MAJOR VERTICAL
Right Flow - Sit Right

STEPS	LEFT HAND	RIGHT HAND
1	right 12	left 20
2	"	left 21
3	"	left 22
4	"	left 13
5	"	left 14
6	"	left 15
7	"	right 1
8	"	right 5
9	"	right 6
10	"	right 7
11	right 2	right 25
12	right 23	"
13	right 9	"
14	right 10	"
15	right high 19	"
16	right middle finger	left 14

MINOR DIAGONAL
Left Flow - Sit Left

STEPS	LEFT HAND	RIGHT HAND
1	left high 19	left 10
2	left 19	"
3	"	left 9
4	"	left 23
5	left 18	"
6	"	left 2
7	left 13	"
8	right 14	"
9	tailbone	"
10	right 1	"
11	left 8	"
12		
13		
14		
15		
16		

MINOR DIAGONAL
Right Flow - Sit Right

STEPS	LEFT HAND	RIGHT HAND
1	right 10	right high 19
2	"	right 19
3	right 9	"
4	right 23	"
5	"	right 18
6	right 2	"
7	"	right 13
8	"	left 14
9	"	tailbone
10	"	left 1
11	"	right 8
12		
13		
14		
15		
16		

Elimination of Fatigue

The Elimination of Fatigue Flow (see charts, pp. 98, 99) is a combination of the Main Central, the Major Vertical, and the Minor Diagonal paths of energy in the body. When these three fundamental flows become disrupted, toxins build up in the body and the immune system doesn't function properly. People become fatigued, sluggish, depressed and heavy. This is a good flow to do when the whole body seems tense and you can barely feel any pulsations anywhere.

Healing Practice #7: Memorize the points.

Learn about different ways to touch, and become familiar with the different sensations you feel on your fingertips and throughout your body.

Practice these four flows with a partner until you feel comfortable giving and receiving a flow.

Give yourself enough time with this section to learn about some of the experiences you'll have after giving and receiving flows.

Learn how to stay grounded by practicing "I can do it" and permitting yourself to feel. When you can do this, you're ready for the next steps in the following chapters. If you start to get overwhelmed at any step along the way, go back to earlier ones and begin again more slowly.

The Pulses

There are six pulses on each wrist. There are three superficial ones and three deep ones on each wrist. The three superficial ones feel lighter than the three deep ones which feel heavier by comparison. These twelve pulses (six on each wrist) represent the twelve main meridians of the body. To read these pulses, have your partner lie down comfortably on her back with her arms relaxed and her hands resting at the base of her rib cage. Then hold her wrists gently by placing your index fingers just below the wrist bone, and your middle and ring fingers along side (see figure 6, page 97).

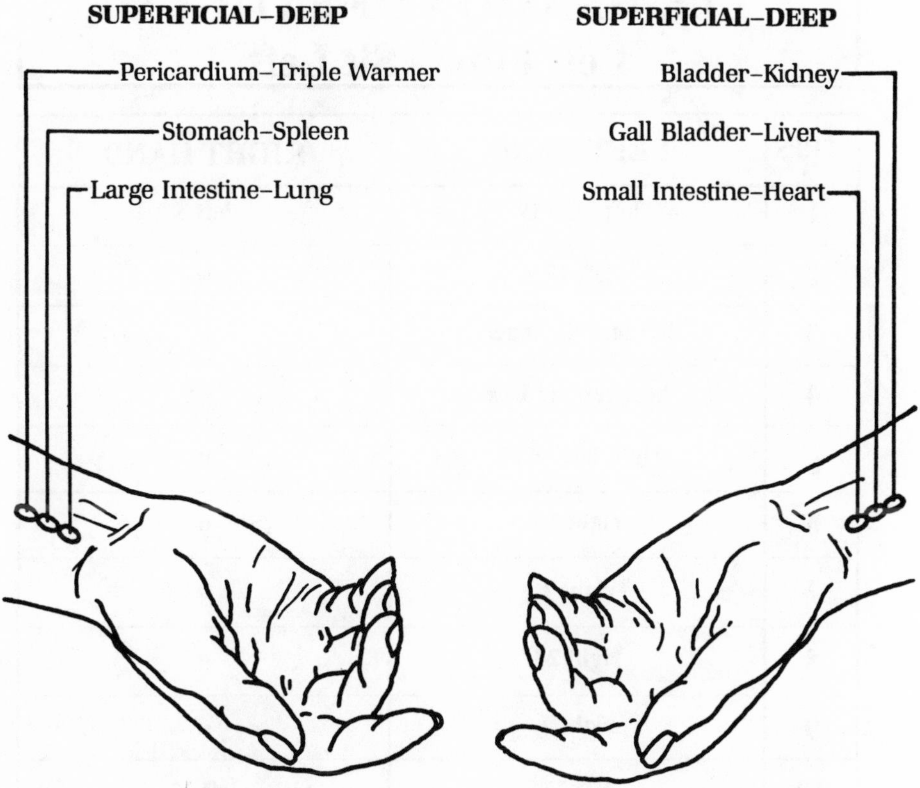

SUPERFICIAL–DEEP

Pericardium–Triple Warmer

Stomach–Spleen

Large Intestine–Lung

SUPERFICIAL–DEEP

Bladder–Kidney

Gall Bladder–Liver

Small Intestine–Heart

RIGHT WRIST

Superficial Pulses (touch lightly)
Index finger–Large Intestine
Middle finger–Stomach
Ring finger–Pericardium
Deep Pulses (touch firmly)
Index finger–Lung
Middle finger–Spleen
Ring finger–Triple Warmer

LEFT WRIST

Superficial Pulses (touch lightly)
Index finger–Small Intestine
Middle finger–Gall Bladder
Ring finger–Bladder
Deep Pulses (touch firmly)
Index finger–Heart
Middle finger–Liver
Ring finger–Kidney

Figure 6: The Pulses

ELIMINATION OF FATIGUE
Left Flow - Sit Left

STEPS	LEFT HAND	RIGHT HAND
1	left high 19	left 3
2	left 17	"
3	left middle finger	"
4	between the 14's	"
5	right lateral 22	"
6	right 15	"
7	right 1	"
8	right 24	"
9	right 7	"
10	left 23	left 12
11	left 9	"
12	between the 13's	crown of the head
13	between the 14's	"
14	top of the pubic bone	"
15	tailbone	between the 9's
16	"	between the 10's

ELIMINATION OF FATIGUE
Right Flow - Sit Right

STEPS	LEFT HAND	RIGHT HAND
1	right 3	right high 19
2	"	right 17
3	"	right middle finger
4	"	between the 14's
5	"	left lateral 22
6	"	left 15
7	"	left 1
8	"	left 24
9	"	left 7
10	right 12	right 23
11	"	right 9
12	crown of the head	between the 13's
13	"	between the 14's
14	"	top of the pubic bone
15	between the 9's	tailbone
16	between the 10's	"

99

First hold lightly, touching each place with the same amount of pressure, and notice if any of the pulses seem to be beating faster or more strongly than all the others. Then hold these same areas a little more deeply still touching each place with the same amount of pressure, and notice if any of these pulses seem to be beating faster or more strongly than all the others. When you're done, look at figure 6, page 97, and write down the heaviest superficial pulse or pulses if there were any, and the heaviest deep pulse or pulses if there were any.

Then hold her wrists one more time and press in on both wrists simultaneously and release to see which wrist seems to be beating the heaviest overall. You may have to check more than once, but when you feel which one seems to feel the heaviest to you, write down which wrist (left or right), which will tell you which flow to do, the left one or the right one. Do not write down *your* left or right hand because you will feel her left-side tension in *her left* wrist with *your right* hand and vice versa.

In the beginning, use the following information to guide you: Do the meridian flows (see chapter four) for the pulses that are beating the heaviest. When you do, these heavy pulses will settle down and those pulses which seemed feeble or missing will become stronger. The end result will be balanced pulses in which all the pulses will be beating harmoniously.

If all the *deep* pulses are heavy on the *right* wrist, and all the superficial pulses are heavy on the left wrist, do the Right Major Vertical Flow. If all the *deep* pulses are heavy on the *left* wrist, and all the superficial pulses are heavy on the right wrist, do the Left Major Vertical Flow. Then re-read the pulses.

If all the deep *and* superficial pulses are beating heavy on the *right* wrist and you can barely feel anything on the left wrist, do the Right Minor Diagonal Flow. If all the deep *and* superficial pulses are beating heavy on the *left* wrist and you can barely feel anything on the right wrist, do the Left Minor Diagonal Flow. Then re-read the pulses.

If all the deep and superficial pulses are beating heavy under both your index fingers, do the 13 Release (see chapter five for Release Flows). If all the deep and superficial pulses are beating heavy under both your middle fingers, do the 14 Release. If all the deep and superficial pulses are beating heavy under both your ring fingers, do the 15 Release. Then re-read the pulses.

If you can't feel any pulses at all, do the Main Central Flow and the Minor Diagonal Flow, or do the Elimination of Fatigue Flow. Then re-read the pulses.

If all the pulses seem chaotic, do the 24, 26 Release and the Main Central Flow, and then re-read the pulses.

If several pulses are heavy and you'd like to narrow it down and discover which meridian needs the most attention, do the 1 Release and the Main Central Flow and then re-read the pulses.

If all the superficial pulses are heavy or chaotic, do the Pericardium Flow. If all the deep pulses are heavy or chaotic, do the Triple Warmer Flow.

The pulses will tell you when the vital energy is moving in a balanced harmonious manner or whether a particular area or meridian needs more touch during another session. Balanced pulses represent wholeness and integrity, and this harmony brings about healing wherever it's needed in the mind-brain-body.

Note: All the fundamental paths or twelve main meridians (except the central ones) flow on both sides of the body. Only one side is shown in all of the figures except for the Major Vertical. Please check Appendix B, pp. 346, 347 to see which side is illustrated.

4

The Rhythmic
Cycles of Healing

Check List for a Healing Session: (read the pulses before and after).

1. Find a quiet room or space that you can use regularly. Rituals are enhanced by familiar objects and surroundings. Vital energy will accumulate in this area.

2. You'll need a cot or table that you can kneel alongside or sit at comfortably in a chair on rollers. There will be less pressure on your hands if you put a foam "egg crate" mattress on top. Cover this with two sheets so you can hold the top one as you slide your hands between the two when you need to touch points on the back. Always have a blanket nearby to cover your partner.

3. Have your partner lie on her back with her spine straight. She will be fully clothed except for her shoes. Some synthetic clothing will distort finger feedback.

4. Put a small clock nearby. Sessions are generally an hour, but may take longer in the beginning. Until you establish your own rhythm, hold the points for each step until the pulses in both points seem synchronous, or for approximately two minutes, and then move to the next step. You can give one or several flows.

5. If you confuse right and left, mark your hands with an "R" on the right one and an "L" on the left one, and mark the right and left sides of the table (partner's right or left shoulder). "Sit Right" means sit to your partner's right. Do the "Right Flow" when your partner's right wrist is pulsing heavier than her left. "Right 9" means to touch point 9 on your partner's right side. Between the 9's is on the spine.

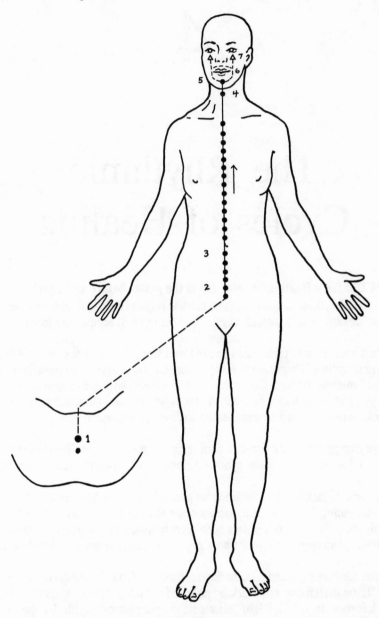

Figure 7: Conception Vessel Meridian

The Conception Vessel Meridian

(Center Front)

The Conception Vessel Meridian (figure 7, p. 104) begins on the perineum (1), ascends through the genitals, the pubic hair, and the hypogastrium (2). It continues to travel upward along the abdominal midline, emerges below the navel (3), and then continues upward to the larynx (4), over the throat and chin and terminates below the lower lip (5). A branch goes around the lips (6) and extends to St. 4 where it enters the eyes (7) joining the Stomach Meridian.

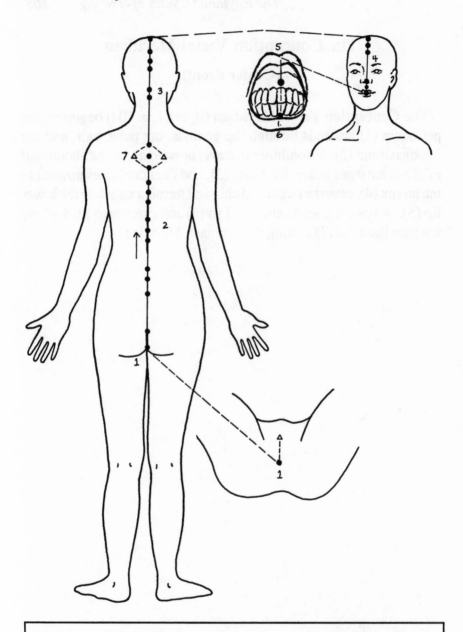

Figure 8: Governing Vessel Meridian

The Governing Vessel Meridian
(Center Back)

The Governing Vessel Meridian (figure 8, p. 106) originates at the tip of the coccyx (1), sending a branch forward on the perineum to CV1. The meridian ascends the spines of the vertebrae at the same time uniting with them (2). It travels to the indentation between the atlas and occipital bone (3), where it penetrates into the brain, emerges at the top of the head, descends over the forehead (4), the nose, the upper lip, and ends on the upper gum between the incisor teeth (5). From there, it sends a branch to join both the Conception Vessel and the Stomach Meridian (6). A branch travels from the spine via Bladder 12 (between second and third thoracics which is between points 3) on both sides (7).

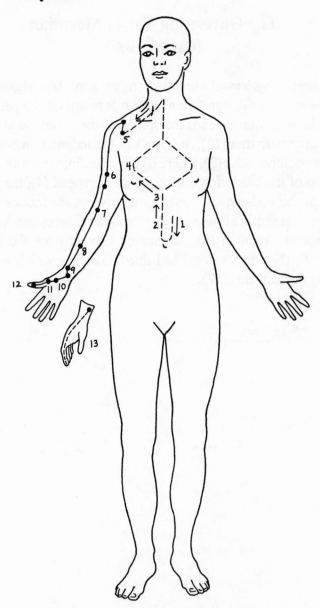

Figure 9: Lung Meridian

The Lung And Large Intestine Meridians
(Surface flow of energy)
Emotions: grief, loss and depression

The Lung Meridian, yin-ascending, (figure 9, p. 108) begins its cycle at 3:00 a.m., peaks at 4:00 a.m., and ends at 5:00 a.m. Its path begins in the stomach (the middle burning space) descends to the large intestine (1) and then turns and moves up (2) along the edge of the stomach to the cardiac orifice (3). It continues to ascend and penetrates the diaphragm and unites with the lung (4). From the lung, the meridian ascends along the trachea and goes sideways through the larynx and reaches the extremity in the axilla (5). Then it passes in front of the Heart and Pericardium Meridians and moves along the inner side (region of the brachium) of the arm downward to the elbow (6, 7) into the ostum pollicare (8, 9) and from there across the thenar eminence to the tip of the thumb (10, 11, 12). A branch travels from the back of the wrist and runs laterally along the inner side of the index finger to its tip where the Lung and Large Intestine Meridians meet (13).

Symptoms of Imbalance

When the Lung Meridian isn't circulating freely, some of the following difficulties may occur: any kind of breathing problem, chest congestion, coughing or lung swelling. Allergies, yawning and hiccoughs. Skin problems such as eczema or changes in pigmentation. Changes in the condition of the hair. Perspiring when sleeping. All kinds of throat and gum problems. Facial spasms. Aching arms and elbows. Feverish palms. Chills in the shoulders and upper back. Paralytic conditions. Low energy. Feelings of melancholy or depression. Shock.

If this meridian has been imbalanced long enough to actually affect the lungs, you'll need to release a variety of different points on the body which may not be on the upper body where this meridian circulates. Many meridians pass through the lungs and affect whether these organs receive energy or not even though none of them are in charge of the total *system* of the lungs like the Lung Meridian is. Check appendix B under *lungs* for more information if the lungs are struggling to heal.

You and Your Friends

The lungs supply oxygen to form oxyhemoglobin for red blood cells. Healthy oxygenation of the blood is related to the blood's ability to cleanse and heal the body. When the lungs aren't receiving enough energy to function properly, you may look pale and washed out with colorless, lackluster skin and hair. You might also be a drag to be around because you're always so down and out , bored and disinterested in life.

You'll probably spend more money on blusher, hair conditioners and skin creams. You could wind up acting like a "couch potato"who yawns a lot even after twelve hours sleep. You'll probably snore and soak the sheets from perspiration which will ruin all the seductive glamour you tried to project before you went to bed and revealed the real you who probably needs to grieve and let go.

If you have a little baby who has colic or just seems fretful and agitated, do the Lung Flow and watch the wee one sleep. Give this flow as a birthday gift to a girlfriend who thinks she needs a facial.

LUNG
Left Flow - Sit Left

STEPS	LEFT HAND	RIGHT HAND
1	left 18	right 11
2	left 19	"
3	left 22	"
4	between the 13's	first thoracic
5	left 14	"
6	right high 1	left 10
7	right 6	"
8	right second toe	"
9		
10		
11		
12		
13		
14		
15		
16		

LUNG
Right Flow - Sit Right

STEPS	LEFT HAND	RIGHT HAND
1	left 11	right 18
2	"	right 19
3	"	right 22
4	first thoracic	between the 13's
5	"	right 14
6	right 10	left high 1
7	"	left 6
8	"	left second toe
9		
10		
11		
12		
13		
14		
15		
16		

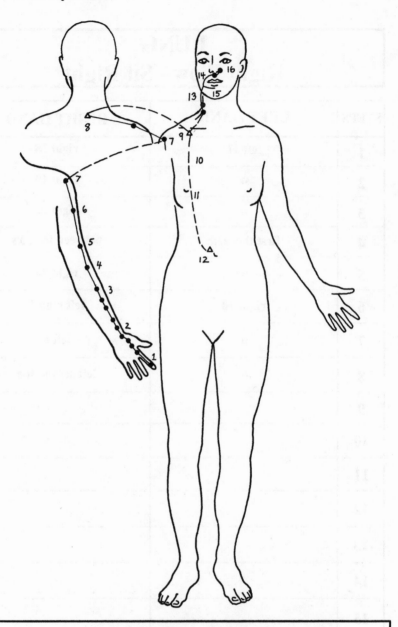

Figure 10: Large Intestine Meridian

The Large Intestine Meridian, yang-descending, (figure 10, p. 114) begins its cycle at 5:00 a.m., peaks at 6:00 a.m., and ends at 7:00 a.m. Its path begins at the tip of the index finger (1) and then travels along the dorsal surface facing the thumb; it continues through the region between the first two metacarpal bones and on into the region between the extensor pollis longus and brevis (2). It then proceeds along the outward side of the forearm (3) to the lateral surface of the elbow (4), continues along the outer side of the upper arm (5) moves through the cleft between the acromion and clavicle (6, 7) to the posterior border of the sternocleidomastoideus to the spinal process of the seventh cervical (the junction of the six yang meridians) (8). It travels through the supraclavicular fossa (9), enters the lungs (10), passes through the diaphragm (11), and terminates in the large intestine (12). A branch of the Large Intestine Meridian diverges at the supraclavicular fossa (9), travels upward across the throat and posterior part of the mandible (13); it then passes through the middle of the cheek (14) and enters into the lower gum (15), and then flows round the upper lip. The left and right flows of the Large Intestine Meridian meet at the philtrum (center of the upper lip) and cross one another. The right meridian crosses to the left side of the face and terminates laterally below the left nostril (16) where the Large Intestine and Stomach Meridians meet.

Symptoms of Imbalance

When the Large Intestine Meridian isn't circulating freely, some of the following difficulties may occur: all kinds of different skin and hair conditions; allergies; swollen cheeks; yellowish eyes; toothaches; nosebleeds; bad breath; numbness in the throat; stiffness in the index finger; swollen, feverish wrists; aches in the upper arms and shoulders; breathing problems; emotional problems such as depression, apathy, and inability to grieve and let go; loss of memory; difficulties in the reproductive organs; problems in the colon such as swelling, blockage, parasites, infection, constipation, diarrhea, gas, pain, and foul smelling stools; abdominal pain and swelling; and hemorrhoids.

You and Your Friends

The function of the large intestine is to remove toxic waste from your body so you won't be poisoned. There are natural intestinal flora which assist in both detoxification and the production of B vitamins. Antibiotics destroy these flora, cause a vitamin B deficiency, and pave the way for female infection. Sugar and nicotine interfere with the natural peristalsis of the large intestine and tend to depress natural evacuation of the colon. Chewing assists peristalsis and gives your saliva time to analyze what you have in your mouth in case it's poisonous so you can spit it out.

If you're given antibiotics from your doctor or dentist, douche once a day with liquid acidophilus and lukewarm water for about three days, which will end all vaginal discharge. Pour a glop (is probably about two tablespoons) of liquid acidophilus into your douche bag, fill the bag with lukewarm water and then douche. Don't use water that's any hotter than this or it will kill the lactobacillus in the acidophilus. Save the rest in your refrigerator. It will keep at the strength on the bottle up until the expiration date. After that, you'll need to use more in your douche bag for it to be effective, or throw it out if it's real old.

When you quit smoking, psyllium seed capsules will help clean the debris from your intestines while you're detoxing from the nicotine. After a period of detoxification, check with your local health food stores for the combination of bentonite and psyllium seed to cleanse the large intestine. When the large intestine begins to function well again, you'll notice a positive difference in your menstrual cycles and period of menstruation as well.

If your Large Intestine Meridian is imbalanced, you may have a terrible complexion that's blotchy, sallow, pale or full of blemishes. You probably have bad breath and gum problems as well. Chances are you're afraid to kiss anyone sensually unless you're holding your breath and standing straight up because your sinuses plug up or you get a runny nose, and besides that you smell and taste funny. Your upper shoulders probably feel like cement which closes your throat and leaves you frigid or non-orgasmic. You may feel like the pits and wonder why no one's attracted to you.

If you have a little baby, this is a good flow to do on him or her if the baby is teething. All mothers know that babies who get cranky during teething also tend to have loose bowel movements. Balance this meridian to facilitate the baby's comfort during teething. Give this flow as a gift to a girlfriend who always avoids eating beans, and seems to spend her paycheck on dental care, throat lozenges, nasal sprays, laxatives, and mouthwash.

LARGE INTESTINE
Left Flow - Sit Right

STEPS	LEFT HAND	RIGHT HAND
1	right 11	left index finger (backside)
2	"	left 19
3	"	left high 19
4	"	right 22
5	"	left 21
6	"	right 13
7	"	right 14
8	"	right high 1
9	"	right 6
10	"	right middle toe
11		
12		
13		
14		
15		
16		

LARGE INTESTINE
Right Flow - Sit Left

STEPS	LEFT HAND	RIGHT HAND
1	right index finger (backside)	left 11
2	right 19	"
3	right high 19	"
4	left 22	"
5	right 21	"
6	left 13	"
7	left 14	"
8	left high 1	"
9	left 6	"
10	left middle toe	"
11		
12		
13		
14		
15		
16		

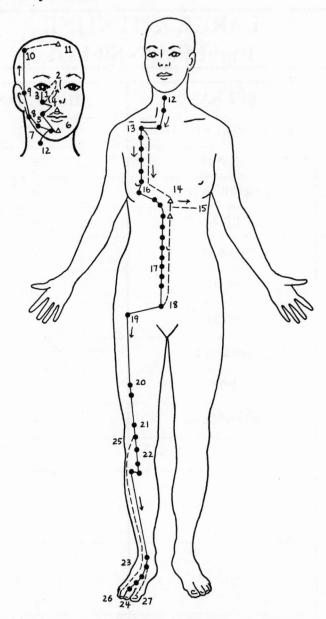

Figure 11: Stomach Meridian

The Stomach And Spleen Meridians
(Surface flow of energy)
Emotions: worry and anxiety

The Stomach Meridian, yang-descending, (figure 11, p. 120) begins its cycle at 7:00 a.m., peaks at 8:00 a.m., and ends at 9:00 a.m. Its path begins at the base of the nose (1) and travels upward along the side of the nose to the root of the nose (2), and from there runs laterally to just below the eye where it unites with the Bladder Meridian (3). It continues downward and then moves laterally to enter and leave the upper gum (4) and travels to the outer corner of the mouth (5) and around to the center below the bottom lip where it meets the Stomach Meridian of the opposite side at CV 24 (6). Then it moves laterally along the lower border of the mandible (7) and proceeds along the angle of the jaw (8) and travels upward in front of the ear (9, reaches the hairline at the temple (10), and travels along the frontal hairline to reach its midpoint (11).

A branch of this meridian emerges from the lower jaw (7) and moves downward along the lateral region of the throat (12) and enters the supraclavicular fossa (13), penetrates the trunk and traverses the diaphragm (14), unites with the stomach and attaches to the spleen (15). A direct extension of the Stomach Meridian continues from the supraclavicular fossa (13) along the mamillary line (16), then medially descends along the sides of the umbillicus (17) and enters the lower abdomen at Stomach 30 (Thoroughfare of Energy) (18) located at the upper border of the inguinal region.

Another branch begins at the pyloric orifice, descends inside the abdomen and joins the original meridian at Stomach 30 (18). From there, the meridian continues to the front of the upper leg (m. rectus femoris) (19, 20), travels through the knee (21) along the antero-lateral aspect of the tibia (22) and extends directly (23) to the dorsum of the foot and moves along the metatarsal of the third toe to the lateral side of the tip of the second toe (24). Another branch leaves the main meridian three inches below the knee (25) and ends at the lateral side of the middle toe (26). Still another branch extends from Stomach 42 and terminates at the medial side of the tip of the big toe where the Stomach and Spleen Meridians meet (27).

Symptoms of Imbalance

When this meridian isn't circulating freely, the following difficulties may occur: insanity (especially when this meridian intermingles with the Bladder Meridian in the eyes); depression; allergies; chapped lips; stuffy nose; nosebleeds; dry mouth; swollen neck; numb throat; goose flesh all over the body; yellowish body; dark complexion; hot, perspiring skin; abdominal bloating; excessive gas; pain: in the stomach, above the breast, in appendix area, in ventral sides of the groin, above the instep, and in back of the dorsal ankle; swollen, aching kneecaps; stiffening of the middle finger; heartburn; nausea and vomiting; gastritis; stenosis (constriction of the opening to the stomach); indigestion; peptic ulcers in esophagus, stomach or duodenum; ptosis (a prolapse of the stomach); the inside of the stomach feels cold and chilly; and excessive talking.

You and Your Friends

The stomach accepts and digests food that is well chewed, compatible with your system and the right temperature. Antacids and alcohol interfere with vomiting spasms and force the opening of the pyloric valve and allow toxic or incompatible substances to enter the intestines. Smoking interferes with the production of gastric juices in the stomach. Marijuana smokers seem to be more susceptible to stomach problems than cigarette smokers, although both are at risk. The stomach and spleen interact to support both digestion and immune processes in the body.

If your stomach meridian is imbalanced, you may be walking around in a state of high anxiety with chapped lips, a stuffy nose, goose bumps and nausea. Besides that, you probably talk too much. You may be a real pain to cook for and wind up drinking your meals at happy hour just to get a few calories and a numb stomach that will accept whatever you feed it. Most people will listen to whatever you have to say for the first few minutes — psychoanalysts will love you.

Give this flow to your roommate if her mouth goes off before her eyes open in the morning and she seems to move frantically about in search of the Malox like it might not be where she left it the night before. She won't have to buy a case of chapstick and nasal inhalents each month, and she'll be able to spend her money for food she can enjoy. Her moods will probably be less cyclical, and when she comes home from work, you can quit throwing your back out from anticipatory ducking. If she's into seizures or insanity, invite several friends and her psychoanalyst over and have a flow party. When her lips get soft and smooth and she can "stomach" eating again, she'll be kinder and more predictable to be with.

STOMACH
Left Flow - Sit Left

STEPS	LEFT HAND	RIGHT HAND
1	left 20	right 21
2	left 21	"
3	left 22	"
4	left 13	"
5	"	right 23
6	left 14	"
7	left 15	"
8	left 8	left 15
9	left middle toe	"
10	left 7	"
11		
12		
13		
14		
15		
16		

STOMACH
Right Flow - Sit Right

STEPS	LEFT HAND	RIGHT HAND
1	left 21	right 20
2	"	right 21
3	"	right 22
4	"	right 13
5	left 23	"
6	"	right 14
7	"	right 15
8	right 15	right 8
9	"	right middle toe
10	"	right 7
11		
12		
13		
14		
15		
16		

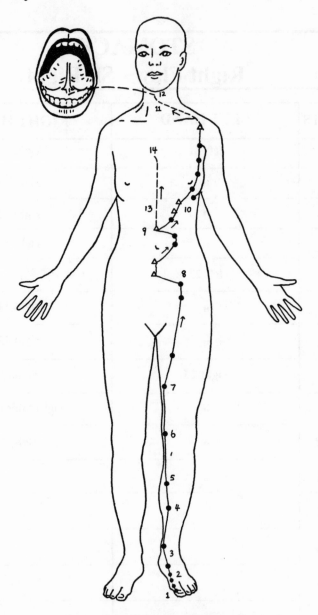

Figure 12: Spleen Meridian

The Spleen Meridian, yin-ascending, (figure 12, p. 126) begins its cycle at 9:00 a.m., peaks at 10:00 a.m., and ends at 11:00 a.m. Its path begins on the medial side of the big toe (1) and runs along the medial side of the foot on the border of the "red and white" skin. After crossing the head of the first metatarsal (2) it reaches the distal edge of the medial malleolus (3) and ascends up the medial front of the lower leg (gastrocnemius m.), (4) along the posterior border of the tibia (5) and crosses and runs in front of the Liver Meridian (6). Then it travels through the anterior medial aspect of the knee and thigh (7) and penetrates the inguinal region into the abdomen (8) where it unites with the spleen and attaches to the stomach (9). From there it passes through the diaphragm (10), and ascending along the esophagus (11) reaches both sides of the root of the tongue and spreads over its lower surface (12). A branch of the Spleen Meridian leaves the stomach (13), passes upward through the diaphragm, and disperses into the heart where the Spleen and Heart Meridians meet (14).

Symptoms of Imbalance

When this meridian isn't circulating freely, some of the following difficulties may occur: pain and hardening of the root of the tongue; problems of the lower esophagus; vomiting right after eating; inconsistent appetite and craving for sweets; acute pains in the stomach; food doesn't seem to descend into the stomach after eating; leucorrhea; reproductive organ problems; pelvic girdle tension; kidney and ureter infections; tumors or inflammation of the uterus; impotency in men; figidity and sterility in women; menstrual irregularities and pain; heavy menstrual bleeding and clotting; constipation; colonic bleeding; parasites; bronchial and lung congestions; allergies; yawning; pneumonia; bad memory; loss of alertness and understanding; cerebral exhaustion (brain fag); excessive imagination; tendency to sleep during the day; body feels heavy; hair falls out; asthenia (low vitality and bodily weakness); white skin (iron anemia); debility; liver, bile, and pancreas ailments; jaundice; enlarged big toes; bunions; odd-shaped toenails; and poor immune function. This meridian is related to vitalization and can be balanced to increase energy in the body.

You and Your Friends

The spleen is the keeper of magnetic iron and hemoglobin, the regulator of red blood cells. It's part of the immune system along with the thymus, lymph nodes and the lymphocyte cells. Together they defend our bodies against foreign or destructive matter and keep us well. The pancreas has a variety of digestive functions and works cooperatively with the stomach, intestines and liver to regulate digestion and sugar balance.

If your spleen meridian is imbalanced, you probably bleed excessively during your periods and may have uterine tumors or endometriosis. There's a good chance that you crave sweets and would rather snack than eat a big meal. Your body may feel heavy and you probably stomp around instead of walking. If this has gone on for some time, you may be losing your hair and feel tired and sleepy all the time.

Give this flow to a girlfriend who yawns all the time and buys Geritol by the case. She'll be more alert the next time you go to dinner, and she'll order a full meal instead of six desserts and four mixed drinks. She'll save money on plumbing bills when there's more hair on her head and less in the drain. Beware — her sex life will improve and she may become pregnant.

This is a great gift for a male friend who's willing but impotent. I don't think this is what they meant when they said, "The way to a man's heart is through his stomach," but what the heck, what's a little retranslation between friends and lovers.

SPLEEN
Left Flow - Sit Left

STEPS	LEFT HAND	RIGHT HAND
1	left 22	right 11
2	left 13	"
3	"	right 23
4	left 14	"
5	left 15	"
6	"	right 25
7	left 1	"
8	"	tailbone
9	left 5	"
10	left 7	"
11		
12		
13		
14		
15		
16		

SPLEEN
Right Flow - Sit Right

STEPS	LEFT HAND	RIGHT HAND
1	left 11	right 22
2	"	right 13
3	left 23	"
4	"	right 14
5	"	right 15
6	left 25	"
7	"	right 1
8	tailbone	"
9	"	right 5
10	"	right 7
11		
12		
13		
14		
15		
16		

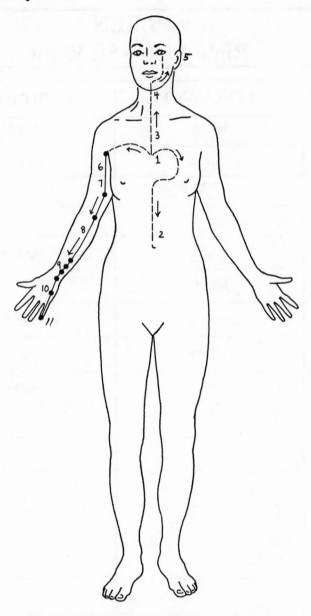

Figure 13: Heart Meridian

The Heart And Small Intestine Meridians
(Deep flow of energy)
Emotions: deep sadness and excessive jolliness from pretense

The Heart Meridian, yin ascending, (figure 13, p. 132) begins its cycle at 11:00 a.m., peaks at noon, and ends at 1:00 p.m. Its path begins in the heart (1) and, after emerging, is connected with the entire system of the heart. The Heart Meridian travels downward from the heart through the diaphragm and communicates with the small intestine (2). A branch originates in the heart (3) and runs upward along the esophagus (4) and joins the eyeball and its surroundings (5). The direct continuation of the Heart Meridian travels upward from the heart into the lung and axilla (6), emerges from the axilla and descends along the posterior border of the medial aspect of the upper arm behind the Pericardium and Lung Meridians (7), crosses the elbow and travels along the medial-posterior region of the forearm (8) to the capitate bone proximal to the palm (9). From there it runs through the medial palm (10) to the inner side of the little finger and terminates at its tip where the Heart and Small Intestine Meridians meet (11).

Symptoms of Imbalance

When this meridian isn't circulating freely, some of the following difficulties may occur: yellowish eyes or red lines in the eyes; difficulty tasting; an enlarged nose that may be red with blemishes and enlarged pores; red on forehead, upper arm and below the eyes; eye congestion; pharyngitis; tonsilitis; yawning; excessive or insufficient perspiration; dry skin; dandruff; loss of hair; pain in axilla, upper arm and ventral elbows; aching, feverish palms; stuttering; speech difficulties; shyness about speaking; lack of keenness and understanding; fear and anxiety; mental exhaustion; phobias; crying and hysteria; oppression (feeling of being weighed down); irritation; dizziness; enlarged, inflamed, or hyperactive heart; blood conditions; ulcers in the small intestine; blocked kidneys; pleurisy; epilepsy; tendency to work strenuously and fast; Parkinson's disease; and many areas of the body are troubled but the focus of the problem can't be pinpointed.

You and Your Friends

The heart pulses as blood moves through it during its rhythmic circulation through arteries and veins. The heart, generally associated with kindness and love, rules and controls the mind. It's considered to be the seat of spiritual faculties and the ruler of wisdom and good judgment. The vascular system is intricately linked with the Triple Warmer and Pericardium Meridians, and together they circulate the vital energy that has been generated within. The effects of "laying-on-of-hands" have been shown to be related to an increase in hemoglobin, the oxygen carrier in the blood. Oxygen and light have long been associated with prana, the life energy.

If your heart meridian is imbalanced, you may have periodic panic attacks and feel somewhat oppressed by the circumstances in your life. If you're still able to bluster your way through life, you may punctuate your speech with laughter that almost sounds musical. Chances are you've begun to accumulate some extra padding on your upper back at the base of your neck, and you may have heavy shoulders and upper arms. If you drink alcohol to get you through it all, you probably have an enlarged nose, ruddy cheeks, broken blood vessels on your face, and tend to perspire excessively.

This is a great gift for a girlfriend who thinks she's important because she knows all the right people, drives a snazzy car, and has a prestigious job. You may have to be there through the grief process when she discovers how inauthentic and empty she's been, and then starts to wonder if she's actually worth anything at all. Kindness, humility and love will heal the pretenses of the past — and save her from high blood pressure and stroke in the future.

HEART
Left Flow - Sit Right

STEPS	LEFT HAND	RIGHT HAND
1	right 3	left little finger (palmside)
2	"	left 19 (little finger side)
3	"	between the 13's
4	"	left 21
5	"	left 20
6	"	left 13
7	right 10	"
8	"	right 15
9	right 23	"
10	"	right 1
11	"	right 6
12	"	right 7
13		
14		
15		
16		

HEART
Right Flow - Sit Left

STEPS	LEFT HAND	RIGHT HAND
1	right little finger (palmside)	left 3
2	right 19 (little finger side)	"
3	between the 13's	"
4	right 21	"
5	right 20	"
6	right 13	"
7	"	left 10
8	left 15	"
9	"	left 23
10	left 1	"
11	left 6	"
12	left 7	"
13		
14		
15		
16		

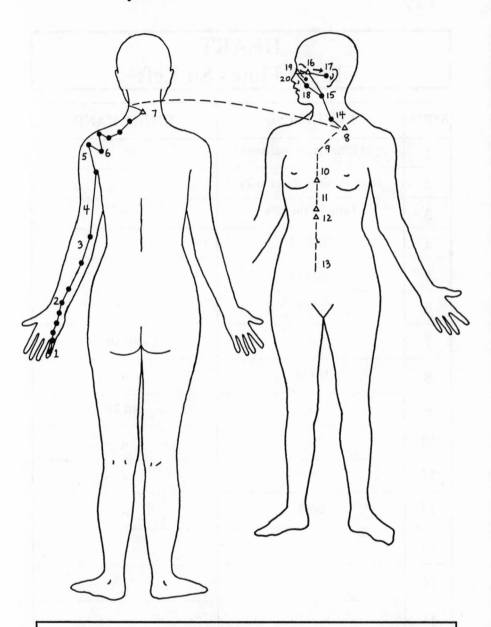

Figure 14: Small Intestine Meridian

The Small Intestine Meridian, yang-descending, (figure 14, p. 138) begins its cycle at 1:00 p.m., peaks at 2:00 p.m., and ends at 3:00 p.m. Its path begins at the tip of the little finger (1) and travels along the lateral dorsal side of the wrist (2). It emerges from the styloid process of the ulna and passes straight upward along the posterior aspect of the forearm to the elbow (3) and passes between the olecranon of the ulna and the medial epicondyle of the humerus to travel along the posterior border of the lateral aspect of the upper arm (4) to the shoulder joint (5). It crosses the scapula (6) and the suprascapular nuchal and cervical region (7) and meets the Governing Vessel Meridian at GV 14 where the right and left Small Intestine Meridians unite. Then the Small Intestine Meridian continues over the shoulder to penetrate the supraclavicular fossa (8) and flows through to be linked with the heart (9). From there it descends along the esophagus (10), passes through the diaphragm (11), to the stomach (12) and finally unites with the small intestine (13).

A branch of the Small Intestine Meridian emerges from the supra-clavicular fossa (8), ascends the neck (14) crosses the mandible (15), continues across the cheek to the lateral canthus (16) and moves to the inside of the ear (17). Another branch emerges from the mandible (15) and travels across the cheek to the infraorbital region and reaches the nose (18). It continues to the medial angle of the eye (19), and then travels laterally to the zygoma (20). At the medial angle of the eye (19), the Small Intestine and Bladder Meridians meet.

Symptoms of Imbalance

When this meridian isn't circulating freely, some the following difficulties may occur: deafness; swollen cheeks; pain in the neck and chin; sore throat; all kinds of ear problems; inability to taste; ringing in the ears; all diseases of the eyes; congestion in the head and neck; pharyngitis; spasms and pains in the throat; an inability to turn the head from side to side; stiff neck; double chin; abscesses in the mouth and upper lip; yellow-tinged eyes that constantly jump about; stiffness and pain in the shoulders and upper arms; colds; bronchitis; asthma; fullness in the chest sometimes accompanied by fever and perspiration; excessive or deficient perspiration; hair problems; skin irritation; dry skin; jaundice; problems in the reproductive organs; impotency and early ejaculation; melancholy; dizziness; nervous breakdown; epilepsy; Parkinson's disease; multiple sclerosis; spontaneous pain in the lower abdomen; and blood conditions.

You and Your Friends

The small intestine analyzes and transforms food into that which will be assimilated and used by the body and that which must be eliminated. In ancient lore, the small intestine is the cauldron in which the gold or elixer of life is made. It's no coincidence that this meridian is linked to the Heart, Pericardium and Triple Warmer Meridians. In astrology, it's a Virgo process of discrimination, and in Tarot, it's the Hermit, card number nine.

If your Small Intestine Meridian is imbalanced, you probably have a double chin, chubby cheeks, difficulty hearing and a stiff neck. You may also wear glasses, and get cold sores and sore throats. People may identify you as the frantic scatterbrain who acts kind of giddy and dizzy at times. You probably have a nice laugh but ramble on like someone cheerfully free-associating. Chances are you've had a hysterectomy.

This is a great flow to do for a chubby-cheeked woman with a hump at the base of her neck who has a double-chin and says "huh?" a lot. She probably lost a husband or a lover years ago and still talks about how lonely she is without a relationship. If she's already wearing a hearing aid (possible long-time imbalance), you may want to give your gift in a series, kind of like a progressive dinner that's eaten and assimilated with change and movement in between each course.

SMALL INTESTINE
Left Flow - Sit Left

STEPS	LEFT HAND	RIGHT HAND
1	left little finger (backside)	right 11
2	left 17	"
3	left 19	"
4	left high back 19	"
5	right 22	"
6	right 21	"
7	right 20	"
8	between the 13's	"
9	right 14	"
10	"	left 9
11	right 15	"
12	right 1 (back of knee)	"
13	right 7	"
14	right fourth toe	"
15		
16		

SMALL INTESTINE
Right Flow - Sit Right

STEPS	LEFT HAND	RIGHT HAND
1	left 11	right little finger (backside)
2	"	right 17
3	"	right 19
4	"	right high back 19
5	"	left 22
6	"	left 21
7	"	left 20
8	"	between the 13's
9	"	left 14
10	right 9	"
11	"	left 15
12	"	left 1 (back of knee)
13	"	left 7
14	"	left fourth toe
15		
16		

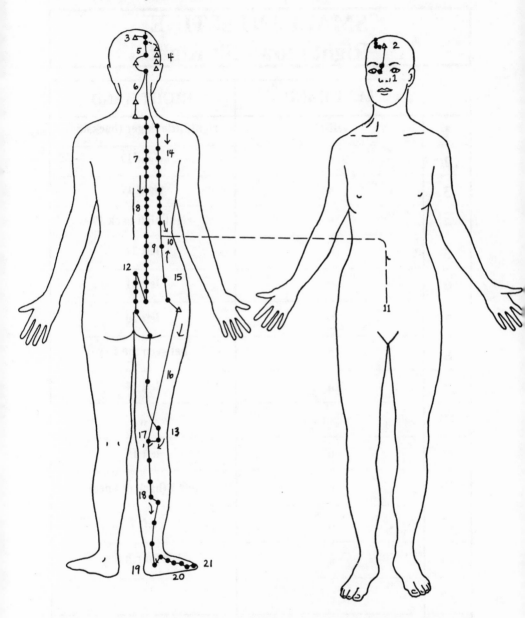

Figure 15: Bladder Meridian

The Bladder And Kidney Meridians
(Deep flow of energy)
Emotions: fear, panic and terror

The Bladder Meridian, yang-descending, (figure 15, p. 144) begins its cycle at 3:00 p.m., peaks at 4:00 p.m., and ends at 5:00 p.m. Its path begins at the inner canthus (1), ascends to the forehead (2) to a junction on top of the skull where the left and right Bladder Meridians meet and communicate with the Governing Vessel at GV 20 (3). From there, a branch moves to the upper rim of the ear (4). The direct continuation of the Bladder Meridian travels from the vertex (3) into the brain (5) and continues through the occipital and nuchal (6) regions to the medial side of the scapula (7), descends parallel to the spine (7) along the medial border of the muscles (8) to the lumbar region (9), where it enters the body cavity through the paravertebral muscles and communicates with the kidney (10), and unites with the bladder (11).

The lumbar branch descends through the gluteal region. At the gluteus maximus, it cuts back (12) and redescends to end in the popliteal fossa (13). The neck branch emerges from the original meridian at the back of the neck and descends along the medial side of the scapula and continues to descend parallel to the spine (14). It crosses the gluteus maximus (15) to the lateral-posterior region of the thigh (16) and continues downward to meet the lumbar branch in the popliteal fossa (17). It then moves downward through the gastrocnemius muscle (18), passes to the lateral side of the lower leg and flows beside the posterior aspect of the lateral malleolus to reach the heel (19). It moves along the fifth metatarsal bone through its tuberosity to the lateral side of the tip of the little toe (20, 21). The Bladder and Kidney Meridians meet at the little toe (21).

Symptoms of Imbalance

When this meridian isn't circulating freely, some of the following difficulties may occur: pressure and pain in the head, especially at the top; migraines; pain in the nape of the neck; aching eyes; nosebleeds; ear problems; myopia and loss of visual acuity; itchy, watery eyes; runny nose; upper jaw pain; eye diseases; tracheal infections; nasal drip; nose ailments; tonsilitis; backaches; hip pain when straightening up; pain in the spine; violent pain in the kidney area; congested kidneys; pain in the anus; hemorrhoids; food doesn't descend properly; vomiting; thighs and calves that are tense and feel as if they're being ripped open; stiff knees; violent pain in the ankles in the achilles tendon; hammertoes; pains in the feet; insanity (especially when it intermingles with the Stomach Meridian); insomnia; crying spells; mental unbalance; little finger bends and won't straighten out; bronchial infections; pneumonia; flu; coughing; muscle cramps; sensitivity to cold and wind; and epilepsy.

Self-Help: For left flow, put your right hand on your left 12 and your left hand on your tailbone, then left center back of knee, then left 16, then left little toe. For right flow, put your left hand on your right 12 and your right hand on your tailbone, then right center back of knee, then right 16, then right little toe.

You and Your Friends

The bladder collects and holds urine between urinations and regulates the flow of water in the body. This system interacts with brain and spine functions as one might guess by the meridian path. If your Bladder Meridian is imbalanced, you probably have backaches, vertebrae that are out of alignment, headaches, hemorrhoids and tight calves. If this has gone on for a long time, you may have hammertoes and migraines. Even if you're tiny, your back muscles probably look like you've been through a Marine boot camp. Chances are you're afraid, even though you try to act like you're not.

Give this flow to a girlfriend who's supporting her local chiropractor. You know, the one with thick glasses who wheezes and clears her throat a lot. You may think she's solid bone when you begin to touch her, so you'll need to keep your anatomy lessons in mind — there are muscles in between the edge of the shoulder blade and the spine, and — no, she's not wearing heavy metal. She'll accuse you of giving her a diuretic during the flow, and may need to excuse herself at least once before you finish. Afterwards, she'll be able to feel her fear, let go, and move in the direction of courage.

BLADDER
Left Flow - Sit Left

STEPS	LEFT HAND	RIGHT HAND
1	right 15	left 25
2	left center back of knee	"
3	left 16	"
4	left little toe	"
5	left 25	left 2
6	"	left 23
7	"	left 9
8	"	left 10
9	"	left 3
10	"	left 11
11	"	left 12
12	"	left 4
13	left 20	"
14		
15		
16		

BLADDER
Right Flow - Sit Right

STEPS	LEFT HAND	RIGHT HAND
1	right 25	left 15
2	"	right center back of knee
3	"	right 16
4	"	right little toe
5	right 2	right 25
6	right 23	"
7	right 9	"
8	right 10	"
9	right 3	"
10	right 11	"
11	right 12	"
12	right 4	"
13	"	right 20
14		
15		
16		

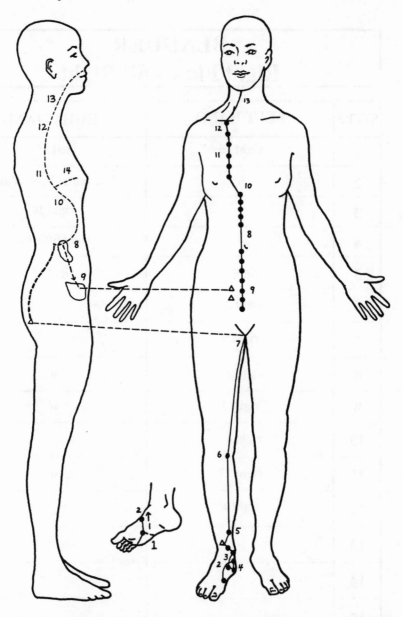

Figure 16: Kidney Meridian

The Kidney Meridian, yin-ascending, (figure 16, p. 150) begins it cycle at 5:00 p.m., peaks at 6:00 p.m., and ends at 7:00 p.m. Its path begins on the plantar surface of the little toe, moves obliquely to the middle of the sole (1), emerges from the inferior aspect of the tuberosity of the navicular bone (2), runs behind the medial malleolus (3), and enters the heel (4). Then it ascends along the medial region of the gastrocnemius muscle (5) and enters the popliteal fossa (6), moves to the medial side and ascends through the medial-posterior region of the thigh (7), penetrates the spine, unites with the kidney (8) and attaches to the bladder (9). A direct continuation of this meridian extends upward from the kidney, passes through the liver (10) and diaphragm, enters the lung (11), and continues along the trachea and larynx (12) up to the root of the tongue (13). A branch emerges from the lung, joins the heart (14) and flows into the chest to connect with the Pericardium Meridian.

Symptoms of Imbalance

When this meridian isn't circulating freely, some of the following difficulties may occur: mouth feels feverish; dry tongue; top part of the esophagus swells; dry and painful throat; all kinds of ear problems; overall face color appears sooty (black) especially on the forehead and the area below the eyes; root of tongue is coated; head and neck congestion; pharyngitis; tonsilitis; eye congestion; feelings of nausea or feeling hungry but no appetite; dizzy feelings upon standing; swollen intestinal walls; pain in the back, buttocks and posterior groin; increased heart pulsation; bloating and water retention; stomach problems; constipation or diarrhea; ascites (fluid in the peritoneal cavity); pain in the navel; gas; fever in the soles of the feet; and icy cold feet up to the knees.

Other symptoms: hysteria; insomnia; nervous breakdown; aversion to speaking; bursts of activity with intense output; inability to stop working; timidity; fear; impatience; suspicion; indecisiveness; lack of will; easily surprised; groaning sounds (sometimes inaudible); all kinds of reproductive problems; air collects in the pelvis; urination is disrupted; all sexual functions disrupted; retention of urine; bladder spasm; dark brown urine (bloody); absence of sex drive; inflammation of sexual organs; hard lumps in the belly; and hernias.

Women: hard and swollen belly like pregnancy; inability to urinate; drooping sexual organs; crooked uterus; sterility; polymenorrhea (frequent menstruation); vulvar pruritis (itching of the vulva); and ovarian infections. Men: involuntary erections; and impotency.

Other symptoms: blood in the expectoration; night sweats; diabetes; jaundice; swelling of parts of the body; frequent yawning; snoring at night; most tranquil and inactive before sundown; early awakening and sleeplessness in early hours; inability to remain seated (fidgets); bones become weak; and functional disruption of the adrenal cortex and thyroid gland. This meridian controls the development of bones, marrow, nails and teeth.

You and Your Friends

The kidneys regulate the quality and quantity of fluid in the body, and select, filter and regulate toxic material in the body as well. But they do much more than this. They also affect all sexual functions, the will-power, and our ability to take action. Ancient lore teaches that the essence of our whole body is released by the kidneys to the semen or ovum during the act of sex.

If your Kidney Meridian is imbalanced, you probably get the fidgets during dinner and find it all but impossible to sit through the movie afterwards. You may have a tipped uterus and feel unfulfilled sexually. Chances are you've never seen your hip bones stick out because your tummy doesn't cave in even when you're slim. More than likely, you bloat at all the wrong times.

Give this gift to a girlfriend who has acne and boils. She'll be the one who's thin with droopy shoulders, and has icy cold hands and feet. Afterwards, she'll quit groaning indecisively as she searches for "white out" for under her eyes, and muk-luks and mittens in the summer. Don't be offended if she restlessly checks her watch, and her legs jerk and twitch through the flow.

KIDNEY
Left Flow - Sit Right

STEPS	LEFT HAND	RIGHT HAND
1	top of the pubic bone	left little toe
2	"	left 6
3	"	left 1
4	left 15	right 25
5	top of the pubic bone	tailbone
6	right 14	"
7	right 13	"
8	right 12	"
9	"	right 20
10	"	right little finger
11		
12		
13		
14		
15		
16		

KIDNEY
Right Flow - Sit Left

STEPS	LEFT HAND	RIGHT HAND
1	right little toe	top of the pubic bone
2	right 6	"
3	right 1	"
4	left 25	right 15
5	tailbone	top of the pubic bone
6	"	left 14
7	"	left 13
8	"	left 12
9	left 20	"
10	left little finger	"
11		
12		
13		
14		
15		
16		

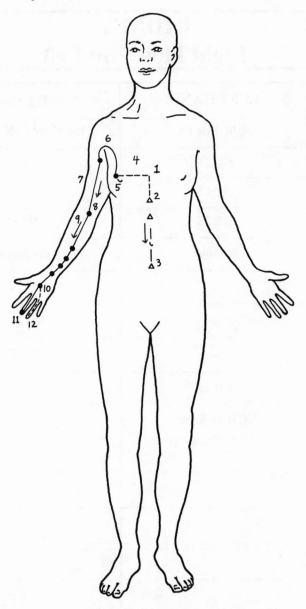

Figure 17: Pericardium Meridian

The Pericardium And Triple Warmer Meridians
(Middle flow of energy)
Feeling States: generation & circulation of vital energy

The Pericardium Meridian, yin-ascending, (figure 17, p. 156) begins its cycle at 7:00 p.m., peaks at 8:00 p.m., and ends at 9:00 p.m. Its path begins in the chest at the middle point between the nipples (if you're flat-chested) (1) and connects to the pericardium, descends through the diaphragm (2) into the abdomen, linking the upper, middle and lower portions of the Triple Warmer (3). A branch travels transversely from the middle point between the nipples through the chest (4) to the ribs and emerges three inches below the axilla (5). It enters the axilla (6), travels along the medial (anterior) aspect of the upper arm between the Lung and Heart Meridians (7) into the hollow of the elbow (8), and continues in the forearm between the tendons of mm. palmaris longus and flexor carpi radialis (9) across the wrist into the palm (10) and along the middle finger to its tip (11). A branch emerges in the center of the palm and runs along the ring finger to its tip (12) where it connects with the Triple Warmer Meridian.

Symptoms of Imbalance

When this meridian isn't circulating freely, some of the following difficulties may occur: arms ache; ventral and/or dorsal elbows tense; underarm swells; palms of the hands become feverish; paralysis of the arms; spasms in the elbows; no feeling in the hands; strong heart pulsations; pricking pain in the heart after a big meal (similar to the feeling of a heart attack); stricture of the heart and death may occur; inflamed heart; and heart feels heavy with sensation of hanging in the chest.

Face becomes flushed; eyes become slanted; face is red and congested; bad breath (rancid); head and neck congestion; weak eyesight; blurry vision; phlegm in the throat; bloody and inflamed eyes; perpetual frown; mouth sores; tongue is swollen and stiff; fullness in the chest and sides; bleeding stomach; soreness in the belly; body literally burns; fever without perspiration; and inability to turn or twist the upper part of the body.

Congested lungs; coughing with aches in the back and chest; paralysis of the legs; incessant thirst; vomiting of phlegm; nausea; strangling apoplexy (stroke); epilepsy; ceaseless and excessive laughter; sudden madness; anger and anxiety for no reason; dazed feeling; shyness; fear of cold and wind; fear of people; cackling, crying or moaning; rambling speech; and sudden loss of speech.

You and Your Friends

This meridian is also known as the organ of Circulation-Sex. It rules the circulation of life energy throughout the body. It also prevents the entry of infectious diseases by promoting the circulation of vital energy throughout the vascular system. This meridian and its inner functions are closely related to the Heart Meridian and the heart itself.

The Pericardium Meridian (called the Diaphragm Meridian in Jin Shin Jyutsu) stabilizes all the superficial pulses and assists all the fundamental, descending flows of energy that move down the front of the body in the Main Central, Major Verticals, and Minor Diagonals. Do this flow when all the superficial (light) pulses are chaotic or beating heavily.

If your Pericardium Meridian is imbalanced, you may look and act like a cackling witch or satanic devil worshiper when you start to laugh and ramble on. If your face gets flushed and people jump when you breathe on them, you may want to get a video of what you looked like at the last party. Your tennis elbow and indigestion may need more attention than you realize.

Good gift for a girlfriend who seems to be going off the deep end. Don't let the enthusiastic talk and excessive jollies fool you; she may be flushed and flustered from more than excitement and fun, fun, fun. She'll be the one everyone's avoiding because she looks and acts weird, and besides, they can't follow what she's talking about. She'll save money on mental health bills and mouthwash, and you'll avoid the hassle of restraining orders when she moves from laughter to rage.

PERICARDIUM
Left Flow - Sit Left

STEPS	LEFT HAND	RIGHT HAND
1	left ring finger (backside)	between the 13's
2	left middle finger (palmside)	"
3	left center of the palm	"
4	left 19	"
5	"	left 14
6	right 25	"
7	right 8 (back of knee)	"
8	right center sole of the foot	"
9		
10		
11		
12		
13		
14		
15		
16		

PERICARDIUM
Right Flow - Sit Right

STEPS	LEFT HAND	RIGHT HAND
1	between the 13's	right ring finger (backside)
2	"	right middle finger (palmside)
3	"	right center of the palm
4	"	right 19
5	right 14	"
6	"	left 25
7	"	left 8 (back of knee)
8	"	left center sole of the foot
9		
10		
11		
12		
13		
14		
15		
16		

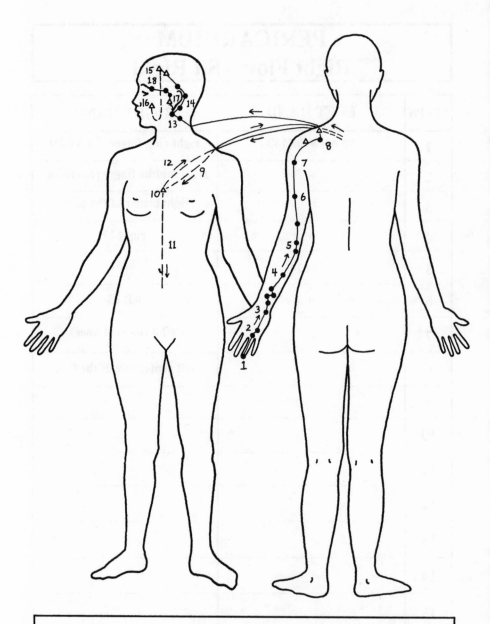

Figure 18: Triple Warmer Meridian

The Triple Warmer Meridian, yang-descending, (figure 18, p. 162) begins at the ulnar side of the tip of the ring finger (1), runs between the fourth and fifth metacarpal bones (2, 3), up the dorsal side of the wrist through the dorsal side of the forearm between the radius and ulna (4) to the tip of the elbow (5). It continues along the lateral aspect of the upper arm (6) to the shoulder (7) where it meets the Gall Bladder Meridian (8). Then it travels to the supraclavicular fossa (9) and penetrates into the chest, particularly its sternal region. Within the chest, it attaches to the pericardium (10), descends through the diaphragm down to the abdomen and successively links the upper, middle and lower parts of the Triple Burning Spaces of the Triple Warmer Meridian (11).

A branch emerges from the sternal region (12), ascends to the supraclavicular fossa (9), moves to unite with GV 14, flows along the lateral cervical and nuchal regions (13), passes along the posterior border of the ear (14), descends in front of the ear (15) and travels downward to the cheek and terminates in the infraorbital region (16). Another branch originates from behind the ear, enters into the ear (17), emerges in front of it, and descends through G.B. 3, and the former branch and turns and ascends to the outer canthus where it connects with the Gall Bladder Meridian (18).

Symptoms of Imbalance

When this meridian isn't circulating freely, some of the following difficulties may occur: headaches; migraines; eyelashes curled inward; white veil on the eyes; upturned eyes (sanpaku); nosebleeds; cervical neck problems; ears with ringing, buzzing or pain; swollen cheeks and throat; numb throat; aching or festering in the outer canthus (outer edge of eye); pain in the cheeks, back of ears, gums and teeth; teeth feel tight; throat infections; dry mouth; unclear hearing; sudden deafness; mastoiditis; infections of middle ear and eustachian canal; red, inflamed eyes; and eye infections.

Pain in the upper arm and dorsal side of the elbows; ring finger stiffens and won't bend; inability to flex or extend elbows; pain and stiffness in the shoulders; backbone pains in the heart region; inability to twist the chest or pain when turning; shoulders feel heavy; sore shoulder blades; duodenal ulcers; internal parasites; moaning; fear; rambling thoughts and fantastic dreams; suddenly unable to speak; and inability to recognize anyone.

Perspiration when sleeping; rheumatism; pain in the joints; arthritis; poor adjustment to temperature changes; icy limbs; fever without perspiration; sudden acute heart pain; epilepsy with vomiting of phlegm; no appetite; empty vomiting; cholera; convulsions; dizziness; fever; inflamed lymph glands and nodes; and flu.

You and Your Friends

This meridian is also called the Three Heaters. It's in charge of generating vital energy in the body through breathing, digestion, and the sexual fires. It works cooperatively with the lungs, small intestine and kidneys to generate vitality, and interacts supportively with the Heart and Pericardium meridians so they can circulate it. This natural process regulates our temperature so we can stay warm in the winter and cool during the summer. Artificial cooling and heating interfere with the functions of this meridian.

This meridian will stabilize all the deep pulses. It's called the Umbilicus Meridian in Jin Shin Jyutsu and is used to balance all the ascending flows of energy in the Main Central, Major Verticals, and Minor Diagonals. Do this flow when all the deep pulses are chaotic or beating too heavily. All flows of energy go to the umbilicus for energy. This area is called the tan t'ien, the hara or the kath. All reproductive energy is supported by this flow. It's the flow of life (light) to fill the fountain of youth.

If your Triple Warmer Meridian is imbalanced, the base of your skull is probably very tight, and your chiropractor keeps adjusting your atlas and axis at the top, and your tailbone at the bottom. You may have astral travels in which you sense a gurgling, rumbling sound at the back of your head, and see very vivid colors and geometric patterns. These travels may leave you feeling sexually aroused. You probably have pain and tension in your upper arms, and see your dentist regularly — or need to. Chances are that your ears ring or you have difficulty listening, or remembering what you've heard.

Give this flow as a gift to a girlfriend who can't get cool in the summer or warm enough in the winter. She'll be the one with aching joints who's considering a hysterectomy after her dental bill is paid. Afterwards, her tennis game will improve and she'll be much more coherent over lunch. As her joints relax, she'll start to let go of past grudges and pain, and be more present when you're together.

TRIPLE WARMER
Left Flow - Sit Left

STEPS	LEFT HAND	RIGHT HAND
1	left ring finger (backside)	right 4
2	left high back 19	"
3	left 11	"
4	first thoracic	"
5	left 20	"
6	left 22	"
7	between the 13's	"
8	right 14	"
9	"	left 14
10	right 23	"
11	"	left 15
12	right 25	"
13	right center back of knee	"
14	right 24	"
15		
16		

TRIPLE WARMER
Right Flow - Sit Right

STEPS	LEFT HAND	RIGHT HAND
1	left 4	right ring finger (backside)
2	"	right high back 19
3	"	right 11
4	"	first thoracic
5	"	right 20
6	"	right 22
7	"	between the 13's
8	"	left 14
9	right 14	"
10	"	left 23
11	right 15	"
12	"	left 25
13	"	left center back of knee
14	"	left 24
15		
16		

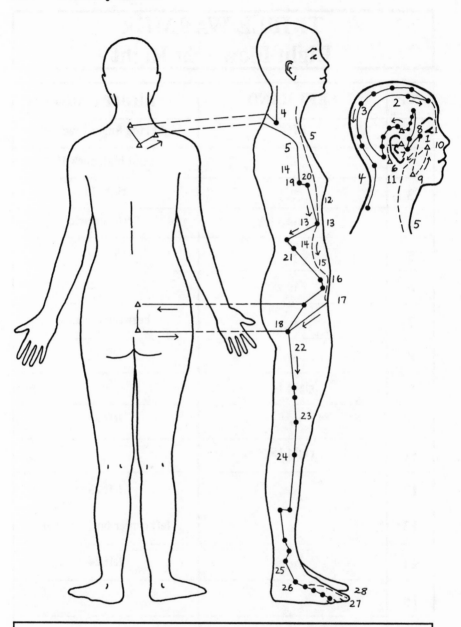

Figure 19: Gall Bladder Meridian

The Gall Bladder And Liver Meridians
(Middle flow of energy)
Emotions: anger, frustration and rage

The Gall Bladder Meridian, yang-descending, (figure 19, p. 168) begins its cycle at 11:00 p.m., peaks at midnight, and ends at 1:00 a.m. Its path begins at the outer canthus (1), travels down then up to the hairline, then zigzags down behind the ear and back up to the hairline and over the forehead where a branch continues to the root of the nose. From the forehead, it moves upward to the hairline (2), first obliquely backward and then descends to a point above the ear (3), continues downward to the region behind the ear and nuchal and lateral cervical regions (4) and arrives at the shoulder, unites with GV 14, meets with the Triple Warmer Meridian and runs downward to the supraclavicular fossa (5).

A branch travels from the region behind the ear, enters the ear (6), emerges in front of it (7) and arrives at the region behind the lateral canths (8). Another branch diverges at the lateral canthus (1) to move downward to St. 5 situated on the mandible (9) and then meets the Triple Warmer Meridian in the infraorbital region (10), descends to again cross the mandible (11) and lateral cervical region into the supraclavicular fossa (5). From there it descends into the middle of the chest, passes through the diaphragm (12), attaches to the liver (13), unites with the gall bladder (14) and then descends along the inner sides of the ribs (15) and the abdominal peritoneum to St. 30 near the femoral artery at the inguinal region (16), then moves in a median direction along the border of pubic hair (17) and travels sideways into the joint of the hip (18).

The original meridian travels straight downward from the supraclavicular fossa (5), passes in front of the axilla (19) and from there, moves along the lateral aspect of the chest (20) passing through the free ends of the floating ribs and the abdomen (21), unites with Bladder Meridian and GV 1, and from there into the hip joint (18). It continues downward along the lateral aspect of the thigh (22) to the lateral side of the knee (23) and passes through the anterior aspect of the fibula (24) directly to its lower end (25), continues anterior to the lateral malleolus (26) along the dorsum of the foot to enter the space between the fourth toe and little toe and terminates at the lateral side of the tip of the fourth toe (27). A branch emerges from the dorsum of the foot and runs between the muscles of the big toe and second toe, and from there it crosses the first and second metatarsals to the distal portion of the big toe at Liv. 1, turns around and passes through the nail across the nail bed to the hair on the second joint of the big toe where the Gall Bladder and Liver Meridians meet (28).

Symptoms of Imbalance

When this meridian isn't circulating freely, the following difficulties may occur: bitter taste in the mouth; goose flesh on the face; pain in the sides of the head, chin and corner of the eyes; bumps like gravel, peas or marbles appear at the top of the neck; poor eyesight; hard to see in the bright daylight; dazzled by bright light; itchy eyes; headaches; migraines; inflamed eyes beginning at the outer corners; bad gums; loose teeth; contracted jaws making it difficult to chew; swollen cheeks; uncontrolled foaming at the mouth; stiff tongue with dry mouth; buzzing in the ears; sudden deafness; nose, ear and eye infections; spasm in the windpipe; tonsillitis; face color is dusty, wan or livid; and tight, bound feeling around the head and chin.

Inability to turn to the side when lying down; pain under the breasts, and in the chest and pleura; enlarged heart; pain in the heart; pain under the liver at the sides and in the heart which prevents twisting around; dorsal sides of legs are hot; pain under the arms, in the hips, dorsal knees, shins, ankles and joints; the ring finger bends and won't straighten out or move; very hot palms and feet without perspiration; swollen armpits; bronchitis; asthma; respiratory diseases; fullness in the chest and difficulty breathing; skin has no luster; jaundice; acute bile duct inflammation; liver ailments; constipation; and problems in intestines and bile ducts.

Constant sadness; madness (the person runs constantly); fear of cold and wind (even cold food and water); uremia; acute kidney infection; hypertension; genital infection; inflamed testicles or uterus; water retention; reproductive organ infection in females which results in a heavy discharge; big sighs (person sighs a lot); perspiring yet cold; muscle problems; muscular dystrophy; apoplexy from blockage of a blood vessel causing loss of bodily functions and paralysis of the four limbs; dizziness; epilepsy; anemia; intermittent fever and chills; profuse perspiration; and low level of activity (lowering of the basal metabolism). This meridian along with the Liver Meridian assists women during childbirth and post partum recovery.

You and Your Friends

The gall bladder stores and concentrates bile for digestion and elimination. When it isn't functioning well, it's nearly impossible to digest fats and meat, and the intestines become foul and unable to void fecal matter properly.

If your Gall Bladder Meridian is imbalanced, you probably look like you're going to bite someone and your chiropractor's getting rich from adjusting your TMJ. Chances are that your hips and lower back ache and you get a tight band of pain around your head. You probably have knots on the back of your neck that get worse as your dental bills get higher. People tend to get out of your way when you get gassey and look like you're foaming at the mouth from saliva that shows when you talk.

Give this flow to a girlfriend with a crooked mouth who sighs a lot and always looks like she's dusty. You know, the one with a hitch in her hip and rocks in her calves who seems to snarl when she smiles and always looks like she's going to punch you. Afterwards, she may wake you at midnight and swear she's in labor even though she's not pregnant, but when she does get pregnant, her delivery will be much easier.

GALL BLADDER
Left Flow - Sit Right

STEPS	LEFT HAND	RIGHT HAND
1	right 12	right 19
2	"	left 20
3	"	left 21
4	"	left 22
5	"	left 13
6	"	left 14
7	right 9	"
8	right 2	"
9	"	tailbone
10	"	left 25
11	"	left 8
12	"	left 16
13	"	left fourth toe
14	"	left 7
15		
16		

GALL BLADDER
Right Flow - Sit Left

STEPS	LEFT HAND	RIGHT HAND
1	left 19	left 12
2	right 20	"
3	right 21	"
4	right 22	"
5	right 13	"
6	right 14	"
7	"	left 9
8	"	left 2
9	tailbone	"
10	right 25	"
11	right 8	"
12	right 16	"
13	right fourth toe	"
14	right 7	"
15		
16		

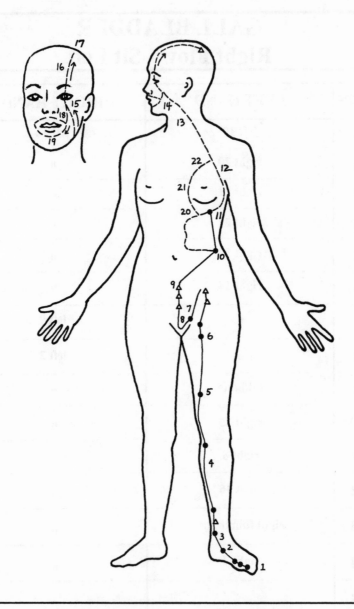

Figure 20: Liver Meridian

The Liver Meridian, yin-ascending, (figure 20, p. 174) begins its cycle at 1:00 a.m., peaks at 2:00 a.m., and ends at 3:00 a.m. Its path begins on the dorsum of the big toe in the hair of its second joint (1), moves across the dorsum of the foot (2) and passes one inch in front of the medial malleolus (3). From there, it crosses the Spleen Meridian and continues upward behind the Spleen Meridian through the medial region of the popliteal fossa (4), travels along the medial region of the thigh (5, 6) up to the pubic hair border in the inguinal region (7), and then travels around the genitals (8). From there it ascends the lower abdomen (9) and travels around the stomach (10), and the left path unites with the liver and attaches to the gall bladder; the right path unites with the spleen and attaches to the pancreas. The meridian then passes through the diaphragm (11), radiates along the ribs (12) and travels along the region behind the trachea and larynx (13) to the pharynx and the fauces (14), connects with the eye (15), then ascends to the forehead (16) and ends at the vertex at GV 20 (17). A branch leaves the eye (15), runs downward to the mandible (18) and surrounds the inner surface of the lips (19). Another branch travels from the liver (20), passes through the diaphragm (21) and ends in the lung where the Liver and Lung Meridians meet (22).

Symptoms of Imbalance

When this meridian isn't circulating freely, some of the following difficulties may occur: dry throat; inability to swallow; nearsightedness; weak and dirty facial color; crooked mouth; yellow-green or greenish complexion; swollen lips; aching hips; chest feels full and tight; females develp swelling and bloating in the lower abdomen; males develop abdominal pains; acute pain in the heart and liver area with an inability to bend forward or backward; unbearable warmth in the chest; pain in the navel; very hard belly; low belly pains which interfere with walking; feeling of a small animal running around in the abdomen; sensation of heat in the lower abdomen; and bloated stomach.

Nausea; vomiting; diarrhea; constipation; dispepsia; gas; increased appetite but food won't digest; pus and blood in the stools; vomiting of blood; bile duct problems; colic; fits of coughing; pleurisy; swollen knees; icy cold arms and legs; aching in internal thighs; all liver illnesses such as hepatitis or cirrhosis; diabetes; gout; excessive sighing; epilepsy; gaunt appearance; great thirst; tuberculosis following excesses and binges; excess or lack of perspiration; and fever.

Constant anger; hysteria; insomnia or sleepiness; enuresis (bedwetting); all kinds of reproductive organ problems. Women: swelling of the lower abdomen and pelvis; urine retention; ovarian infections; vulvar pruritis; uterine hemorrhage; post-partum infections; black blood discharge after childbirth; and difficult childbirth delivery. Men: small hernias in the genitals; infection in the penis; and absence of sperm.

You and Your Friends

If your Liver Meridian is imbalanced, you probably have two scowl lines between your brows, a hard little mound for a belly and PMS. There's a good chance that you're nearsighted and like to stay up late and sleep in a bit in the morning. You probably get defensive when someone says "good morning," and sometimes your friends think you're a bitch. You may scratch your crotch when no one's looking and sigh a lot when you're trying to make a point.

Do this flow on a girlfriend who thinks it's funny to watch you hit the deck from her biting wit and well-timed delivery. She's the one with paranoia, hysterics, and a "pissed-off" attitude during PMS who probably needs a Kidney Flow as well. Remember to touch lightly—don't dig in with your nails. Your friendship will improve immensely and you may even discover she's likable. Afterwards, she'll think a miracle happened, because if she's out of her teens, she's probably as tired of her "Jekyl and Hyde" behavior as everyone else.

This is a great gift for a pregnant girlfriend before she delivers and again after the baby is born. Include a Gall Bladder Flow before and after as well.

LIVER
Left Flow - Sit Right

STEPS	LEFT HAND	RIGHT HAND
1	top of the pubic bone	left 7
2	"	left 5
3	"	left 1
4	right 14	left 15
5	"	left 9
6	right 13	"
7	left 12	"
8	"	right 22
9	"	left 20
10	"	between the 14's
11		
12		
13		
14		
15		
16		

LIVER
Right Flow - Sit Left

STEPS	LEFT HAND	RIGHT HAND
1	right 7	top of the pubic bone
2	right 5	"
3	right 1	"
4	right 15	left 14
5	right 9	"
6	"	left 13
7	"	right 12
8	left 22	"
9	right 20	"
10	between the 14's	"
11		
12		
13		
14		
15		
16		

5

Releasing Tension: Dissolving Trauma

Release work is another phase of the magical process of doing Flows. Whenever we practice the Touch of Silence, we become present in the light and come into contact with our inner teacher. Whenever we touch ourself or others with kindness, everyone who has been touched becomes changed. The art of healing is a meditation on the art of living.

Three Fundamental Flows: To recap a bit, the first part of this work begins with knowledge about the three fundamental flows of energy in the Main Central, the Major Verticals, and the Minor Diagonals. At the most basic level, we're working toward a balanced movement of energy in these paths, and we're using the points along the Main Central and Major Verticals to do this. These paths of energy are responsive to a life-cycle rather than a twenty-four hour phase of motion.

Fourteen Main Meridians: The next part begins with a recognition that other paths of energy are born out of these three fundamental ones. These paths move through the tissues and cells of organs, muscles and nerves to work cooperatively as total organ-systems, and are named accordingly the Liver Meridian, the Bladder Meridian, and so on. All of these paths of energy circulate constantly, but each one has a two-hour phase within a twenty-four hour cycle in which energy is more available to it for repair and maintenance of its total system.

Although we're always touching the points along the Main Central or Major Verticals, when we touch certain points in different sequences or patterns, we're able to restore a balanced circulation of energy in the fourteen meridians.

Release Tension In Blocked Points: As we touch, sometimes we'll notice extreme tension in certain areas. These points will feel dead, hard and unyielding. When we discover areas like this, it helps to release these points first and then go back and read the pulses. Sometimes one or two blocked points will interfere with the flow of energy in five or six meridians. Once these points are relaxed, it's easier to discover which meridian is the source of the problem by re-reading the pulses.

Release Tension In Lower Body First: The purpose of all flow work is to restore a balanced circulation of energy in the mind-body. Whenever we're releasing areas of tension, we must first check to see if the energy is flowing in the legs and lower body. Then we need to check for a free flow of energy down the front of the body. And finally, we can release the back of the body. All of the fundamental flows of energy move up the back and down the front of the body.

Some Points Are More Controlling Than Others And Must Be Released Last: The major control points (4, 12, 11 and 3) are in the head and neck, and the major crossroads for deep tension (3, 9 and 10) are in the upper back and shoulders where the vertical flows of energy cross the horizontal ones. If these are deep-released first, the energy will try to move up the back and over the head, and it might not be able to flow freely down the front of the body into the legs. It's best to release the legs first (1, 5, 6, 7, and 8), and then take a quick touch check of points 13, 14, and 15 on the front if you're not sure. If some of these front points are blocked, do a quick release of the ones that need it.

Tension Everywhere: If a person seems tense all over, you may need to focus primarily on the legs and front of the body, and get the back during another session. If they're *real* tense all over, work lightly all over the body using any of the three fundamental Flows or the meridian Flows that seem to be out of balance. Aim for movement to restore a balanced circulation in the body rather than deep releasing which may add to their distress.

How To Touch: The way you touch is the same no matter which Flows you're doing. Your touch is always one of kindness. It's the "touch of silence" that's barely perceptible if at all. You should not be poking, grabbing, digging, wiggling, forcing, coercing and violating. When you touch someone very lightly with kindness, your mind-body will fill with the light of creative energy until it overflows to surround you and come into contact with the other person. When this happens, their mind-body will fill with the creative light and it will begin to move within them. This creative light will recognize itself and seek a union with itself in the light from your fingers as you touch the points.

Hands Like Jumper Cables: As soon as this happens, movement will begin because your hands are like jumper cables when you use them simultaneously to touch. Your right hand sends the energy and your left hand receives it. You'll know when this movement happens because you'll be moved deeply and compassionately by the experience. It will feel like a gentle rhythmic dance that's peaceful and endless. You may even breathe a sigh of relief when the tension releases in them, and eventually you'll learn *that it will always release in them whenever the energy is able to move freely through you.*

What Your Fingers Will Feel: It will feel different on your fingers as well. Before movement begins, the area will feel dull, lifeless, and possibly hard and tense. As movement does begin, you'll feel little pulsations, and possibly squiggles, electrical buzzes and shocks. When it's moving well, it will feel more like a smooth continuous flow that feels peaceful to the fingertips. As it begins to deep-release, the area will sink in and pull at your fingertips like a vortex of energy. Unless you're relaxed, it might be difficult to keep touching the area. If you're tense, it will be hard for you to handle the increased movement of energy and you'll become hot or feel very taut, which will cause your fingers to be repelled instead of attracted to the spot. The energy may begin to back up into your arms and leave them feeling heavy and numb.

When you're relaxed, you can stay in touch with the area that is deep releasing and you'll begin to feel the differences between a surface flow of energy, the middle flow, and the deep one that goes clear to the bones and back out to the surface. While the area is releasing, you may feel little stingy, scattered stuff at your fingertips that usually means the person's system is toxic. Or you may feel actual pain in your fingertips which means that real pain is releasing somewhere in the body even if the person can't feel it yet. This pain usually feels like sharp, acute flashes on the fingertips rather than the one long, continuous, knifelike feeling which occurs at the bottom depth of deep releasing.

Relaxation: As tension releases, you'll feel the shift in your body and at your fingertips, and the person you're touching will look, feel and behave differently as well. She'll feel the energy move through her body like squiggles, warmth, a flow of warm water, twitches, or like a little bug crawling across her cheek. As a deep release occurs, her diaphragm will relax and her breath will move into her abdomen. You'll hear gurgles in her abdomen. She may feel and/or hear her vertebrae move into alignment. Other areas may reposition themselves as well when muscles relax. She may move in and out of sleep. Visions and memories will surface into her awareness like a dream state. She will be easily startled by abrupt movement or noise just like someone in deep meditation would be.

Read The Pulses And Observe: Afterwards, her pulses will be smooth, balanced and pleasingly rhythmic. She will feel deeply relaxed and will appear to have had a refreshing nap. Her face will look soft, youthful and relaxed. She'll be a bit spacey and not in touch with conversation that requires logic and data processing. She may want to nap afterwards, and she'll probably sleep much more deeply and restfully that night.

Twenty-Four To Forty Eight Hours After The Session: Within twenty-four to forty-eight hours afterwards, she'll be more sensitive because she'll have feelings in those areas that were blocked and tense, and because she'll be more conscious and aware of everything than she was before. Her senses may seem more acute, and she may have pain and discomfort as tissues heal and toxins leave her body. Some people are sleepier than usual for several days. Other people have dramatic shifts in posture, skin tone, elimination of waste, or moods and insight. Pain and discomfort, and shifts in appearance and feeling may continue as long as three to seven days. The most acute stage is within the first three days, and the obvious part of the process almost never continues past a week.

What can you expect? Almost anything. The body is rather ingenious about what it needs to do to heal. Each person is unique and aside from the fairly common examples above, I've seen almost as many different ways to heal as there are people. If you tell people to expect something specific, you may influence the outcome unnecessarily.

Remain positive and supportive, and inform them that they may or may not be uncomfortable for a couple days. I usually tell people to call me if anything happens that seems strange and unfamiliar enough to concern them. Almost always, just knowing they can call me is enough for them to feel safe.

Medical Questions: When I get calls from people who have medical concerns, I ask them to call their physicians. Questions like, "What if I have cancer?" or "Do you think I have a bleeding ulcer?" or "Is it possible that I have a tumor in my brain?" should be referred immediately to a physician. The question itself is enough to let me know that the imagery is there even if the ailment isn't — and the Touch of Silence is not about trying to cure disease. When people heal, it's a total mind-body process. Any focus upon a specific disease is inappropriate unless that person has been diagnosed with having that disease and wishes to address that diagnosis within the context of total healing. Healing is focused upon health and wellness, not on disease and illness.

People who wish to rule out certain diseases in their bodies should do so, and if they need medical assistance, they should get it. But when they seek support through something like gentle touch healing either as an adjunct to medical intervention or instead of regular medical treatment, they're seeking contact with their inner light and wisdom and trusting that as they become whole and healthy, their bodies will know exactly what to do to heal. They're learning something different about themselves by giving and receiving kindness, and their decision to heal and the way they choose to do this must be made by them, not by someone else. Never tell someone not to seek medical assistance if that's what they choose to do, and never make that decision for them if they're having difficulty deciding for themselves.

What's Holding And What's Releasing?

When someone releases tension from trauma and conditioning, what's actually happening? The most obvious physical changes are muscle relaxation. When muscles relax, the skeletal structure moves into a more normal position, and blood circulates more freely and moves into tissues to cleanse them of debris. The central nervous system is affected as well. People begin to think and behave differently, and their moods and attitudes shift. Overall, people become more flexible in their brain-body and discover new perspectives in thinking and new options for behavior.

There's a temptation to rely solely on some obvious methods to relax the muscles (massage), re-align the vertebrae (chiropractic), and alter the brain (drugs). Almost everyone has at one time or another used all of these methods to relax and for immediate relief from physical or emotional pain. Very often, these methods are appropriate and expedient. However, if you've come to rely on these methods as the sole solution for healing, you might miss the total picture.

You can relax a muscle over and over, or see your chiropractor three times a week, or take drugs or nutrients to stabilize your brain-body chemistry, and all of it will work up to a point, but none of it will replace your need to shift and heal more fundamentally. It's both expedient and wise to stabilize the brain-body system the best you can while you also heal the mind-body system. However, you can't use external interventions exclusively or to an extreme and expect to heal. For example, if you're abusing drugs, you can practice meditation, prayer and kindness forever and ever and still create a mess in your life, because the subliminal messages about yourself and how you really feel still get projected into your mind field even though you appear to be tranquil or stable.

When we release through gentle touch healing, we're releasing illusions about reality so we can become sane, healthy and conscious. Lies and distortions about reality get reflected in our bodies. We can travel the earth in search of great physicians and healers and never get well. Others can catalyze us so we can catch a glimpse of the light and then begin to move along its path of wisdom and healing, but no one can do the moving for us.

Tell your story a thousand times if you have to. Whatever happened probably hurt terribly, and I'm sure it wasn't fair. But someday knock on other doors and begin to listen. Then reach out your hands and your heart in kindness wherever you go. Suffering is a universal human condition that only feels solitary when we lock ourselves into a darkness sustained by resentment and fear. No one escapes suffering and each of us needs and deserves compassion from one another. Our anger and hatefulness toward one another are little more than our recognition of a personal pain reopened by fresh injuries to a universal wound (the struggle for simultaneous individuation and connectedness) shared by all human beings.

As spiritual beings birthed into flesh, we live in a physical womb that sometimes feels like a prison without chance for parole. Seeking release, one day we discover, *My mind, not my body, leaves me imprisoned. This warden of limits separates me. This guardian of my fantasies hold the keys to flight and freedom. Loosed from its bondage, I now see that all movement is ultimately of the mind, not the body.*

If release is in the mind-body and movement continues by living in the light, why touch with the fingers at all? Touching not only provides a focus of attention for both people and real human contact, it also embodies the principles of magic through two physical vehicles in a non-doing process. It's a ritual that enables both people to get out of the way so magic can happen. However, it's not just a fanciful ritual, a harmless pastime. It's a ritual organized around fundamental principles that silently teaches both people about life.

It's also like the ritual dance between lovers who say, *Oh touch me where I dare not, know not. I give you permission to awaken me to the mystery of myself. In turn, I touch your darkness and illuminate your soul. I trust you as I reveal myself to you and delight in knowing you are more than what was known before.*

As you feel, light enters your areas of darkness and dissolves your physical and emotional pain. As you feel, dark attitudes, memories and judgments dissolve in the light of consciousness. As you feel, dark images from denial, fear and revenge release into the light of healing and melt like a dream barely remembered. As you feel, you become spiritually connected with yourself and others *and* able physically to care for yourself and others. When you practice the silent ritual of touch healing, you will practice the steps we all take when we begin our journey on the path that returns to the light.

Touch Of Silence As A Way Of Life

Let's look at some examples of how "flow work" is similar to living and the ways in which we relate with ourselves and others.

1. When you touch someone, you touch softly and then gently pull back ever so slightly as you become kind and receptive — and the energy begins to flow between you.

Like life, you reach out and touch others with kindness and then gently pull back just a bit to listen and be receptive — and the energy flows between you.

2. If you push and poke when you touch, the area tenses more and the energy stops flowing between you. To create a polarity between you now so the energy can flow, one of you will have to be more than, better than, bigger than or more forceful, and the other person will have to be less than, inferior, smaller, or weak.

Like life, if you begin to push on people to get your way, they'll resist and you'll become spiritually disconnected. To recreate a polarity between you so you can connect, one of you will have to violate and the other be violated — or one of you will become the nurturing caretaker and the other one will become needy and dependent.

3. When you're touching someone during a healing session, your mind field interacts with the mind field of the other person, and your thoughts get reflected in the person you're touching. We've experimented with this one in class and the results are astounding. Try it for yourself with a partner who is willing to experiment. Hold thoughts and attitudes of anger and hatred, and afterwards, ask your partner what they felt and picked up from you. Then try it with love and kindness or sexual seduction, or thoughts about how fat and ugly the other person is. You can't get away with a thing!

Like life, whatever's in your mind field will get reflected in the way people treat you and the image they walk away with after being with you. You may bring out the worst in people who are generally kind, or you may reveal the nasty side of people who might never have treated *you* that way if you hadn't invited it through your mind field.

4. When we release through touch healing, we discover that our bodies hold distorted patterns because our thoughts and attitudes have been destructive, and that our bodies will heal when we quit judging, blaming and resenting.

Like life, we discover that our circumstances and relationships become distorted when our thoughts and attitudes are destructive, and that our relationships heal and our circumstances improve when we quit judging, blaming and resenting.

5. Touch healing is more apt to reveal the ways in which we've participated in our tension and distress, while absent healing (prayer offered from a distance) may leave us with the notion that we can continue to think and act unkindly without realizing the connections between our distress and our behavior.

Like life, we tend to wake up when we're faced with real life crises, while we may fantasize and theorize indefinitely when we successfully remove ourselves from the arena, and miss the connections between our crises and the way we think and feel.

6. During healing, we discover that when we release the tension and grieve and let go, we heal.

Like life, we discover that when we release judgment, anger and blame, grieve and let go, our relationships heal.

7. When you touch another with kindness, the energy moves through both of you and you both heal and transform.

Like life, each time you're kind to people, you receive the very experience you're giving, and both you and the people around you begin to transform and heal.

8. When we practice touch healing, we notice that as we release tension, old pictures of pain and self-destructive imagery also release. We discover the relationship between our imagery and our health when we begin to recognize that destructive images get stored in the cells of our bodies.

Like life, we soon discover that the ways in which we picture ourselves and others eventually come true in our relationships and circumstances. We also learn that our imagery shifts as our attitudes change, and along with a positive shift in attitude and imagery, our relationships and circumstances become healthier and more satisfying.

9. When we touch others who are tense, we discover that their tension dissolves when we're relaxed and kind, but if we're unable to relax, they probably won't give up their tension either.

Like life, when we judge and blame, people continue to be destructive toward us, but when we release and let go in forgiveness and kindness, they become kind and forgiving toward us as well.

10. When we touch people who are continually drugged, we often notice their difficulty in sustaining healing changes in their bodies even though the pulses may become balanced after each session. Already dependent upon drugs, they become dependent upon being touched by someone else, because they're unable to integrate the experience consciously and let it come from within.

Like life, when we continue to take drugs we are avoiding the experience of pain, grieving and letting go. When this happens, we become dependent upon external soothing and relief, which leads to addictive relationships with others.

11. When we touch people and they begin to release and heal, it's virtually impossible not to share in the joy of this experience. However, if we become too excited, or too informative about what they can expect, we inadvertently externalize their experience and deprive them of the opportunity to internalize their own healing process. No real healing takes place if we do anything that simulates external rewards — like approval, overly enthusiastic encouragement or too much direction. This is perhaps the hardest one for me to remember — to just be there and share in the experience *and* to stay out of the way so it can happen uniquely within them.

Like life, when we reward, approve, and cheer people on to

encourage them in their behavior or success, we rob them of the experience of *feeling* both their successes and their failures. Until people can *feel* what anger and irresponsibility costs them inside themselves, they'll have a tendency to project their successes and failures onto others.

Sometimes external punishment and reward can be similar to using a drug, because it's the most expedient method to stabilize an acute situation. Also, external reality can be a feedback for success or failure, but it won't work with people who never internalize any connection between what they feel and think about themselves and others, and what they say and do to themselves and others.

Fundamental Tension Results From
A Spiritual-Physical Dichotomy

Fundamental tension happens when we attempt to view the world as if it were a spiritual-physical dichotomy, thereby polarizing a basic creative rhythm. Although we're almost always spiritually connected, we're also almost always physically separate — but like the yin-yang symbol, the spiritual and physical are so interrelated that as one emerges, the other recedes in a never-ending dance that must be cooperatively balanced. All tension begins here when we try to hold back the cooperative rhythmic dance in favor of having *either* no boundaries or expectations to simulate the spiritual *or* all rules and predictability to simulate the physical. There are boundaries, expectations, probabilities, rules and predictability in both the spiritual and physical realms of existence, but there is more merging, dissolving, creating and healing in the spiritual realm than there is in the physical one.

Dysfunctional families are microcosms of larger socialized human dysfunctions with regard to this balance. For example, some families run like well-oiled machines — all function and no heart. The members of these families seem unable to merge spiritually. Instead, there's a spiritual rebelliousness, and cooperation and cohesiveness are established by following the rules, doing what's right, and putting on a good show to achieve worldly or familial success. Other families seem to share a relaxed camaraderie, lots of love and acceptance between each family member, and total chaos when it comes to getting anything done well or on time. The people in these families may forego any need for orderliness, time commitments, responsibility to work, or any adherance to social or legal ethics. Here, there's a kind of physical rebellion in favor of spiritual merging.

Healthy families produce healthy individuals. Dysfunctional families produce people who continue to dichotomize these principles within themselves, which results in flip-flop attitudes, behaviors, circumstances and relationships as they attempt to achieve a balance which will enable them to feel whole and healthy. All tension results from this simple fundamental imbalance, but by the time it gets chaotically expressed as ill health, loss of work and broken relationships, it looks like a complex mess. It's complicated further by projection and blame when people attempt to distance themselves from the confusion so they can sort it all out and organize it in a more manageable fashion.

And horror of horrors, when people do begin to see what's real, they're often overwhelmed by what they've done to themselves and others, and they feel such deep sadness that they sometimes begin to feel tremendous guilt and shame and want to go back and "undo" what happened. This is the critical point in awakening that calls for the utmost in kindness, forgiveness, grief and letting go. It's the point at which you'll be able to recognize what it has cost you to live the way you have, and to make a choice about whether you want to continue paying that price for the rest of your life. If you don't, you'll at the very least need to be *willing* to live your life differently and to *allow* change to happen.

The Tree of Life and Our Awakening

On the Tree of Life (see chapter eight), these are the experiences represented in paths 15, 16, 17, 18, 19, 20 and 21. In path 15, we realize that appearances are deceptive, and we must look beyond them to discover the truth. In path 16, we discover the destructive separativeness that may occur through speech and action. In path 17, we awaken to the realization of our spiritual connectedness with others, even though we're still individual expressions of being as well. In path 18, we begin to rebirth ourselves from within as we incorporate spiritual wisdom. In path 19, we come to realize courage, identity, self-respect and our purpose for being. In path 20, we awaken to our past attitudes and behaviors as we arise from our slumber and move into the light. In path 21, we become a human member of the universe who is organized in a new way.

The awakening on path 20 is called the path of Judgment, and the biblical reminder, "Judge not lest ye be judged," applies to judgment of yourself as well as others. If you judge yourself or anyone else at this point in your healing, you'll stop your healing process. The Tree of Life is a geometric representation of the principles inherent in the 26 points on your body. The 26 points are part of a primordial language that fundamentally links the existence of a Divine Macrocosm with the human microcosm.

Making Amends

The juncture of awakening is the one in which you'll either let go and let God, or you'll try to turn around and "undo" or "fix" so you won't feel so guilty and ashamed or lose those people whom you care about so deeply. If you let go and let God, you'll begin to live in the light, and all the rest will take care of itself. If you turn around and try to fix it, you'll become tense and dysfunctional again and begin to believe that this is all there is to living. The action of making amends to others is not the same as turning around to fix it, while making amends with the expectation that others will welcome you back or treat you differently is.

Make amends physically and spiritually the best you can without hurting yourself or others. Then take a careful look at yourself and notice where you have difficulty cooperating and being human. If you shut off your feelings, think all the good ideas in the world belong exclusively to you, and believe you've got a private line between you and God, you're spiritually rebellious and uncooperative even if you act like the most responsible, organized, thoughtfully cooperative person in the world. If you refuse to say what you mean, arbitrarily alter your agreements with others so they never know what to expect, and act as though rules and order pertain to everyone but you, you're physically rebellious and uncooperative even if you're the most delightfully loving, playfully accepting, uncritical person in the world.

Physical cooperation enables us to get the job done and to function well in the physical world, but it doesn't feel satisfying and joyful when we disconnect spiritually, and act out of a sense of *duty and obligation*. Spiritual cooperation enables us to feel connected and supported and gives us the opportunity to feel love, but our work won't get done just because we feel good if feeling good is dependent upon *limitless time and unconditional performance*.

Many codependents are like machines that get the job done but — who wants to hang around a machine with no heart. People who become machines feel spiritually lost, unattractive and lonely. Many addicts become addicts so they won't feel and act like machines. Some people are charming, attractive drifters who can talk their way in or out of anything because there's always someone who'll take care of them. Machine-like people tend to live off the spiritual presence of charmers.

The Star
In release work, the last five points (22, 23, 24, 25 and 26) are points of reference that open us up to the light. When these points become

illuminated simultaneously during acceptance and letting go, a geometric pattern of light forms around and within the mind-body in such a way that a star of light appears above the crown of the head, a balanced focus of energy can be felt in the umbilicus, and the dichotomy between spirit and form disappears. It's as if there are two major focal points, one above the crown and one in the umbilicus, and then light begins to radiate everywhere. The star above the head is sometimes visually like a dodecahedron and a star shifting back and forth, and sometimes like a ball of radiance or a point of light that radiates.

A Release Described Through Analogy and Metaphor
The total release is like the one that occurs during full orgasm minus the drama, and the experience afterwards is similar to feeling peace, love and total spiritual merging. The pelvic basin releases in such a way that a circle of light may appear like a tunnel or a doorway into another realm, and the rim of the pelvic basin may feel like it merges with the opening in the throat and the rim of the lower jaw. The crown of the head may feel vibrant and seem to fill with light. There may be a sense of timelessness and total wisdom and love. There may be other sensations and visuals as well, but like any healing, it's better to say too little than to risk setting up expectations that may get in the way of each individual's unique experience.

It's a little like the sexual experience. We all tried to share something about it with one another to shed some light on the truth and to dissolve destructive superstitions and lies. We did the best we could, but some people tried to go too far, and the essence of making love got lost in the cookbook manuals on sex. It's not always easy to know when to speak and when not to. Physicians are faced with the same dilemma now that they recognize that some people die from the diagnosis alone, and others get well just because they believed the person who said they would.

Spiritual truths are more apt to be revealed through silence, experience, parables and koans than they are through precise data and facts. I've described the most consistently common experiences to provide guidance without disrupting your own personal discoveries. Both the visuals and the direct mind-body experiences are clues for further exploration about mind-body interactions and the ways in which they differ from brain-body physiology. These truths are similar to the ones that inspired great scientists to formulate theories that led to applied mathematics and physics.

Release Points

Use the following flow patterns to release areas of tension that may be disrupting the overall balanced circulation of energy. The following is a list of some of the difficulties that may occur when these points are blocked. One area of tension can disrupt several meridians that flow through that point. Other information about the points can be found in the appendices.

1 Release

Points 1are located on the inner knees at the joint. High 1's are located on the inner thighs in a pocket approximately four inches above the knee joints. This Flow harmonizes the ascending and descending flows of energy in the body. As the central flow of energy moves up the center back and down the center front, it makes its first separation to move through points 1. This release will help problems from the waist up, such as the ones that may occur in the liver, heart, lungs, and head. When these points are released, your digestion will improve and so will conditions of obesity. This is a good flow to do and then follow with re-reading the pulses.

Women sometimes lock the inner knees to stop the free flow of feeling in the pelvis. This tension in the inner knees interferes with three meridians (Spleen, Liver and Kidney) that flow from the feet, up the inner legs and into the pelvic organs to assist with menstrual periods, fertility, pregnancy, sexual responses, and the maintenance of healthy reproductive organs. Tension in points 1 affects all the urogenital organs and their function. Urinary problems can be either urine retention or incontinence, or infection or inflammation any-where along the urinary tract.

When you won't allow feeling to flow through your pubic bone and down your inner thighs and knees, the cost may be a swollen, distended abdomen, overweight, smelly discharge, cramps, infertility, frigidity, and water retention.

Quick Flow: Cross your hands and hold your high 1's for digestion. Hold your high 1's with uncrossed hands for obesity.

1 RELEASE
Left Flow - Sit Left

STEPS	LEFT HAND	RIGHT HAND
1	left 1	left 2
2	left 5	"
3	left 6	"
4	left 7	"
5		
6		
7		
8		
9		
10		
11		
12		
13		
14		
15		
16		

1 RELEASE
Right Flow - Sit Right

STEPS	LEFT HAND	RIGHT HAND
1	right 2	right 1
2	"	right 5
3	"	right 6
4	"	right 7
5		
6		
7		
8		
9		
10		
11		
12		
13		
14		
15		
16		

2 Release

Points 2 are located on the lateral midlines of the lower back at the top of the pelvic crest on either side of the spine (fourth lumbar). When point 2 is painfully sore, the symphysis pubis is blocked and must be released first before you release the 2 or the pain will persist. To release the tension at the pubic bone, do a Main Central Flow or the fifteen release. The 2 release helps all leg problems such as varicose veins, gout, and injured ankles. It releases the tension from the legs so new energy can flow in. When points 11 are tense, they affect the same side 2 and opposite side 15.

When women shut off feelings that flow through the pubic area into the inner knees, they will have tension in their 2's as well. This results in problems such as inflammation of the uterus, tubes, ligaments, and ovaries; painful or irregular menstruation; urine incontinence; inflammation of the urinary tract; urine retention; diarrhea or constipation; intestinal spasms or inflammation; hemorrhoids; edema; or lower back problems. The spinal area between the 2's may become tender, swollen or out of alignment.

When you won't allow your feelings to flow through the pelvic region, the cost may be chronic lower back pain, knee pains, PMS, constipation and chronic bladder infections. The Hip Flow (pp. 277, 278) will help release tension in these areas. Then check the pulses to see which meridians are out of balance.

Quick Flows: Hold the 26 and opposite 24. Hold the same side 2 and 15.

2 RELEASE
Left Flow - Sit Left

STEPS	LEFT HAND	RIGHT HAND
1	left 6	left 2
2	left 7	"
3	left 8	"
4	left 25	"
5	right 5	"
6	right 15	"
7	left 2	left 9
8	"	left 26
9	"	left 3
10	"	left 12 or 4
11	right 22	"
12		
13		
14		
15		
16		

2 RELEASE
Right Flow - Sit Right

STEPS	LEFT HAND	RIGHT HAND
1	right 2	right 6
2	"	right 7
3	"	right 8
4	"	right 25
5	"	left 5
6	"	left 15
7	right 9	right 2
8	right 26	"
9	right 3	"
10	right 12 or 4	"
11	"	left 22
12		
13		
14		
15		
16		

3 Release

Points 3 are located at the upper inner edge of the scapula between the spine (third thoracic) and the shoulder blade. This release helps the lymph system function and therefore it assists with problems like infections and fevers from colds and viruses. It also helps relieve chronic bladder problems and difficulties in the arms. When points 3 are relaxed, the legs and back will relax as well. Release of the left 3 will help alleviate stuttering. Step one can be used to reduce fevers.

Points 3 are located at a crossroads for the fundamental Central, Vertical and Diagonal flows in the body. They're also located adjacent to the spine where the Governing Vessel and Bladder Meridians interact. These points are critical to immune system functioning, and release of fatigue from tension and toxins in the body.

Women who have tension in the 3's often get heavy arms and shoulders, and begin to form a fat pad on the spine at the base of the neck. Tension in the 3's and 11's interferes with the free flow of energy in the six arm-chest meridians. This results in difficulties with breathing and digestion, results in water retention and fatigue, and often leads to a hysterectomy.

If you're unwilling to have feelings in these areas, the cost may be chronic sore throats, fatigue and bouts of colds and flu. You may begin to look swollen and puffy, and feel sad and depressed. Eventually, you may form a dowagers hump at the base of your neck and have a double chin. The worst of it may be that you just never feel very vital and energized.

Quick Flow: Hold same side 15 and 3.

3 RELEASE
Left Flow - Sit Right

STEPS	LEFT HAND	RIGHT HAND
1	left 3	left little & ring finger (palmside) middle & index finger (backside)
2	"	right 21
3	"	right 19
4	"	right index, middle, ring, & little fingers (palmside)
5	"	left high 1
6	"	right 15
7	"	right 7
8		
9		
10	**NOTE**	
11	Touch each finger one at a time in steps one and four.	
12		
13		
14		
15		
16		

3 RELEASE
Right Flow - Sit Left

STEPS	LEFT HAND	RIGHT HAND
1	right little, ring finger (palmside) middle & index finger (backside)	right 3
2	left 21	"
3	left 19	"
4	left index, middle, ring, & little fingers (palmside)	"
5	right high 1	"
6	left 15	"
7	left 7	"
8		
9		
10	**NOTE**	
11	Touch each finger one at a time in steps one and four.	
12		
13		
14		
15		
16		

4 Release

Points 4 are located at the base of the skull on either side of the top of the spine (atlas and axis). This release relieves pain and problems in the tonsils, sinuses, throat, heart, knees and legs. It opens the chest cavity so energy can pass through. It's helpful for people whose legs feel heavy. When points 4 are tense, they affect tension in the same side 10 and opposite side 13. To relieve someone who is unconscious from any cause, start from step nine and work backwards.

Points 4 are favorites for anyone who has ever decided to hold on and defend a position no matter what. The longer you hold on, the more your face will change along with everything else in your head — like your brain. You can control almost any feeling in your body by tensing the 4's and freezing them in place. However, you'll have headaches, eye, ear and nose problems and a locked jaw. In the end, you'll suffer from hypertension and almost any mental disorder imaginable.

While you're defending your position and working on a build-up of tension, your face may start looking strange from crooked jaw, fixated or wild-looking eyes, and a face that twitches. If that's not enough, you may begin to lose your sense of hearing, and be more or less unconscious most of the time even when you appear to be awake. No amount of make-up is going to help your face — not even a complete makeover.

I once worked on a man who could barely shuffle his way into my office. He appeared dull and his body felt heavy and lifeless. He hadn't been able to make love with his wife for almost two years. His 4's were blocked solid. After several sessions, his wife called to thank me and let me know that they were lovers again.

When these points get blocked, they interfere with the Triple Warmer, Gall Bladder and Bladder Meridians. When this combination of tension goes too far, it also interferes with the Conception Vessel, Governing Vessel and Stomach Meridian, and then the person looks, feels and acts real crazy. A condition of acute insanity can occur. Quick Flow: Hold opposite 4 and 9.

4 RELEASE
Left Flow - Sit Left

STEPS	LEFT HAND	RIGHT HAND
1	right 20	left 4
2	right 21	"
3	right 13	"
4	left 13	"
5	left 1	"
6	left 7	"
7	left 15	"
8	"	left 22
9	left 10	"
10	left middle finger	"
11	"	right 4
12	"	tailbone
13	"	between the 23's
14	"	between the 9's
15		
16		

4 RELEASE
Right Flow - Sit Right

STEPS	LEFT HAND	RIGHT HAND
1	right 4	left 20
2	"	left 21
3	"	left 13
4	"	right 13
5	"	right 1
6	"	right 7
7	"	right 15
8	right 22	"
9	"	right 10
10	"	right middle finger
11	left 4	"
12	tailbone	"
13	between the 23's	"
14	between the 9's	"
15		
16		

5, 6, 7, 8 Release

Points 5 are located on the inner ankles in the pocket below the ankle bone. Points 6 are located on the inner edge of the instep just below the ball of the foot. Points 7 are located in the middle of the pad on the big toe. Points 8 are located at the outer edge of the knees at the joint (also check back of the knee and the area of tension that forms at the outer edge just below the knee joint). Low back 8's are in the center of the calves, and low front 8's are midway between the knees and the ankles, just lateral to the shin bone.

This release relieves opposite side, waist-up problems on the front or back. It helps open points 15 and 2 so the energy can flow through the pelvis into the legs. This releases the diaphragm and upper body tension which affects, for example, the chest, liver, gallbladder, spleen, and upper back. This Flow also helps with opposite side hip problems and same side crooked toes that overlap one another. If someone has emphysema, do this flow first and then follow with any of the Lung Flows or the Breathing and Digestive Flow (page 269).

Points 5 assist the groin and throat. Points 6 help relieve varicose veins, open the groin, and relax the shoulders. Points 7 help headaches, hot palms and small intestine. Points 8 assist with problems of elimination and constipation, and help reproductive and rectal areas.

This amazing little flow will move energy through the pelvis, release the diaphragm and open the throat. It will also relieve problems such as convulsions, nightmares, insomnia, hysteria, madness, and stupidity. Sometimes you can tell there's tension in the feet and toes just by looking, and sometimes you won't know until you touch the points.

I once worked on a woman whose large toes overlapped the second and middle ones on both feet. They'd been like that for eighteen years. During our one session together, I did this release on both feet. Each time I reached step eight and touched point 8, her leg cramped up with a "charley horse" and her large toe lifted up and moved into its proper place. I saw her a year and a half later at a conference and her toes were still straight.

5, 6, 7, 8 RELEASE
Left Flow - Sit Left

STEPS	LEFT HAND	RIGHT HAND
1	left 5	right 15
2	left little toe	left 5
3	left fourth toe	"
4	"	left 6
5	"	left 5
6	left 7	"
7	left little toe	"
8	"	left 8
9	"	left 25
10	"	left 2
11	right 15	"
12		
13		
14		
15		
16		

5, 6, 7, 8 RELEASE
Right Flow - Sit Right

STEPS	LEFT HAND	RIGHT HAND
1	left 15	right 5
2	right 5	right little toe
3	"	right fourth toe
4	right 6	"
5	right 5	"
6	"	right 7
7	"	right little toe
8	right 8	"
9	right 25	"
10	right 2	"
11	"	left 15
12		
13		
14		
15		
16		

9 Release

Points 9 are located at the bottom inner edge of the scapulae between the spine (seventh thoracic) and shoulder blades. In many ways, tension in this point is the beginning of all problems in the body. Releasing the left one helps the liver and gall bladder; releasing the right one helps the pancreas and spleen. The opposite 9 and 14 are interrelated. When the 12's are tense, they affect tension in the same side 9 and opposite side 14. This flow will release tension in the opposite side chest when it's, for example, hard and swollen, or the opposite back or hip. It will also release the same side foot and ankle and relieve, for example, callouses, bunions and corns or assist with sprains. Release the 9's if your baby is fussy and can't keep milk down.

Most people you touch will need to have their 9's released. People tense these areas so they can hold their breath and avoid feeling. Also, tension in the 9's is so related to what we eat that almost no one escapes the damages that occur from a poor diet and adulterated food. Smoking cigarettes or marijuana will create tension in this area as well as the 10's. All manner of digestive and respiratory problems occur when these areas are tense.

Little babies need to be held and cuddled. When they're touched with warmth and love, they breathe and digest their food more easily. When they feel insecure and afraid, they become tense in the 9's and 10's and develop respiratory and digestive problems.

Quick Flow: Hold same side 12 and 19 (little finger side).

9 RELEASE
Left Flow - Sit Left

STEPS	LEFT HAND	RIGHT HAND
1	left 19 (little finger side)	left 9
2	left 17	"
3	left ring, middle, & index fingers (backside)	"
4	right 1	"
5	right 5	"
6	left 15	"
7	right 14	"
8	left 9	left 12
9	right 21	"
10		
11		
12	**NOTE**	
13	Touch each finger one at a time in step three.	
14		
15		
16		

9 RELEASE
Right Flow - Sit Right

STEPS	LEFT HAND	RIGHT HAND
1	right 9	right 19 (little finger side)
2	"	right 17
3	"	right ring, middle, & index finger (backside)
4	"	left 1
5	"	left 5
6	"	right 15
7	"	left 14
8	right 12	right 9
9	"	left 21
10		
11		
12	**NOTE**	
13	Touch each finger one at a time in step three.	
14		
15		
16		

10 Release

Points 10 are located at the middle inner edge of the scapulae between the spine (fifth thoracic) and shoulder blades. Lateral 10's are located in the center of the scapulae on the shoulder blades. This release may be used to help heart mitral disease; heart acceleration; tuberculosis; bronchopneumonia; asthma; dizziness; poor memory; high blood pressure; hoarse voice or loss of voice; lack of strength in the thumb; swollen knee on the opposite side; pain and stiffness in the same side hip; stiffness in the neck or shoulder on the opposite side; children who aren't speaking; stuttering; speech problems in general; and to balance the ascending flows (up the back).

As you can see, it relieves difficulties in the chest and throat, and releases tension in the opposite side limbs. It's important for all speech and heart problems, and all lung tensions. When the 10's release, you may notice changes in the size and shape of your breasts. Some people cough up phlegm or appear to develop a cold as mucous gets released from the lungs following release of tension in these areas. Your voice may seem fuller and more resonant when tension is released. If you're a singer, you need to be free of tension in the 10's, pelvis and feet, and any of the more obvious areas that may constrict the throat such as the 11's, 12's, 3's and arms.

Quick Flow: Hold same side 15 and 1. Hold 18's. Hold 4's.

10 RELEASE
Left Flow - Sit Left

STEPS	LEFT HAND	RIGHT HAND
1	right 1	left 10
2	"	left 9
3	right 7	"
4	right 16	"
5	right 8	"
6	left high 19	left 10 or 3
7	left 18	"
8	left index finger	"
9		
10		
11		
12		
13		
14		
15		
16		

10 RELEASE
Right Flow - Sit Right

STEPS	LEFT HAND	RIGHT HAND
1	right 10	left 1
2	right 9	"
3	"	left 7
4	"	left 16
5	"	left 8
6	right 10 or 3	right high 19
7	"	right 18
8	"	right index finger
9		
10		
11		
12		
13		
14		
15		
16		

11, 12 Release

Points 11 are located at the base of the neck where it curves to join the shoulder on either side of the spine (first thoracic). Points 12 are located on the back of the neck in line with the bottom of the ear lobes on either side of the spine (third cervical).

When points 11 are blocked, same side 2 and opposite side 15 tend to be blocked as well. When points 12 are blocked, same side 9 and opposite 14 tend to be blocked as well. When points 4 are blocked, same side 10 and opposite 13 tend to be blocked as well. When points 3 are blocked, they may involve other points in any of the above combinations.

When points 11, 12 and 4 become tense and strain toward point 3, it's due to overuse of the opposite arm and hand. Overuse of the arm will result in an inability to turn the head to the opposite side. If, for example, this is a result of overuse of the right arm resulting in an inability to turn the head to the left, then release the right 10 and opposite neck area by placing your right hand on the right 10 while you move your left hand sequentially up the left 3, 11, 12 and 4, holding each one long enough to release it. Do exactly the opposite if tension results from overuse of the left arm.

For whiplash, you may want to release the back as well as the neck. Place your left hand on the left 11 while you move your right hand up the right 23, 9, 10, 3 and 11, holding each point long enough to release it. Then leave your right hand on the right 11 and repeat the process with your left hand on the left 23, 9, 10, 3 and 11. Follow this with the example above for releasing tension in the arm and neck.

Most of the time, you'll feel pain or stiffness in the upper body (head, neck, arms or trunk) when these points are blocked, and you may develop lower body difficulties, especially in the pelvic area, because the energy can't flow freely through the pelvis into the legs. Sore throat and respiratory problems eventually result when tension persists. Tension in these points affects many other areas because all meridians must be able to flow through the neck into the head. Release of the 11's and 12's assists the thyroid and parathyroids.

11, 12 RELEASE
Left Flow - Sit Right

STEPS	LEFT HAND	RIGHT HAND
1	left 12, 11, & 3 (as one releases, go to the next)	left high 19
2	"	left 18
3	"	right 21
4	"	right 20
5	"	right 22
6	"	right 9
7	"	right 25
8	"	right 15
9		
10		
11		
12		
13		
14		
15		
16		

11, 12 RELEASE
Right Flow - Sit Left

STEPS	LEFT HAND	RIGHT HAND
1	right high 19	right 12, 11, & 3 (as one releases, go to the next)
2	right 18	"
3	left 21	"
4	left 20	"
5	left 22	"
6	left 9	"
7	left 25	"
8	left 15	"
9		
10		
11		
12		
13		
14		
15		
16		

13 Release

Points 13 are located on the lateral midlines of the upper chest just below the third ribs. The point between the 13's is located in a little indentation on the breast bone. This release corrects intermingling of the Triple Warmer, Large Intestine, Small Intestine and Main Central. This flow helps all reproductive problems such as irregular menstruation; leucorrhea discharge; ovary bleeding; prostate; general sexual problems; and hormone balance. Use with Leg Flow (page 269) for cramps. It assists the thyroid gland; chest congestion; nausea; abdominal pain; back head pain; neck and shoulder tension; digestion; breathing; elimination; and balances metabolism and appetite.

One woman who hadn't had a menstrual period for over a year, started her period within twenty-four hours after one session from this release. Another woman who had had colitis for eighteen months, no longer had any signs of it within three days after one session from this release. People who are constipated will usually have a very thorough bowel evacuation within hours after this release.

The combination of pulses for the three meridians listed above tend to become imbalanced and intermingle over and over again when a woman is still mourning the loss of a relationship — even if it's years later. Very often, both Lung and Heart Meridians will be imbalanced as well. This combination is far more prevalent in females than in males. The person needs to accept, grieve and let go.

If this intermingling has gone on for a long period of time, the person's wrists will feel tight and swollen and they'll probably be fatigued. If this is the case, you'll need to do the Minor Diagonal and the Main Central, and release points 3, 9, 10 and high 19 as well.

The Triple Warmer is the power house for all twelve meridians. The 13 release opens the three belts (13, 14 and 15). It harmonizes and balances the mind. It's the fountain of youth. This is a wonderful flow to do before and after surgery to reduce or eliminate pain.

Quick Flow: Do Main Central self-help. Hold high back 19's.

Self-Help: Do any of the meridian Flows that intermingle, especially the Triple Warmer.

13 RELEASE
Sit Right

STEPS	LEFT HAND	RIGHT HAND
1	between the 10's	between the 13's
2	first thoracic	"
3	"	right high back 19
4	"	left high back 19
5	"	between the 14's
6	"	right little & index finger
7	"	left little & index finger
8	"	top of the pubic bone
9	between the 9's	"
10	between the 23's	"
11	tailbone	"
12		
13		
14	NOTE	
15	Touch each finger one at a time in steps six and seven.	
16		

14 Release

Points 14 are located on the lateral midlines of the rib cage at the base of the last ribs which can be felt on this midline. The point between the 14's is in the center pocket at the base of the sternum. This release will assist with snoring; senility; epilepsy; convulsions due to indigestion (usually in children); unconsciousness; valvular diseases of the heart; same side knee pain and lung and diaphragm problems; same side arm tensions or dorsal thigh pain; opposite side brain or kidney problems; and low fever. Left 14 assists the spleen; right 14 assists the liver. When there's tension in the left 14 and the rib cage is high on that side, the carbohydrate intake is too high. If the opposite is true in the right 14, protein assimilation is bad. The 14's are the main breathing and digestive flow area and they're related to the opposite 9's and 12's.

People who have been traumatized tend to hold tension in the 9's and 14's. When these areas are held tight, it's easier to avoid feelings. When these areas (especially the 14's) begin to release, I've seen many people start to laugh. Sometimes they'll begin to laugh uncontrollably. If this happens while you're touching someone, just stay quiet and continue touching. This isn't laughter because something's funny. It's the first stage of tension releasing and generally precedes deep sobbing and letting go.

When the 14's release, the person may become aware of abdominal pain or sensitivity. As release continues and energy is able to move through the pelvis into the legs, pain or swelling in the abdominal area will disappear. The upper and lower body will become integrated and the person will feel much more "grounded." Long time tension results in all kinds of digestive disturbances such as vomiting, stomach disorders and loss of appetite. Tension in these areas also results in throat spasms, an inability to swallow and hiccoughs.

Quick Flow: Hold both 12's. Hold 12 and opposite 21 for snoring. Hold both middle fingers. Hold first thoracic and thumb if there's pain in the 14's.

14 RELEASE
Left Flow - Sit Left

STEPS	LEFT HAND	RIGHT HAND
1	left high 1	right 9
2	left 24	"
3	left 25	"
4	"	left lateral 10 (on the shoulder blade)
5	left 17	"
6	left middle finger	"
7	"	left 9
8	right 15	"
9	right 5	"
10		
11		
12		
13		
14		
15		
16		

14 RELEASE
Right Flow - Sit Right

STEPS	LEFT HAND	RIGHT HAND
1	left 9	right high 1
2	"	right 24
3	"	right 25
4	right lateral 10 (on the shoulder blade)	"
5	"	right 17
6	"	right middle finger
7	right 9	"
8	"	left 15
9	"	left 5
10		
11		
12		
13		
14		
15		
16		

15 Release

Points 15 are located on the lateral midlines of the lower trunk in the pockets of the groin where the legs join the body. Low 15's are located on the front of the body approximately four inches below the groin in the center of the thigh. The point between the 15's is in the center at the top edge of the pubic bone.

This release will assist all heart ailments, and all breaks, sprains and swelling in the legs. If the person has bone problems as well, also do the Kidney and Bladder Flows. Steps 1, 2 and 3 will help: same side abdominal discomfort, hip pain, painful and swollen knee, cold foot and swollen lower leg. Swelling results when the energy becomes stagnated and doesn't flow freely into the legs.

If there's tension in point 11, it blocks opposite 15 and same side 2. If the 15's are blocked, release them before releasing points 2 or 3. When the 15's are blocked, sometimes the shoulders will be rounded and pulled forward as if the person is slumping. When this happens, there's tension centrally at the top of the pubic bone as well as in the groin.

When the groin and pubic bone are blocked, people get the fidgets and when they try to relax, their legs jerk and twitch. Release these areas and check for tension in the 23's, 25's and Kidney and Bladder Meridians as well. All types of urogenital problems begin from tension in these areas and are generally preceded by lower back pain and lower abdominal distention.

Quick Flow: Hold same side 15 and 6; 15 and 3 or 15 and 1. Hold 19's; little fingers; or 17's.

15 RELEASE
Left Flow - Sit Left

STEPS	LEFT HAND	RIGHT HAND
1	left 6	left 15
2	left 8	"
3	"	left 2
4	right 25	"
5	right 15	"
6	left 25	"
7	"	left 9
8	"	left 3 & 11 (as one releases, move to the next one)
9	left 19 (little finger side)	left 10
10	left 15	right 18
11		
12		
13		
14		
15		
16		

15 RELEASE
Right Flow - Sit Right

STEPS	LEFT HAND	RIGHT HAND
1	right 15	right 6
2	"	right 8
3	right 2	"
4	"	left 25
5	"	left 15
6	"	right 25
7	right 9	"
8	right 3 & 11 (as one releases, move to the next one)	"
9	right 10	right 19 (little finger side)
10	left 18	right 15
11		
12		
13		
14		
15		
16		

16, 17, 18, 19 Release

Points 16 are located on the outer ankles just below the ankle bones. Points 17 are located are located on the outer edge of the hands (little finger sides) just above the wrist joints. Points 18 are located on the palms of the hands in the mound at the base of the thumbs just above the wrist joints. Points 19 are located in the crook of the elbows on the thumb side. High 19's are midway between the shoulders and the elbows on the side of the upper arms. High back 19's are midway between the shoulders and the elbows on the backside of the upper arms opposite the biceps.

This release will help same side chest problems such as the breast, skeletal structure, pain, or fullness and swelling. For example, it's good for lumps in the breast, healing from mastectomy, protruding ribs, or to assist the heart. It will assist opposite side back problems such as stiffness or paralysis, and it will help the opposite arm when it is bent and stiff. Steps 1, 2 and 3 are part of the Bladder Flow. Release of points 16 and 17 will assist the ascending flows that move up the back of the body. Release of points 18 and 19 will assist the descending flows that move down the front of the body.

This is a good release to use for all kinds of cerebral difficulties; headaches; and eye, ear, nose and throat problems. Difficulties can be as serious as meningitis; migraine; epilepsy; facial neuralgia; loss of speech; deafness; inflammation of the lymph nodes in the neck and armpits; vertigo; conjunctivitis; inflammation of the cornea; or chronic nosebleeds. All manner of mental disorders may occur such as depression; schizophrenia; hysteric aphasia (sudden loss of the ability to express or comprehend speech or written language); hysteria; phobia; insanity; or loss of consciousness.

16, 17, 18, 19 RELEASE
Left Flow - Sit Left

STEPS	LEFT HAND	RIGHT HAND
1	left 16	left little toe
2	"	left 8
3	"	left 25
4	left 25	left 19
5	left 17	"
6	left 18	"
7	"	left high back 19
8	"	left high 19
9	right 15	left 18
10	right 1	"
11		
12		
13		
14		
15		
16		

16, 17, 18, 19 RELEASE
Right Flow - Sit Right

STEPS	LEFT HAND	RIGHT HAND
1	right little toe	right 16
2	right 8	"
3	right 25	"
4	right 19	right 25
5	"	right 17
6	"	right 18
7	right high back 19	"
8	right high 19	"
9	right 18	left 15
10	"	left 1
11		
12		
13		
14		
15		
16		

20 Release

Points 20 are located on the lateral midlines of the face just below the frontal eminence. The point between the 20's is the area generally referred to as the "third eye" in the indentation between the brows. This release is good for chronic tension, pain and discomfort in the general frontal area. It also helps to relax the whole body. It assists all eye problems, and will relieve some headaches and facial neuralgia.

Quick Flow: Put your right hand on the left 20, and your left hand on the right 20 while the person being balanced hold's her 14's. Then put your right hand between the 14's and your left hand on the pubic bone while the person being balanced holds her 15's.

20 RELEASE
Left Flow - Sit Left

STEPS	LEFT HAND	RIGHT HAND
1	left 20	left 12
2	between the 14's	"
3	left 23	"
4	left ring finger	"
5	left 19 (little finger side)	"
6	top of the pubic bone	left 20
7		
8		
9		
10		
11		
12		
13		
14		
15		
16		

20 RELEASE
Right Flow - Sit Right

STEPS	LEFT HAND	RIGHT HAND
1	right 12	right 20
2	"	between the 14's
3	"	right 23
4	"	right ring finger
5	"	right 19 (little finger side)
6	right 20	top of the pubic bone
7		
8		
9		
10		
11		
12		
13		
14		
15		
16		

20, 21, 22 Release

Points 21 are located on the lateral midlines of the face in the pocket just below the cheekbones. The point between the 21's is the tip of the nose. Points 22 are located on the lateral midlines of the upper trunk in the pocket below the clavicle. Lateral 22's are located in the pocket below the clavicle closer to the shoulder joint. The point between the 22's is at the little cleft in the breast bone at the base of the throat.

This release will help coughing and phlegm from colds; dizziness; anemia; high blood pressure; and autism in children. It assists same side head pain and earache; and opposite side brain problems and eye shape. It helps all types of facial difficulties and relieves tension in the eyes, ears, nose and throat. Difficulties may express themselves as facial paralysis; facial abcesses; migraines; glaucoma; cataracts; eye spasms or loss of tone in the eye muscles; chronic runny nose; boils on the nose; inability to use the sense of smell; asthma; pleurisy; or diaphragm spasms.

Left side tension occurs when the left 9 tenses from overusage of the right arm and right 14 tension. In this case, the liver and gall bladder are affected. The opposite is true for right side tension, and the spleen, pancreas, right 9 and left 14 are affected.

The interaction between these three points reveals more than an inspection of each individual point. When you draw two diagonal lines from points 20 through the opposite points 22, you'll form a central point at the root of the nose between the brows, and the line which extends through the 22's will pass through the 26's. When you draw two diagonal lines from points 20 through the opposite points 23, you'll form a central point in the throat. When you draw two diagonal lines from points 21 through the opposite points 23, you'll form a central point at the base of the throat. When you draw two diagonal lines from points 22 through opposite points 23, you'll form a central point on the chest between the breasts. According to Qabbalistic symbolism, twenty-two is the conventional symbol for any circle, a sign of wholeness and unity.

20, 21, 22 RELEASE
Left Flow - Sit Left

STEPS	LEFT HAND	RIGHT HAND
1	left 20	right 4, 12, 11, & 3 (as one releases, move to the next)
2	left 21	"
3	left 22	"
4	left index finger (palmside)	"
5	left 18	"
6	right 14	"
7	right high 1	"
8	right 5	"
9	left 10 or 9	"
10	"	right 17
11		
12		
13		
14		
15		
16		

20, 21, 22 RELEASE
Right Flow - Sit Right

STEPS	LEFT HAND	RIGHT HAND
1	left 4, 12, 11, & 3 (as one releases, move to the next)	right 20
2	"	right 21
3	"	right 22
4	"	right index finger (palmside)
5	"	right 18
6	"	left 14
7	"	left high 1
8	"	left 5
9	"	right 10 or 9
10	left 17	"
11		
12		
13		
14		
15		
16		

23, 25 Release

Points 23 are located on the back lateral midlines in the pocket just below the rib cage at the waist on either side of the spine (twelfth thoracic). Points 25 are located at the base of the buttocks up against the bones you sit upon on either side of the spine (tailbone).

This release will help all blood conditions such as blood pressure, hypoglycemia, leukemia and anemia, and all addictive problems such as smoking and drugs. It assists with infections, chills and fevers, hyperactivity, thyroid gland function, and the fidgets. This Flow is very energizing and revitalizing. The 23's are the key blood collection center. Release same side 23 and 9 to assist with blood problems. Triple Warmer and Pericardium Flows will assist the release of tension in these areas.

The interactive tension between the 23's and 25's is much more revealing than tension in the individual points. Interactive tension results in abdominal distention and lower back problems, and prevents a coordinated central point of balance from forming in the umbilical region just below the navel. This point is free to exist during total balance between the central and peripheral flows of energy, and results in an inner transformation that occurs when wholeness and balance are present.

When you draw two diagonal lines from points 23 through the opposite points 25, you'll form a central point in the umbilicus near the navel. When you draw two diagonal lines from points 26 through opposite points 23, you'll form a central point at the base of the sternum.

Quick Flow: Hold ring fingers. Hold same side 25 and 3.

23, 25 RELEASE
Left Flow - Sit Left

STEPS	LEFT HAND	RIGHT HAND
1	left 5	left 25
2	"	left 2
3	"	left 23
4	right 15	"
5	right little toe	"
6	right fourth toe (sole side)	"
7	"	left 9
8	left high back 19	"
9	left ring finger	"
10		
11		
12		
13		
14		
15		
16		

23, 25 RELEASE
Right Flow - Sit Right

STEPS	LEFT HAND	RIGHT HAND
1	right 25	right 5
2	right 2	"
3	right 23	"
4	"	left 15
5	"	left little toe
6	"	left fourth toe (sole side)
7	right 9	"
8	"	right high back 19
9	"	right ring finger
10		
11		
12		
13		
14		
15		
16		

24, 26 Release

Points 24 are located on the lateral midlines on the top of the feet midway between the base of the toes and the ankle. Points 26 are located at the outer edge of the body where the arms join the shoulders on the little finger side. The sixth thoracic on the spine is a midpoint.

When all the pulses are chaotic, do the Main Central Flow first to balance the left and right bodily flows and then do this release three times and re-read the pulses. If you can't reach the 24, go to the 8 and 15. If there's pain in the 26, have the person hold the same side 17 on herself as the 26 you're holding. The person will switch sides as you switch sides.

Like the 23-25 release, the interaction between these two points reveals more than tension in the individual points. Interactive tension results in chaotic pulses and prevents central points from forming in the umbilical region just below the navel or in the central groin (perineum). When you draw two diagonal lines from points 26 through the opposite points 24 when the legs are spread wide apart, you'll form a central point in the umbilicus. If you do the same thing when the feet are separated a shoulder width apart, you'll form a central point in the groin (perineum).

24, 26 RELEASE
Left and Right Flows - Sit Left

STEPS	LEFT HAND	RIGHT HAND
1	right 24	left 26
2	"	right 26
3	left 24	"
4		
5		
6		
7	**NOTE** If the person has pain in the 26's, have her hold the same side point 17 on herself as the point 26 you are holding, and have her switch sides when you do.	**NOTE** Do the Main Central Flow first, then do this Release three times, and then re-read the pulses.
8		
9		
10		
11		
12		
13		
14		
15		
16		

26 Release

Point 26 is the point of no beginning and no end. The number 26 = completion. This release makes a complete circle from point 1 to 26. It assists all the limbs (arms, hands, fingers, legs, feet and toes). It's a good release for arthritis.

When you draw two diagonal lines from points 26 through the opposite points 23, you'll form a central point just below the base of the sternum. When you draw two diagonal lines from points 26 through same side 22's and opposite 20's, you'll form a central point at the root of the nose between the brows. Lines from 26's through opposite 24's will form central points in either the umbilicus or groin depending upon the position of the feet. Points 26 coordinate with one another and the sixth thoracic to create a central point on the breast bone. The chest coordinate, along with the interaction via the 20's, 21's and 22's that forms a central coordinate at the root of the nose, produces a midpoint coordinate in the throat. Many different coordinates that surround and interpenetrate the body all come together to form the crown chakra which extends just above the center top of the head.

26 RELEASE
Left Flow - Sit Left

STEPS	LEFT HAND	RIGHT HAND
1	left little & ring finger (hold one & then the other)	left 26
2	left 12	"
3	right 21	"
4	right 19	"
5	right 15	"
6	left high 1	"
7		
8		
9		
10		
11		
12		
13		
14		
15		
16		

26 RELEASE
Right Flow - Sit Right

STEPS	LEFT HAND	RIGHT HAND
1	right 26	right little & ring finger (hold one and then the other)
2	"	right 12
3	"	left 21
4	"	left 19
5	"	left 15
6	"	right high 1
7		
8		
9		
10		
11		
12		
13		
14		
15		
16		

We are a moving design within a symbol so multifaceted that although we're all the same, each of us is unique. Sometimes reading about symptoms that result from tension may make us aware of the cost we pay for being tense and rigid. However, symptoms don't reveal the hidden truth about these points. Difficulties of all kind occur when these points are blocked, but the absence of tension that occurs when wholeness and balance are present is more than the absence of symptoms — it's the Touch of Silence where wisdom begins.

6

Special Flows

Fifteen years ago when I first studied Jin Shin Jyutsu (see Notes, pages 373 and 374), I learned many quick self-help flows and several longer ones to relieve specific frequently occuring conditions. I've included the ones I use most often.

The Fatigue Flow
The Fatigue Flow is a combination of the fundamental central, vertical and diagonal flows in the body. It brings these three flows into balance, supports immune function, assists in the elimination of toxins, and alleviates fatigue. Points 3 are the main focal points for releasing fatigue.

Quick Flow: Place hands side by side on the crown of the head with the fingers pointing toward the forehead.

Self-Help:
1. Simultaneously place your left thumb over your left ring finger nail and push down (clears the thoracic cavity and allows the energy to flow through); and place your right 6 on your left 1 (pulls the energy down); and place your right hand on your left 3 (pulls the energy up). Then reverse to assist the right side.

2. For leg tension: simultaneously place your left thumb over your left ring finger nail and push down; and place your right 6 on your left 1; and place your right hand on your left 25 or coccyx (pushes energy up); and then move your right hand to your left 23 (for energizing). Then reverse to assist the right side.

3. For back tension: simultaneously place your left hand on your left 25; and place your right hand on your left 23 (for energizing and for all blood conditions); and then move your right hand to your left 3; and then move your right hand to your left 12 (good for all hip and leg problems). Then reverse to assist the right side.

4. Middle Finger: hold, to balance ascending and descending flows in the body. This opens lungs, clears the eyes, and adjusts the chemistry (acidity and alkalinity) of the body. Hold with thumb on palm side to strengthen descending flows, or press pads of middle fingers together. Hold with thumb on back side to strengthen ascending flows, or press middle fingernails together.

5. Bend middle finger and press on its nail with the thumb of the opposite hand. Helps ascending and descending flows, and physical, emotional, mental and digestive problems.

6. Press back of ring fingernail with thumb of same hand. This clears the chest cavity and assists breathing, emotional problems, allergies and asthma.

7. Hold base of ring and little fingers simultaneously with palms of hands together, thumb of opposite hand between the middle and ring fingers of hand being held. Calms the nerves.

8. Hold middle and index fingers and thumb simultaneously at the base. Put the thumb of the opposite hand between the middle and ring

fingers of the hand being held. The palm of the holding hand should be against the back side of the hand being held. Good for digestion, physical fatigue and blood. Middle finger for breathing; index finger for elimination; thumb for breathing, blood, physical fatigue and head.

Depth Flows

The longer the Minor Diagonal flows remain imbalanced, the deeper the tension in the body. Tension begins near the surface and usually progresses more deeply with age, but you may find deep tension in a young child or surface tension in an elderly person.

1st depth (childhood): affects mouth, teeth (teething), stomach (colic), spleen (fatigue), diarrhea (2's), lungs (breathing). Hold little babies across the shoulders and across the coccyx (bottom and 2's). This puts the diagonals and verticals in balance with the central flow and helps babies get a good start from birth. Can use this flow for hyperkinetic children.

2nd depth (teens): affects nose, lungs (asthma, allergies, coughing, phlegm — tension in shoulder blades and 2's), skin (acne).

3rd depth (30's-40's): affects eyes (glasses), liver, gall bladder (tension in 14's).

4th depth (50's): affects ears (ringing, hearing loss, dizziness), kidney, bladder (urine retention or incontinence), reproductive organs (hysterectomy), bones, nails (brittle), stiff limbs and joints (rheumatism), rectum (elimination, hemorrhoids), and sleep at night. Do this flow first and all the other depth flows begin to fall into place.

5th depth (60's): all combined which causes pains from the combination of 1st through 4th depths. Overall numbness, tenseness, blackouts and visits to all the medical specialists.

6th depth: loss of consciousness (One or both 4's close up — when both close, blackouts, coma, death).

To reverse the aging process, do the depth flows in reverse by beginning with the 4th depth flow and ending with the 1st depth flow.

DEPTH FLOWS 1-4
Left Flows - Sit Left

STEPS	LEFT HAND	RIGHT HAND
1	*steps 2 - 4 for first depth* *steps 5 - 9 for second depth*	*steps 10 - 12 for third depth* *steps 13 - 16 for fourth depth*
2	right 2	left lateral 10 (on the shoulder blade)
3	"	left 21
4	"	left 19
5	right 24	left 2
6	left 14	"
7	right high 1	"
8	left 2	right 13
9	"	left 21
10	left lateral 3 (on the top of the shoulder blade)	left 4 or 12
11	right 4 or 12	"
12	right 21	"
13	right high 1	left 2
14	right 15	left 23
15	left high back 19	left 12
16	left 23	"

DEPTH FLOWS 1-4
Right Flows - Sit Right

STEPS	LEFT HAND	RIGHT HAND
1	*steps 2 - 4 for first depth* *steps 5 - 9 for second depth*	*steps 10 - 12 for third depth* *steps 13 - 16 for fourth depth*
2	right lateral 10 (on the shoulder blade)	left 2
3	right 21	"
4	right 19	"
5	right 2	left 24
6	"	right 14
7	"	left high 1
8	left 13	right 2
9	right 21	"
10	right 4 or 12	right lateral 3 (on the top of the shoulder blade)
11	"	left 4 or 12
12	"	left 21
13	right 2	left high 1
14	right 23	left 15
15	right 12	right high back 19
16	"	right 23

Intermingling Of The Diagonal Flows

Lung tension develops when the Diagonal Flows become imbalanced. When this happens, points 4, 12, 11 and 3 become blocked. This results in shoulder tension, coughing and phlegm. A person may have a heavy, uncomfortable feeling in the stomach area at the base of the sternum, and experience intermittent feelings of hunger. Tension develops at the base of the rib cage, in the hips and around the tail bone. Knots may develop along the shoulder blades from the 3's to the 9's. The fingers may become stiff and crooked. The feet may get cold from the instep to the toes, bowel movements may be hard or runny, the hips may become painful and stiff, and the area near the spleen may throb.

Lung Flows I, II and III will correct intermingling and restore balance to the Diagonal Flows in the body.

Lung Flow I

This will assist lung and shoulder tensions and restore normal consistency to the bowel movements. Steps one, two and three will correct a high fever and restore balance. Charts on pages 255, 256.

Lung Flow II

Use this Flow if the pulses are all heavy on one side. This Flow assists breathing, digestion and elimination, and may be used for low or high fever. Charts on pages 257, 258.

Lung Flow III

This Flow will restore balance to the appetite, relieve tension in the stomach and abdomen, aid digestion, assist normal bowel function, aid breathing, increase circulation to the feet, and help ulcers to heal. Chart on page 259.

LUNG FLOW I
Left Flow - Sit Left

STEPS	LEFT HAND	RIGHT HAND
1	left 22	left 11, 3, 12, & 4 (as one releases, move to next)
2	right 14	"
3	left little, ring, & middle finger (backside) - hold in sequence	"
4	left index finger & thumb (palmside) - hold in sequence	"
5	right 2	"
6	left 8	"
7	left 25	"
8	left 10	"
9		
10		
11		
12		
13		
14		
15		
16		

LUNG FLOW I
Right Flow - Sit Right

STEPS	LEFT HAND	RIGHT HAND
1	right 11, 3, 12, & 4 (as one releases, move to next)	right 22
2	"	left 14
3	"	right little, ring, & middle finger (backside) - hold in sequence
4	"	right index finger & thumb (palmside - hold in sequence
5	"	left 2
6	"	right 8
7	"	right 25
8	"	right 10
9		
10		
11		
12		
13		
14		
15		
16		

LUNG FLOW II
Left Flow - Sit Left

STEPS	LEFT HAND	RIGHT HAND
1	left 15	left 2
2	"	left 20
3	"	left 21
4	"	left 22
5	"	between each left rib from left 22 to left 14
6	"	left 1
7	"	left 23
8	"	left 10
9	"	left 3
10	"	left 4 or 12
11		
12		
13		
14		
15		
16		

LUNG FLOW II
Right Flow - Sit Right

STEPS	LEFT HAND	RIGHT HAND
1	right 2	right 15
2	right 20	"
3	right 21	"
4	right 22	"
5	between each right rib from right 22 to right 14	"
6	right 1	"
7	right 23	"
8	right 10	"
9	right 3	"
10	right 4 or 12	"
11		
12		
13		
14		
15		
16		

LUNG FLOW III
Sit Left

STEPS	LEFT HAND	RIGHT HAND
1	between the 13's	tailbone
2	"	between the 23's
3	"	between the 9's
4	"	between the 10's
5	"	first thoracic
6	"	crown of the head
7	between the 14's	"
8	top of the pubic bone	"
9		
10		
11		
12		
13		
14		
15		
16		

Vertical Harmony Flow

This is referred to as "everlasting life" in the Bible. It's the cup that runneth over. It's the breath of life, ours alone, always there, the oneness that we are, our essence, the universal flow of what is and we are. It's different from the Main Central Flow, and our free will and choice can interfere with it. You can experience this Flow by breathing ever so softly and gently straight up to the crown of your head.

This Flow descends centrally from just below the nose through the front ribs and abdomen to the pubic bone and connects in the perineum with the Governing Vessel. From the center of the forehead (third eye), it moves to the center top of the head and descends along the spine to the tailbone and connects in the perineum with the Conception Vessel.

You can assist this Flow by placing your right hand at the base of the head (4's) and then move your left hand by touching between each vertebrae all the way down the spine until you reach the coccyx (tailbone). If you discover a vertebra that seems to be out of alignment, hold the place alongside it and the opposite 11 or 3 area, or the opposite high 19. Then do the Main Central Flow to support balance.

Thumb Flow

A quick Flow to do when Lung and Large Intestine Meridians intermingle. Hold same side 3 and pulse area on the wrist (thumb side). Helps release tensions causing lung congestion; heart palpitation; eye irritation; perspiring when sleeping; nosebleed; stuffy nose; swollen cheeks or throat; or pains in breast, upper arms, elbows, teeth, and throat.

Self-Help: Three tense knots may appear in the armpit. Put one hand on the knot on the thumb side and the other hand on the same side point 14 or on the opposite side points 3 or 11.

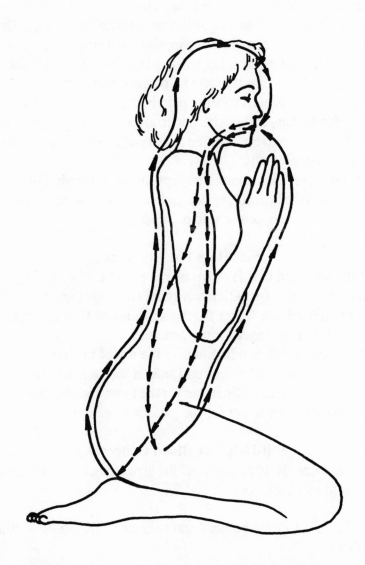

Figure 21: Vertical Harmony Flow

Little Finger Flow

A quick Flow to do when Heart and Small Intestine Meridians intermingle. Hold same side point 10 or 10 in the center of the shoulder blade and pulse area on the wrist (little finger side). Or hold pulse area on the wrist (little finger side) and first, third or seventh thoracic. The first thoracic helps digestion; the second thoracic helps breathing; and the third thoracic helps the diaphragm.

Helps release tensions causing pain in the heart, appendix, ventral arms, solar plexus, shoulders, upper arms and elbows; and assists feverish palms; cold feet; swollen throat and cheeks; and eyeballs that seem to be popping out.

Self Help: Three tense knots may appear in the armpit. Put one hand on the knot on the little finger side and the other hand on the same side point 14 or on the opposite side points 3 or 11.

Self-Help For Digestion

Put the left hand upside down on the top of the head. Right hand holds the left thumb for the left side of the stomach; then the right hand holds the left middle finger for the spleen; and then the right hand holds the left little finger for the pancreas.

Put the right hand upside down on the top of the head. Left hand holds the right thumb for the right side of the stomach; then the left hand holds the right middle finger for the liver; and then the left hand holds the right little finger for the gall bladder.

Self-Help For Blood Congestion

Hemorrhoids: Hold points 8 and the area along the opposite side of the rectum. Release points 8 and 25.

Nosebleeds: Release points 4 and balance the Kidney and Bladder Meridians.

Menstruation: Release points 2, 15, 8, and 16, and the pubic and tailbone areas.

Bleeding ovaries: Release points 25.

Vomiting of blood: Clear the neck and shoulder area and do the Fatigue Flow. Release points 3, 11, 12, and 15.

Blood in the bowel movements or urine: Release points 15, 25, and 2 and the pubic and tailbone areas. Do the Central and Diagonal Flows, and balance the Kidney and Bladder Meridians.

Coughing up blood from the lungs: Do the Major Vertical Flow and balance the Bladder Meridian. Release points 3, 10, 9, 23, 25, and 2.

Varicose veins: Release points 8 and 15.

Hold points 2 and and opposite points 1 to assist abdominal areas. Hold points 2 and opposite points 8 or 24 to assist lower back.

To Reverse The Movement Order
Of Progressive Patterns Of Illness
Tension, pain and illness often come and go or move along in a cyclical rhythm similar to other rhythms in our bodies. This quick little Flow signals the body to stop the destructive cycle. Use this and then restore balance where it is needed. Hold same side points 6 and little toe.

Spinal Vertebrae And Their Relationships To The Body
As you read this, think of the words "contract" and "expand" as words related to "tense" and "relax" respectively. Also think of the words "stop" and "assist" as representing actions intended to restore balance. When one acts out of an intent to restore balance, things decrease and increase, lower and raise, contract and expand, end and

renew more in the manner of rhythms and cycles rather than fixed conditions.

Cervicals:

1st - Lowers fever, revives unconscious person, and regulates pulse. Thumb.

2nd - Stops nausea, stimulates teeth, and opens pupils. Index finger.

3rd - Stops elbow pain, contracts lungs, and corrects diaphragm. Middle finger.

4th - Contracts veins of the heart, liver, kidney, spleen and lungs. Ring finger.

5th, 6th and 7th - Contracts veins of the teeth, throat, thyroid and esophagus. Little finger.

Thoracics:

1st - Assists all digestive difficulties and all organs, stops heart and stomach pain, and decreases lung blood. Thumb.

2nd - Corrects mitral difficulties in the heart. Index finger

3rd - Assists lungs and breathing, and makes milk in the breasts. Middle finger.

4th - Keeps upper thoracic open, expands esophagus, and contracts kidney. Ring finger.

5th - Contracts the heart and stomach, balances blood pressure, and opens pylorus. Little finger.

6th - Expands the trachea. The hollow at the base of the thumb at the wrist (palm side).

7th - Assists the diaphragm, expands the kidneys, and contracts all internal organs. Thumb.

8th - Index finger.

9th - Assists liver. Middle finger.

8th and 9th - Increases function of the heart, expands gall bladder, and stimulates the bladder.

10th - Assists gall bladder. Ring finger.

11th - Assists spleen. Little finger.
12th - Assists stomach. Hollow at the wrist.
10th, 11th, and 12th - Expands stomach, intestines, liver, gall bladder, uterus, lungs, and ureter, and assists leg ailments.

Lumbars:
1st - Thumb.
2nd - Assists kidney. Index finger.
3rd - Assists large intestine. Middle finger.
4th - Assists small intestine. Ring finger.
1st through 4th - Contracts veins of stomach, intestines, liver, kidney, spleen, uterus and bladder.
5th - Shrinks bladder. Little finger.

Sacrum:
1st - Is called a thoroughfare. Thumb.
2nd - Index finger.
3rd - Middle finger.
1st, 2nd and 3rd - Assists reproductive organs.
4th - Ring finger.
5th - Little finger.
4th and 5th - Assists toes and soles of feet.

Chest-Back Expanding And Contracting Flow
Our attitudes and emotions become expressed through our bodies. Sometimes our shoulders curve forward and droop and our chests cave in, and sometimes our shoulders raise up and back and our chests puff up and our rib cages becomes high and rigid. This Flow brings balance to these areas and helps vertebrae return to their natural positions, restores easy breathing, rejuvenates the body, adjusts metabolism and revitalizes.
If your shoulders are back and your chest is expanded, contract the

shoulders by putting your right fingers on your left foot (on the ball of the foot midway between points 6 and 7), and your left fingers on your right foot (same area).

If your shoulders are forward and your chest is caved in, expand by putting your right fingers on your right foot (same area as above on ball of foot) and your left fingers on your left foot (same area).

Diagonal Muscle Flow

When we become extremely tense and rigid, it's difficult for our bodies to remove waste and heal the tissues. This quick Flow helps relax all the muscles and rejuvenate the body, adjusts metabolism and aids muscle tone. (Note: The Liver and Gall Bladder Meridians also assist the muscles in the body).

If you're very hard and tense but also thin, put your right fingers on your right outer knee one inch down and one inch in from the right point 8, and put your left fingers on your left outer knee one inch down and one inch in from the left point 8. (Hands uncrossed).

If you're very hard and tense but also heavy, put your right fingers on your left outer knee one inch down and one inch in from the left point 8, and put your left fingers on your right outer knee one inch down and one inch in from the right point 8. (Hands crossed).

Skin Surface Ascending Flow

The skin is the largest organ of elimination in the body, and it helps regulate body temperature. This quick Flow helps to remove fatty substances, regulate body temperature and perspiration, and to correct extreme hairiness and complexion problems such as acne.

Hold same side little toes and points 6 in the center of the foot. Hold one foot until the energy feels balanced and then hold the other foot. To locate the point, find point 6 and then move from the inner edge of the foot toward the pocket in the center.

Deep Skin Descending Flow

This quick Flow regulates body temperature, is good for hot flashes, relieves gaseous toxins, clears the complexion, assists the lymph system, and helps with difficulties such as hives, scars, pockmarks and psoriasis. It assists mental and emotional difficulties, headaches, migraines, breathing, digestion and elimination. For good results, hold twenty minutes a day for two weeks — pulsing should occur in all fingers.

Self Help: Spread palms and fingers of right hand on the right calf of the leg, and spread palms and fingers of the left hand on the left calf of the leg. (Hands uncrossed). Then switch and spread palms and fingers of left hand on the right calf of the leg, and spread palms and fingers of the right hand on the left calf of the leg. (Hands crossed).

Five Quick Flows To Assist Various Common Difficulties

Quick Flow One: This Flow releases tension that may result in hepatitis (liver), gall stones, appendicitis, abdominal pain, dysentary, large and small intestine difficulties, breathing, breast problems or growths in the reproductive organs.

Right Flow: Hold the right point 11 with your left hand, and move your right hand to right point 25, then to left point 2, and then to right point 15.

Left Flow: Hold the left point 11 with your right hand, and move your left hand to left point 25, then to right point 2, and then to left point 15.

Quick Flow Two: This Flow releases tension that may result in tonsilitis, asthma, bronchitis, menstrual pain, nausea, neck spasms, callouses on the bottom of the feet, corns on the big toe, or leg pain from the knees down on the dorsal side. This Flow assists all feet and throat difficulties.

Left Flow: Put your right hand on left point 16 and your left hand on left point low 8 (center of the calf).

Right Flow: Put your left hand on right point 16 and your right hand on right point low 8 (center of the calf).

Quick Flow Three: This Flow releases tension that may result in neuralgia, rheumatism, infantile paralysis, joint pains, arthritic conditions, migraines, various paralyses, or when the arms and legs become stiff and bent. This Flow assists every joint in the body.

First hold the left point 5 with your right hand and the left point 16 with your left hand. Then switch to the other foot and hold the right point 5 with your right hand and the right point 16 with your left hand. Notice that the right hand always holds points 5.

Quick Flow Four: This Flow releases tension that may result in hip imbalance, spinal curvature, general misalignment of the body, or paralysis anywhere in the body. This Flow assists temperature regulation, reproductive organ function, and relaxes the hips.

If both shoulders are tipped forward, put your right hand on the left point 8 and your left hand on right point 8 and hold both points simultaneously until the energy feels balanced.

If the right shoulder is high and the person seems pulled toward the left, put your right hand on the left point 8 and hold it. This helps to cool the body.

If the left shoulder is high and the person seems pulled toward the right, put your left hand on the right point 8 and hold it. This helps to warm the body.

Quick Flow Five: This Flow releases tension that may result in fatigue, an accumulation of toxins in the body, stiff limbs and joints, arthritis, nearsightedness and liver difficulties.

Left Flow: Put your right hand on left point 19 and your left hand on left point 3.

Right Flow: Put your left hand on right point 19 and your right hand on right point 3.

Breathing And Digestion

This Flow (pp. 271, 272) balances the ascending and descending flows in the body. By releasing tension in points 9 and 10, it corrects eating and breathing problems and therefore assists such things as asthma, chest congestion, allergies, emphysema and digestive difficulties. It also relieves tension that may result in back problems and in leg problems such as varicose veins, and it assists the lungs, neck, pelvic girdle, heart, arms, breast and chest. After drug abuse has ended, this Flow will help the body get rid of toxins. It's an excellent Flow for deep emotional tension, and will help people complete the grieving process and let go.

Quickie self-help: Make a circle with thumbs over same side ring fingers, press slightly and hold.

Dizziness

This Flow (pp. 273, 274) balances the vertical and diagonal flows in the body. Dizziness results from imbalance between the right and left 9's and 10's. Points 18 and 19 help restore equilibrium in the body and balance to the right and left 9's and 10's.

Back Of Leg Pain

This Flow (pp. 275, 276) relieves tension in the arms, legs, shoulders, breasts and pelvic girdle. It assists people who have been unable to lift. Leg pain results from tension in the opposite arm and shoulder. This Flow helps relieve varicose veins. Use with the 16, 17, 18, 19 Release for good results. If there is sciatica pain, the 12's and 15's must be free of tension before pain will subside.

Self-Help: For left leg pain, put your left hand on left point 25, and put your right hand on left center back of knee, then on left point 24, and then on left point 3. For right leg pain, put your right hand on right point 25, and put your left hand on right center back of knee, then on right point 24, and then on right point 3.

Hip Pain

This Flow (pp. 277, 278) is excellent for sciatica and lower back problems. It generally relieves pain no matter how severe. I have personally witnessed some rather astounding one-session healing in people who previously had years of chronic lower back problems and in several people who couldn't walk at all. When you begin this Flow (step one), hold each toe one at a time until you feel the energy flow and then hold them all at once until you feel the energy flow smoothly. As you move to step two, continue holding all three toes and do so as you proceed from step two through step fourteen.

Self-Help: For right side hip pain, hold little, ring and middle toes of left foot with your right hand, and put your left hand on the right side of the pubic bone, and then move it to right point 12.

For left side hip pain, hold little, ring and middle toes of right foot with your left hand, and put your right hand on the left side of the pubic bone, and then move it to left point 12.

Eyes

If the lungs are clear, the emotions are clear, and then the eyes become clear. When points 20 and 21 are clear, points 23 will open. The right point 10 affects the left eye. Specific steps in this Flow (pp. 279, 280) are related to tension affecting other parts of the body. For example:

Steps 1, 2: (10 area) - lung congestion.

Steps 3, 4: (20, 21 area) - blood pressure and same side eye tension.

Steps 5, 6, 7: Epilepsy, pancreas, heart palpitation, and constipation.

BREATHING AND DIGESTION
Left Flow - Sit Left

STEPS	LEFT HAND	RIGHT HAND
1	left 18	left high 19
2	left 14	"
3	right high 1	"
4	"	left 15
5	left 6	"
6	left middle toe	"
7	left 8	"
8	left 15	left 2
9	"	left 23
10	right 25	"
11	right 13	left 10
12	left middle finger	"
13		
14		
15		
16		

BREATHING AND DIGESTION
Right Flow - Sit Right

STEPS	LEFT HAND	RIGHT HAND
1	right high 19	right 18
2	"	right 14
3	"	left high 1
4	right 15	"
5	"	right 6
6	"	right middle toe
7	"	right 8
8	right 2	right 15
9	right 23	"
10	"	left 25
11	right 10	left 13
12	"	right middle finger
13		
14		
15		
16		

DIZZINESS
Left Flow - Sit Left

STEPS	LEFT HAND	RIGHT HAND
1	right 21	left 12
2	right 22	"
3	right 19	"
4	right 18	"
5	left high 1	"
6	"	left 9
7	"	left 10
8		
9		
10		
11		
12		
13		
14		
15		
16		

DIZZINESS
Right Flow - Sit Right

STEPS	LEFT HAND	RIGHT HAND
1	right 12	left 21
2	"	left 22
3	"	left 19
4	"	left 18
5	"	right high 1
6	right 9	"
7	right 10	"
8		
9		
10		
11		
12		
13		
14		
15		
16		

BACK OF LEG PAIN
Left Flow - Sit Left

STEPS	LEFT HAND	RIGHT HAND
1	left 24	left 25
2	"	left 9
3	left 25	"
4	"	left 12
5	"	right 11
6	"	right 19 (little finger side)
7	"	right 17
8	"	right 15
9		
10		
11		
12		
13		
14		
15		
16		

BACK OF LEG PAIN
Right Flow - Sit Right

STEPS	LEFT HAND	RIGHT HAND
1	right 25	right 24
2	right 9	"
3	"	right 25
4	right 12	"
5	left 11	"
6	left 19 (little finger side)	"
7	left 17	"
8	left 15	"
9		
10		
11		
12		
13		
14		
15		
16		

LEFT HIP PAIN
Left Flow - Sit Right

STEPS	LEFT HAND	RIGHT HAND
1	left 2	right little, fourth, & middle toe (hold in sequence until flow
2	left 23	comes in & then hold together) "
3	left 9	"
4	left 10	"
5	left 3	"
6	left high back 19	"
7	left ring finger	"
8	right 2	"
9	right 23	"
10	right 9	"
11	right 10	"
12	right 3	"
13	right high back 19	"
14	right ring finger	"
15		
16		

RIGHT HIP PAIN
Right Flow - Sit Left

STEPS	LEFT HAND	RIGHT HAND
1	left little, fourth, & middle toe (hold in sequence until flow	right 2
2	comes in & then hold together) "	right 23
3	"	right 9
4	"	right 10
5	"	right 3
6	"	right high back 19
7	"	right ring finger
8	"	left 2
9	"	left 23
10	"	left 9
11	"	left 10
12	"	left 3
13	"	left high back 19
14	"	left ring finger
15		
16		

278

EYES
Left Flow - Sit Right

STEPS	LEFT HAND	RIGHT HAND
1	right 10	right center of the armpit
2	right index finger	"
3	right 4	"
4	left 20	"
5	left 21	"
6	left 20	"
7	"	left 14
8	"	left 1
9	"	left second toe (sole side)
10		
11		
12		
13		
14		
15		
16		

EYES
Right Flow - Sit Left

STEPS	LEFT HAND	RIGHT HAND
1	left center of the armpit	left 10
2	"	left index finger
3	"	left 4
4	"	right 20
5	"	right 21
6	"	right 20
7	right 14	"
8	right 1	"
9	right second toe (sole side)	"
10		
11		
12		
13		
14		
15		
16		

7

Coming
Full Circle

We began our journey by identifying trauma and abuse and some of the ways they affect our mind-brain-body. We continued with the healing ritual and ways to practice touch. And now we'll finish where we began by putting it all together.

It's easy to lose sight of our purpose if we get caught up in all the ways to "fix" our fat bodies, PMS, wrinkles, headaches, bloated bellies, and bad tempers. In fact, it's amazingly easy to lose sight of the truth if we begin to believe in the ritual itself rather than what it reveals.

The ritual of healing reveals the following:

1. All of the Flows are a teaching.

2. The wisdom is in the practice rather than the method.

3. Each instruction is a guide.

4. The points may be special or ordinary.

5. Touch can be empty or full.

6. Some people will listen for the silence and others will be content with the noise.

7. All problems can be captured in the question.

8. All difficulties can be resolved within.

9. Learning is an inner process that results from practice.

10. All healing results from learning that leads to wisdom.

11. People who listen for the silence will hear the voice of the Divine.

12. People who practice kindness will be moved from within into a new way of being.

One of the most fundamental truths to remember from this book and during the ritual of healing is that we're touching ourselves from the inside out. We heal from the inside out, and healing continues as we learn to live our lives from the inside out. All problems arise when we reverse this process and try to live from the outside in.

The Flows As A Teaching

Each time you touch yourself or someone else, you'll accomplish little or nothing if you focus on the external part of the ritual. The moment you focus upon the Divine, the confusion (noise) will cease and you'll touch into the silence that teaches and heals.

Circle Practice #1: Do the same flow several different ways until you realize from within what you are learning each time you practice a flow on yourself or someone else. For example:

1. Go through all the steps and touch each point with indifference.

2. Repeat the same steps and quickly poke at each point.

3. Repeat the same steps and hold each point with a firm pressure for two or three minutes.

4. Repeat the same steps and hold the attitude about how wonderful you are for healing this sick person.

5. Repeat the same steps with kindness.

6. Repeat the same steps as an opportunity to learn from a Wisdom that moves in the silence and stirs those who are still.

Circle Practice #2: Do this same process in your everyday life.

1. Spend several hours treating everyone you meet with indifference.

2. Then spend several hours poking at people by being abrupt. Act as if people don't count except in terms of their usefulness to you — like getting the job done quickly, or waiting on you first, or immediately giving you the answer you want.

3. Then spend several hours firmly controlling everyone you meet by asking just one more question, taking just a little longer than you need to when there's a line of people behind you, or by holding someone in a tight, gripping hug.

4. Then spend several hours acting positively wonderful, benevolent, brilliant or righteously obligated toward everyone you meet while you hold the attitude of how much better they feel when you're around, and how much you do for them.

5. Then spend several hours just being kind to yourself and everyone you meet. (Note: if you flip back into #4 behavior of being nice, sweet, good and right — this isn't kindness. Kindness isn't visible or obvious).

6. Then spend several hours walking around doing whatever you're doing with a sense of humility and gratitude for being able to be reached, touched and taught by a nurturing Wisdom that follows you wherever you go.

The Wisdom Is in the Practice Rather Than the Method

Many students learn different methods of healing and immediately want to teach these methods. When a spiritual ritual is secularized by people who haven't been touched and moved by its spiritual essence, the ritual eventually becomes associated with nonsense or failure. Spiritual truths and inner wisdom can be communicated from one person to another through hundreds of different rituals. But the ritual itself is empty unless the teacher overflows and the students are willing to be filled with silence.

Circle Practice #3:

1. Read the symptoms for several meridians that seem to describe the difficulties you're experiencing. Close the book, hope the symptoms go away, and notice if they do.

2. Get together with a friend and discuss symptoms, points, data, theory and method. End your meeting and notice if either one of you feels any better.

3. Read this book, get some realizations, and write them in your journal. After about a week or two, notice whether you feel any better or are still just getting realizations.

4. Spend five or ten minutes each night feeling new feelings in different parts of your body. Ask to be received in the Light and guided and protected by Father-Mother God or your Higher Power or the nurturing Wisdom of the Divine and then — go to sleep. Notice if you begin to feel any different and if anything seems to shift in your life.

5. Get together with a friend, pick a Flow that seems right, get comfortable and safe, keep it soft and simple, and take turns giving and receiving one Flow. Notice what's different immediately afterwards and during the next couple days.

Circle Practice #4:
1. Read a good book about something like healing, cognitive therapy, or getting along in relationships. Mark all over the book, discuss it with others, or make a few notes in your journal. Notice whether your life changes or you feel any better.
2. Go take some classes, attend several conferences, and get together with others to discuss what you've learned and what it means. Notice whether your life changes or you feel any better.
3. For several days, discuss your realizations with everyone you meet and tell your story about being abused and what you realize about that now. Notice if your life changes or you feel any better.
4. Spend several days just feeling whatever you're feeling wherever you go. Act like someone who doesn't know very much but that's okay because all you're expected to do is to be willing to feel whatever you feel in your body.
5. Get together with a friend, allow at least two hours to play together, get comfortable and safe, keep it soft and simple, and take turns choosing and accepting which game you'll play for each hour.

Each Instruction Is A Guide
When someone tells you to meditate on a mandala, gaze at a flame or enter the house of God, they're giving you instructions that guide. Most people follow obediently for awhile until they're distracted or bored, or they refuse because they already know it won't work because it's utter nonsense. If you'll use instruction and discipline like a guide and let it penetrate you within, you'll discover the mandalas of the mind, and the flame that overflows like a fountain, and the architecture of the Divine. You'll follow your own star and become the brilliance you see.

Circle Practice #5:
1. Find a little book of parables or koans and read it.
2. Take several classes in Hatha Yoga, T'ai Chi, Chi Kung, Feldenkrais or Alexander Method and ask yourself what moves more when you move less. Also ask yourself what happens in focused movement that doesn't happen when you move without being focused.
3. Do one Flow on someone without focusing on what you're doing, why you're there or who you're with. Then do the next Flow with focused attention (i.e., I'm doing a Bladder Flow on Susie to help her release tension in her calves and lower back). Notice which way was kinder for both of you.
4. Do one Flow on someone with a very pointed, alert, attentive focus upon your fingertips (your eyes will feel like they're fixed and focused right at the spot you're touching). Then do the next Flow in a dreamy, meditative state of attentive presence in your fingertips (your eyes will feel like they're gazing peripherally even though you'll be aware of changes in the points you're touching). Which way is more like kindness?

Circle Practice #6:
1. Write down three things that are bothering you and reverse them, and then notice what shifts (i.e., poisitions, attitudes, actions) if the reversal is true. For example: Switch — Lisa is avoiding me; Tom says I'm a slob; and I don't like Betty to, I'm avoiding Lisa; I say I'm a slob; and Betty doesn't like herself.
2. Spend fifteen minutes exercising just because you know you should, and then spend fifteen minutes moving to Motown or some music of your choice. Notice whether anything's different.
3. Go to your next meeting just because you're supposed to be there and righteously show up on time. Then go to another meeting with some idea about what you're doing and why you're there, and say hello to the people you're with.

4. The next time you're with someone, stare right at them, get a little intense so they'll know you're paying attention, and laugh, cough, wiggle, or comment on everything they say and do, so they'll know you're right there with them. If you survive this one, go find someone else to be with and spend a few minutes talking with them softly and gently in a state of kindness.

NOTE: As you do the homework, see if you can discover which patterns are abusive and which ones aren't. How did you know the difference?

The Points May Be Special Or Ordinary

A piece of wire is ordinary until it's part of a violin. When people go to a hardware store, they don't associate wire with music. A violin may appear to be just wood and wire until it's played, but its value is revealed by the artist, not by someone who isn't trained or skilled. An artist is someone who can hear the music before she learns to play the instrument, and in the playing she learns to create music she never heard before.

Circle Practice #7: Do one Flow on someone and be aware of them as flesh, muscles and bones in a body that is either tense or relaxed. Then do a second Flow on that person and be aware of them as a moving pattern of light. Notice whether the points feel different when you're different.

Circle Practice #8: Have sex with someone as if you're two physical bodies getting together to have an orgasm, and do all the right things so that will happen. Then make love with that same person as if you're two moving patterns of light. (Read chapter eight on Tantra in *Sex, Pleasure and Power: How To Emerge Spiritually Without Going Nuts.* — see Notes).

Touch Can Be Empty Or Full

The wilderness of a crowd becomes background when your lover crosses the room to greet you.

Circle Practice #9:

1. The next time you give a Flow, think of all the things you could be doing if you weren't sacrificing yourself for that person. Notice whether the person gets restless and wants to get up and leave. Then give another Flow to the same person while you think about the opportunity to discover something about life because that person is there with you while you give her a Flow. Notice what's different for both of you.

2. Give someone a Flow while you worry about yourself and whether or not you're doing it right. Does the energy flow from your fingers? Then give that person another Flow while you trust that you're both being guided by a Higher Power throughout the whole session. Does the energy flow between you?

Circle Practice #10:

1. Hang all over the person you love so they'll know you care. If your relationship survives, spend a couple days just flirting, glancing, listening, and moving about softly with presence.

2. Give someone exactly the right gift for the right reason at the right time. At another time, give this person something you bought spontaneously in a moment filled with love.

Some People Will Listen For The Silence
And Others Will Be Content With The Noise

You can always tell a tourist by the way she moves about and what she carries with her — eyes darting here and there, lists of things to do, and a camera to record the important things that happen. A tourist pays for noise to relieve the stress from boredom. She dies between events and awakens long enough to board the next bus. Just passing through — here today, gone tomorrow.

Circle Practice #11:

1. Try to do ten Flows on someone in an hour so you won't miss anything. Notice if her pulses are balanced when you finish. The next time, pick one or two Flows that seem just right and take your time. Check her pulses afterwards.

2. Do a Flow on someone and hold the thought that if you're really good, she'll get well or feel better right away. Notice how you both feel afterwards. Then do a Flow with the same person and just be kind. Notice how you both feel afterwards.

3. After you've received a Flow, you'll be more sensitive and feeling. Every time your feelings remind you about the ways you've been hurt and abused, get angry, cry, and talk a lot about everything that happened to you. The next time you receive a Flow and you begin to have feelings that remind you about the ways you've been hurt, go into your body and consciously feel those feelings. Let the anger and sadness move through you and don't talk about it with anyone. Notice what happens.

Note: If you continue to let your emotions move through you no matter what, notice what else happens. One of the best ways to help someone become aware of their posture or muscular tension is to have them exaggerate that posture or the tension in the muscle and then relax and let go. Each time you start to become emotional, pause and focus upon what you feel (a very subtle "emotional flex"), and while you focus *and* feel, relax and let it melt away.

Circle Practice #12:

1. Write down all your achievements, awards, degrees, and monumental feats of accomplishment. Spend the next several days 'name dropping' yourself and talk about what you've done, what you can do, and how hard it's been for you. If you have any friends left, spend the next few days carrying on conversations that are newsy, bantering and flirty, primarily listening to what others say to you, or conversations that are action-oriented to accomplish a task. (What about exchanging ideas? — notice your intent first).

2. The next time you're bored and restless, call a friend and talk about anything, gossip and exchange hard-luck stories, or go to the movies with someone, or go shopping. Notice if you feel less bored and restless afterwards. Then the next time you get bored and restless, stretch out flat on your back on your bed and take a "feel trip" through your body while you describe the experience to yourself in "feel talk." Then call a friend, go to the movies, or go shopping if you still want to and notice whether you feel less bored and restless afterwards.

All Problems Can Be Captured In The Question

A good question captures the essence of a problem in such a way that the solution becomes evident within the process of questioning. The question itself reveals the nature of the problem. For example, the question, "Does Bob still love me?", reveals that something was evident to you before that is no longer evident now. What did you use for evidence? Is just the evidence missing, or is love absent as well? The solution may depend upon what you used — the evidence — as criteria for love.

A question provides boundaries for the mind. We are the questioner, the quest, and the origin of the question. Overachievers who compete and judge can't formulate good questions because they already know it all. Emotional people who whine and blame can't fomulate good questions because they've already decided how it is. People become abusive when they haven't learned how to question.

Circle Practice #13:

1. The next time you receive a Flow, if you're sensitive or uncomfortable afterwards, you may find yourself asking, "Why am I in pain? How come I have diarrhea? How long will I feel this way?"

Assuming you know that the first stages of healing may be uncomfortable, what really underlies all of these questions? Isn't there an assumption that something's wrong and you wish it were right?

What if you assumed that the pain and diarrhea were signals that your body was waking up, healing, and eliminating toxins and waste from your system? If so, you might ask the question, "What can I do to support my comfort without interfering with the healing process?"

2. If you've been raped, battered or cruelly abused in other ways, what questions do you ask? Why did he, she, or they do that to me? Why do people act that way? What do people expect from me after the way I've been treated? How would he, she or they feel if someone did that to them? When will he, she or they realize how badly they've hurt me? Will he, she or they ever realize how cruel they've been to me?

These can be self-defeating or even dangerous questions if they're the only ones you ask. Try a few others like: Can I heal? If I can heal, what do I need to know so I can do it? When I heal, how will my lifestyle change? Even though I don't understand why people do cruel things to other people, am I willing to turn this question over to a Higher Power and get on with my life?

Circle Practice #14:

1. The next time you're in a restaurant and the waitress seems distracted and thoughtless, ask yourself if her child's in the hospital, or her husband just left her, or she can't pay the rent that month. Notice how these questions affect the way you treat her.

2. The next time you're tempted to laugh at or shun a woman who looks washed out, unkempt and addle-brained, ask yourself if she's been battered and abused. Notice what the question does to your perception of her.

3. The next time you run into one of those tough executive bitches, ask yourself if perhaps she was raised with four brothers and her parents wouldn't send her through college because they didn't want to waste their money on a girl. Did your question enable you to be kind?

4. If your last three lovers left you, ask yourself: Why or in what way did I want them to leave? How did I insure that they would leave? If a new lover comes along, what can I do to make him or her leave me?

All Difficulties Can Be Resolved Within

When someone we love is ill, injured or mean and we're physically and spiritually bonded with them, we suffer for them and ourselves. Suffering results when the spiritual bond is disrupted because both people are focused on pain. Pain is a signal of separation. Pain shows up in the physical world when the physical body separates from itself as a cooperative physical-spiritual unit.

Physical-spiritual disruption often occurs during illness or injury, or when people separate from one another by being mean and abusive. We all seek union within ourselves and with others. This union gets expressed as health, wholeness, and sanity. Serious disruption in the physical signifies a breakdown in the spiritual. Suffering results when we can't *express* our spiritual union within.

Answers and reasons won't undo the absolute pain and terror some people have experienced at the hands of others or from illness and injury. The stories are endless and reflect a nightmare of horror from cruelty and darkness. Restraint, punishment, crisis intervention, social services and health care are all necessary but — they're not enough. Healing begins with each individual who is willing to express kindness, courage and self-respect.

Circle Practice #15:

1. The next time you receive a Flow from a friend, wiggle around a lot, talk about your work, other people or the state of the nation, and get up to go to the bathroom or get a drink of water at least twice. Assuming you were good friends to begin with, how is your friendship after the session? Reverse this by being quiet and receptive.

2. Get a Flow from a friend and complain about your pain at least a dozen times during the session. Then call your friend everyday for the next week and tell her how bad you feel physically, emotionally and mentally since the session. Ask her to give you another Flow and notice what happens — does she cancel, forget, start the session late, or tell you her troubles and how hard things are for her during your second session? What happens to the friendship (spiritual bonding and physical cooperation)? Reverse this by noticing movement and change in your body, and acknowledging your friend for her support.

Circle Practice #16:

1. Decide that love is unconditional because it's spiritual. Call someone who loves you and arrange to meet that person for a picnic or (your choice).

Now, based on your decision about love, do things like the following: Show up late. Dish up your own food, cover the dish, move it out of reach and begin eating. When your friend starts to eat, get a magazine and read it. Don't speak to your friend for an hour or two, but talk to your dog and other people in the park. When the person asks you why you're treating him or her the way you are, tell them you aren't doing anything or say something sensible like, "My father raped me when I was two," or close them off completely by telling them, "This is just the way I am." If your friend gets upset or leaves, tell him or her that he or she obviously doesn't love you.

Note: The next time you're with someone who acts this way, try to make things better from the outside in by doing things like: Smile a lot. Carry on a conversation whether the other person talks or not. Cheerfully eat in silence. Offer the person some food and tell him or her how much fun you're having. Tell a joke, or say something nice.

Probably none of this will work. Kindness, courage and self-respect are much more apt to show up when you're willing to get up and leave. It's okay for someone to be miserable, but it's not a license to abuse others.

2. Pick a problem that has a simple solution like, "I haven't fed my cat for three days and she keeps meowing."

Call several friends, a veterinarian, the humane society, a neighbor or two and a couple of relatives. Tell each person your problem, and when they tell you to feed your cat, give them lots of reasons why you can't: I can't feed her until I know exactly what she should weigh. She may need dental work and I don't want to risk her swallowing a tooth. My husband beats me. I fed her three days ago. I don't think that's why she's meowing. Siamese cats meow more than Calico's. People blame me for everything. Migraines make me confused. Why can't she just curl up and keep quiet?

Afterwards, do you have any friends left? Is anyone still willing to talk with you about your cat? Is the problem still there?

Now write down several problems that may reveal where you cry out. What are you hungry for? Do your reasons and excuses feed you? What feeds you and relieves your pain from hunger?

For example, are you hungry for revenge? If so, go get revenge on someone and then notice if your hunger decreases or increases.

List everything you expect from others so you won't feel so miserable. Write out exactly how they have to be and what each person must do (i.e., what do you expect from them and what can they expect from you).

For example: I will only get a job done if I feel well, and I expect you to realize this and be willing to wait for my work. Sometimes I'll hand it in an hour late, sometimes a week late, and during severe crises, it may take me several months.

I'll only talk to you if I feel like it. I never make love until I haven't been upset for several days and feel certain I won't be upset in the near future. Then tell the other person that it's difficult for you to know when you'll be upset because it just happens and it's not always the same.

When you're finished with your list, notice whether or not anyone can ever express love or friendship toward you. Notice how this is like abusing and being abused. If you can't see it, switch roles.

Learning Is An Inner Process That Results From Practice

We learn about the world around us in many ways. Sometimes we learn by memorizing rules and data, and we tend to remember what we've learned as if it's separate from us. Other times we learn when something about what we're learning moves us inside ourselves and encourages us to act on what we feel. When we feel something about what we're learning, we tend to give it meaning and value and make it part of ourselves.

When what we learn seems separate from ourselves, things like rules and data become behaviors we're obligated to do or sterile ideas that someone else said were right. We then tend to act mechanically or stubbornly resist because we feel like we're being pushed around by others. We also tend to project our difficulties onto others and blame them for our failures and the way we feel.

When what we learn seems like part of ourselves, it becomes meaningful and valuable in our lives. We tend to protect and nurture what we've learned and act upon it with confidence. When we do this, we're able to be introspective about our attitudes and behaviors, and from this inner examination, we're able to make changes.

Inner learning provides us with inner boundaries and limits. We feel confident about what we'll accept and what we'll reject in our lives. We develop courage, self-confidence and self-respect. We develop our own identity and out of this, our work and our relationships become meaningful, valuable and satisfying.

Inner learning never stops. It continues every moment of every day for the rest of our lives. It's the process of looking within to see how we really feel about something and then reflecting that feeling in our behavior. It's looking within at our feelings, putting them into language, and then taking action in accordance with what we really say and how we really feel. This calls for non-judgmental, total honesty with ourselves to the best of our ability each day.

Circle Practice #17:

1. Give a Flow to someone and pretend that you're only doing it because I said you should, and that the most important part of giving the Flow is to do it right.

When you're finished with the Flow, tell the person that you did it because that's the one Jan Kennedy said you should do, and then tell the person everything you did that was right (i.e., you followed the instructions in the book, located all the points precisely where they were, held each point exactly the right amount of time, got through the Flow faster than the last time, didn't let your mind wander, and never thought a bad thought).

Notice how you feel. Notice if your friend feels warm and nurtured now that she knows how right, perfect, and obedient you are.

2. Then give another Flow to your friend and choose the one you feel is best. Do the Flow the way it feels the best to you (i.e., feel for the points and when it feels right, pause in that spot. Move in your own rhythm by some kind of inner sense that lets you know when to move on to the next point. Think about whatever feels right at the moment, and go ahead and have a "bad" thought or two if that happens).

Notice how you feel. Ask your friend how she feels and what happened within her while you were touching her. Then think about whether there's anything you might like to do differently the next time.

Circle Practice #18:

1. The next time you take a "feel trip" through your body, if your "feel talk" shifts into emotionally charged memories, write down at least three revenge scenarios or retaliatory actions that these memories prompt. For example, if you recall when your mother pulled your hair and spit in your face while she was drunk, which reminds you of when she locked you out in the cold all night because she and her boyfriend passed out and couldn't hear you knocking, what action comes up from within you? Is there anything, even a teensy bit, about wanting to grab her by her hair and smash her head against the wall, clobber her with the damn booze bottle she emptied, take her to Siberia in November and dump her from the car, or burn the house down with them in it so you can all be warm? Tell the truth.

Okay — if your list looked like material for "Crimes of Our Times" or "Memoirs of A Rotten Child," pause, breathe, feel and look again. You have some inner values that may provide you with some clues about your very own boundaries — rather than what society says about right and wrong or whatever your mom may have taught you. It's just that most of them may have come into being from unpleasant feelings rather than pleasant ones. However, it's at least a place to start.

If you leave these inner values (feelings) in the action form that wound up on your list, you can't act effectively because: a). The event is over. b). You'll need to recreate the hurt so you can do this to someone else. c). The cost is enormous for acting this way. d). If you're basically kind and law abiding, you'll need to split off from yourself so you can "forget" and deny ever having done or thought about doing something so dastardly. But most of all — e). You'll never have the chance to really learn something real sane and healthy about yourself.

2. Let's look inside of you and see what might be there. a). You have an inner value all your own about someone pulling your hair and spitting in your face. This is a pretty universal value among sane, sober human beings. So value number one, *no matter what,* I will not spend time with people who deliberately pull my hair and spit in my face. Now you can take action by putting this into practice in your daily life, and you can stick to this decision so long as it's still a deep inner value that's meaningful to you. It's one of your limits to begin establishing some boundaries for the person identified as you.

b). Value number two might be, "I will not live with anyone who does not respect my needs for warmth and shelter and my right to have them in my own home, or while I'm staying with them." Now you can take action and put this into practice in your daily life.

Looks simple now, but it hasn't been so simple if you've been abused, because the abuse itself taught you that you have little or no value and so you have no rights. Setting your own limits is the same as having rights, and coming from within yourself (your feelings) to set those limits, is an establishment of the value you place on you. These limits and values are the most important measures you can use to reveal your success, satisfaction, self-respect and well-being.

Circle Practice #19:

1. Spend the next few days comparing yourself with everyone to see which one of you is better or worse than the other. Check with your friends to see if anyone is getting better faster than you.

Then get out your journal and lie about how well you're doing, make up reasons for any failures you can't lie about, and judge yourself harshly for any failures you can't either lie about or make up good reasons for.

Vow to try harder to be better than anyone you know, and so perfect that no one can find fault with you ever again. Are you having fun yet? How are you sleeping? How's your blood pressure? What else do you need to learn so you can know it all the best and never make a mistake? Which people in your life regularly vote on you to let you know if you're better or worse? (Notice if you can spot any abuse of self or others.)

2. Now reverse this and at least pretend that you know that no one on the face of the earth has ever walked in your shoes. Spend the next few days noticing how you've changed through the years.

Notice if there's anything about you that never seems to really change even though you put it on your New Year's resolutions list every year. Spend a few minutes each day going on a "feel trip" to see if you can discover any values you have about one of these unresolved resolutions.

Break the *big change* you want into *little changes* that are related to it. Take a couple of "feel trips" on one of the little changes and see how that feels to you. If it feels right, put it into "I can do it" action language. Do this for a couple months without checking in with anyone but yourself, and only journal the truth about the gentle pitty pat from your own shoes.

All Healing Results From Learning That Leads To Wisdom

Whenever we learn something, we're changed by what we learn. As we learn and change, we develop an inner reference book called "wisdom."

Memorizing what's right or wrong is not the same as learning. This kind of thinking — "I'll have lots of friends and everyone will think I'm wonderful if I'm always right and know all the answers" — does not result in wisdom.

All learning is not equivalent to wisdom, but it does take a certain kind of learning to develop it. Very often, health and sanity depend upon knowing the difference between the two.

Circle Practice #20:

1. The next time you give a Flow, tell that person everything you're doing and why, so she'll understand and learn what it takes to get well. Afterwards, write down one or two Flows for her so she can do it herself. Notice how she looks and acts after the session, and ask her how she feels.

2. The next time you give a Flow to that person, say absolutely nothing except to gently murmur, "Hmmmm, that feels good," when you read her pulses at the end of the session. Notice how she looks and acts after the session, and just listen to whatever she has to say.

Circle Practice #21:

1. The next time someone tells you about something they've accomplished, tell them enthusiastically how great they are, mention several other important people who've accomplished something similar and suggest emphatically that your friend is in the big leagues now. Then knowingly remind that person what other people will probably think when they hear about it. Notice whether the person gets kind of plastic looking.

2. Then try something different the next time someone tells you about something they've accomplished: Just listen. Maybe ask them a question or two. Then listen. Or perhaps say something like, "You sound like you feel wonderful about X." Then listen. Notice whether the person relaxes and goes beyond the initial opener about accomplishment and says something deeper and more meaningful to her.

Note: If you still don't get a sense of what happened inside these people, have a friend role-play both roles with you after you tell that friend about something you've accomplished. Then notice the difference in learning that takes place inside of you. Which way leaves you anxious and which way leaves you confident? Can you spot why?

Also, when we're anxious, we don't feel safe—just like when we're abused. Is it possible that abuse is something that separates you from yourself, something that takes you away from an awareness of your own inner rights and limits and leaves you dependent upon the external world around you?

People Who Listen For The Silence
Will Hear The Voice Of The Divine

When I was little, I was taught to listen for the "still small voice" when I prayed. I thought this meant that God spoke in a tiny, little voice. Many years later when I read *The Teachings of Don Juan*, and Don Juan spoke about looking for the truth in the space between the cracks, I had a sense of what he said, but it didn't fully live inside me yet. Then one day something began to move inside me as a way to live and be — and I called it, "listening for the silence," or the "touch of silence." When it fully lives in you, you may call it by another name.

Circle Practice #22:
1. Give one Flow while your attention is on all the details about how to do a Flow.
2. Then give another Flow while you just follow the instructions the best you can and have your attention on an invisible, healing presence that seems to fill the room. Notice anything different between the two Flows.

Circle Practice #23:
1. Make plans to go somewhere with a friend. When you get together, act as if the most important part of getting together is where you're going to go, getting there on time, seeing everything there is to see, what it's going to cost, and how much you can do in the first hour.
2. During the second hour, act as if whatever happens is an opportunity to be together and interact in different ways. Notice whether you get to know your friend differently in the second hour than you did in the first one.

People Who Practice Kindness Will Be Moved From Within Into A New Way Of Being
Kindness is not something you can "send" or try to be or do for someone. Kindness already lives within you. When it's present, abuse is absent. Generally the word "kindness" is enough to evoke a feeling within so that your state of being will be one of kindness. If this word doesn't evoke something within you, try other words like gentleness or softness until you feel a shift within yourself.

When you discover the right word for you, you'll know it, because as long as you're aware of what that word means to you inside, you'll be unable to treat yourself or anyone else unkindly (abusively).

"Practicing kindness" means the willingness to put what you've learned (inside) into action. You'll know if you're putting it into practice because you'll begin feeling, and when you begin feeling, you'll realize how much courage it takes to be kind. Courage will dissolve the fear within you and you'll begin to feel safe.

Once you begin to feel safe, you won't need to step back to simpler ways of being and acting (regression) nearly as often. When you don't need to step back as often, you can begin going forward more often. When you can begin going forward, you can learn something new.

Circle Practice #24:

1. Give a Flow and make all the right gestures so the person will know you're being kind to them (i.e., smile a lot, use a tone of voice that will let them know how nice you are, ask them how they've been in a tone to let them know you're a kind, caring person, hold your face and body like a kind person would).

2. Then give a Flow while you're feeling kind within yourself. Notice any differences between the two Flows.

Circle Practice #25: The next time you're in a situation where you would normally smart off or act aloof, defiant, or defensive, pause, breathe, shift inside by becoming kind to yourself and everyone around you. Notice what happens. When you can do this, it's the beginning of the end and a doorway into the light.

We Heal From The Inside Out

The mind is a spiritual field of light and vital energy that surrounds us and moves within our bodies. We learn from the mind through feeling.

Circle Practice #26: All the facets of healing are interwoven, but generally we need to:

1. Get safe.

2. Be kind.

3. Feel whatever we can feel inside our bodies.

4. Practice being safe, kind and feeling, and the "I can do it" process.

5. Discover what gives us pleasure and bring these things or ways of being into our daily lives.

6. Continue this creative way of living to establish meaning, values and self-respect within ourselves. With these, we can form our limits and boundaries, our unique, individual identities.

> *Eventually, we become living beings*
> *who move in the light*
> *with serenity, courage and wisdom.*

8

The Mythology
Of Being

It's never been easy to talk about the essential nature of life or of being human. Many wise, enlightened beings have done their best to express principles of Truth through stories, parables, poetry and koans. Symbolism has always been used like a picture to convey a gestalt (all parts are unified) of information that is interrelated rather than linear (information that's sequential). All of the mysteries or sacred spiritual teachings have been passed from one person to another in these narrative and visual forms.

The Qabbalists (ancient Hebrew mystics) developed an exquisitely intricate geometric symbol called *The Tree of Life* (see figure 22, p. 306). Within this symbol, they incorporated the mystical wisdom of letters, numbers, and geometry. This mystical wisdom encompasses the symbolism used in astrology, tarot, and acupuncture. Like other symbols and stories, *The Tree of Life* was used to pass sacred teachings from one generation to another.

The healing ritual, *Touch of Silence,* is another way to impart wisdom from one person to another. The points are intricately related to letters, numbers, geometry, astrology, tarot, and acupuncture.

Touch softly and listen for the silence.

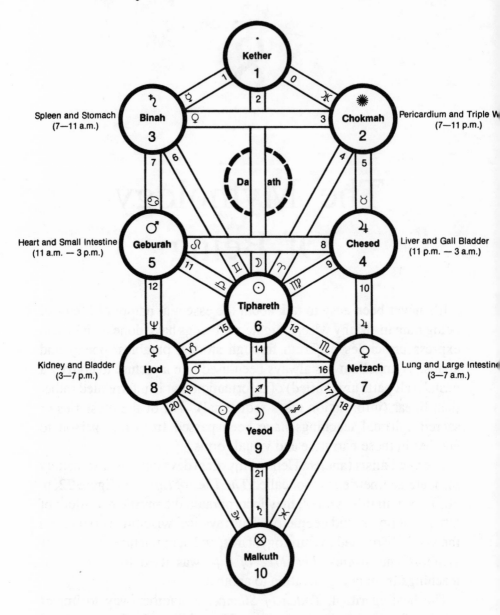

Figure 22: The Tree Of Life

The Points In Touch Of Silence

As a story, the points are like the paths on the Tree of Life. As symbols, the points are like the pictures expressed through the symbols of Hebrew letters, numbers, tarot and astrology. As a ritual, the touching of the points is similar to the rituals of laying on of hands, acupuncture and magic. As wisdom, the unfolding of healing is intended to reveal something about the essential nature of being human, and The Way or Tao of Life.

When the central points are tense, we become rhythmically imbalanced and devitalized, and tend to lose our Spiritual Will and feel empty within. When these points release, we begin to feel the Breath of Life, and we start to become creative, vital, and spiritually fulfilled. The central points correspond to path zero on the Tree of Life and to the principles symbolized by The Fool in tarot and the planet Uranus in astrology.

When points one are tense, we tend to be focused in a separative way as observer and object observed, and we rarely recognize ourselves as creators of our conditions. When these points release, we begin to focus as observer merged with that which is observed, and we start to notice that the essence of anything externalized already lives within us and becomes focused into manifestation through our thoughts and feelings. Points one correspond with path one on the Tree of Life and the principles symbolized by The Magician in tarot and the planet Mercury in astrology.

When points two are tense, we tend to reproduce ourselves by associating our self-imagery with painful, destructive memories. When these points release, a form of rebirthing starts to occur as we begin to recognize and remember ourselves in new ways. Points two correspond with path two on the Tree of Life and the principles symbolized by the High Priestess in tarot and The Moon in astrology.

When points three are tense, we tend to have difficulty creating new imagery to form a healthy self-image, and we may feel depressed and unattractive. When these points release, we begin to see new alternatives and we start to relax and become less defensive. Points three correspond with path three on the Tree of Life and the principles symbolized by The Empress in tarot and the planet Venus in astrology.

When points four are tense, we tend to have difficulty setting limits and regulating ourselves and thus, we tend to react rather than organize ourselves thoughtfully. When these points release, we begin to come from mental imagery into a conscious structure of speech and action. Points four correspond with path four on the Tree of Life and the priniciples symbolized by The Emperor in tarot and the sign Aries in astrology.

When points five are tense, we tend to have difficulty getting still and going within to listen to our inner teacher. When these points release, we begin to be kinder and start to develop inner meaning and values for ourselves and our life. Points five correspond with path five on the Tree of Life and the principles symbolized by The Hierophant in tarot, and the sign Taurus in astrology.

When points six are tense, we tend to organize ourselves into polarized categories such as up-down, good-bad, right-wrong, and we have difficulty realizing that our inner unity gives rise to opposition and differences so we can learn about our wholeness. When these points release, it's easier for us to perceive the unity and reciprocity in all things that initially may seem polarized, and it's easier for us to know about our own wholeness. Points six correspond with path six on the Tree of Life and the principles symbolized by The Lovers in tarot, and the sign Gemini in astrology.

When points seven are tense, we tend to seek nurturing and protection from people, places and things outside ourselves. When these points release, we begin to nurture and support ourselves from within, and as we feel safe, we become willing to take action in the world. Points seven correspond with path seven on the Tree of Life and the principles symbolized by The Chariot in tarot, and the sign Cancer in astrology.

When points eight are tense, we tend to stubbornly cling to false ego desires and petty attachments, and we may behave pretentiously or narcissistically with others just to get our way. When these points release, we begin to release ego attachments and petty willfulness as we discover the infinite nature of our being as a purposeful ray of light. Points eight correspond with path eight on the Tree of Life and the principles symbolized by Strength in tarot, and the sign Leo in astrology.

When points nine are tense, we're generally holding on to something that needs to be completed so we can let go and begin again, and we probably need to be touched with love and kindness so our inner light can transform us from within. When these points release, we begin to feel a sense of renewal and rejuvenation as our inner light forms a union with our blood to heal and revitalize our bodies. Points nine correspond with path nine on the Tree of Life and the principles symbolized by The Hermit in tarot, and the sign Virgo in astrology.

When points ten are tense, we tend to become arrogant, pretentious and grandiose. When this happens, we tend to perpetuate old patterns of behavior and repeat past mistakes until we begin to feel a deep sadness from expressing a false self within. It's said in ancient wisdom that the heart is the seat of the mind and the place of true wisdom. When these points release, we begin to rely less on outer knowledge and human law, and start to grasp the truth about wisdom and the laws of change. Points ten correspond to path ten on the Tree of Life and the principles symbolized by The Wheel of Fortune in tarot, and the planet Jupiter in astrology.

When points eleven are tense, we tend to take action out of a sense of duty or obligation, or we react to external conditions and tend to project blame onto others. When these points release, we start to generate action from a cooperative harmony that exists, within and without, prior to any action we take. Then our action begins to be an extension of our imagery and harmonious relatedness within, and it reflects the ritual of healing as a practical expression of wholeness. Points eleven correspond to path eleven on the Tree of Life and the principles symbolized by Justice in tarot, and the sign Libra in astrology.

When points twelve are tense, we tend to be caught up in brain-body reality and to try to effect change by seeking cause and effect in the physical world. When these points release, we begin to be aware that all change begins in the mind before it shows up in the physical, and that changes depend upon what we think and feel. Points twelve correspond to path twelve on the Tree of Life and the principles symbolized by The Hanged Man in tarot, and the planet Neptune in astrology.

When points thirteen are tense, we tend to separate the feelings in our hearts from the feelings in our genitals, and when we want to express love, we act as though we're nurturing or caretaking. We also tend to have difficulty renewing ourselves because we refuse to forgive and let go. When these points release, our sexual energy begins to join with our heart and brain centers, and we start to experience the magic of Love and the Wisdom of the Divine as our bodies become magnetized in a new way. Points thirteen correspond to path thirteen on the Tree of Life and the principles symbolized by

Death in tarot, and the sign Scorpio in astrology.

When points fourteen are tense, we tend to act as if we knew it all by interfering with the moving breath of life, which will bring us new knowledge and feeling if we let it. When these points release, we become more willing to test the waters so we can verify our thoughts and feelings and learn what's really true about them. Points fourteen correspond to path fourteen on the Tree of Life and the principles symbolized by Temperance in tarot, and the sign Sagittarius in astrology.

When points fifteen are tense, we tend to be humorless and to feel stuck, as we identify all our failures and limitations outside ourselves in the physical world. When these points release, we begin to see the humor in things that seemed so ominously permanent and real, and we quit taking ourselves so seriously by being less judgmental and punitive. Points fifteen correspond to path fifteen on the Tree of Life and the principles symbolized by The Devil in tarot, and the sign Capricorn in astrology.

Path fourteen, called the Angel of Light, leads us right into path fifteen, called the Angel of Darkness, and path fifteen is the first stage of spiritual unfoldment. When the fourteens release and we become aware of what we think and feel (light), we may, at first, blame others for how that is rather than continuing in our awareness and learning from within (darkness). The Angel of Light leads us to the Angel of Darkness to teach us to laugh and play whenever we're tempted to believe in the appearances of darkness and assign cause and blame in the physical world.

When points sixteen are tense, we tend to focus on old beliefs and prejudices to formulate our goals and take action, and as a result, we repeat destructive behaviors. When these points release, we may feel out of control and unsafe at first, as our old notions about reality break down and disintegrate, but eventually we become receptive to new ways of thinking and feeling. We learn to say what we see and have it agree with reality, which enables us to take positive, conscious action. Points sixteen correspond to path sixteen, the second stage of spiritual unfoldment, on the Tree of Life and the principles symbolized by The Tower in tarot, and the planet Mars in astrology.

Once we see the illusion in appearances outside ourselves (path fifteen), we are given the opportunity to destroy the illusions within ourselves through speech and action (path sixteen).

When points seventeen are tense, we tend to defend our thoughts and feelings as if they represented our identity of self. We may act as if we're just physical positions in time and space, disconnected from other selves. We also tend to join or lead groups as if we're unique and separate from the others, and thus, we may feel lonely and unsupported. When these points release, we begin to be "light in motion" and to live our lives like a meditation. We learn to "fish" by choosing a problem, posing a clear question, casting into our inner consciousness, and then waiting and listening. By questioning and listening, we become humble and realize our connection with others in every group we join or lead, and we begin to feel the warmth and support of genuine friendship. Points seventeen correspond to path seventeen, the third stage of spiritual unfoldment, on the Tree of Life and the principles symbolized by The Star in tarot, and the sign Aquarius in astrology.

When we destroy the darkness within ourselves through speech and action (path sixteen), we're given the opportunity to become humble about our success so we won't ruin it by thinking ourselves superior or special (path seventeen).

When points eighteen are tense, we may reproduce negativity unconsciously. Our sleep and dream cycles are periods in which we reproduce habitual thoughts and feelings and incorporate them within the cells of our bodies, and when points eighteen are tense, we have no awareness about what we're incorporating. When these points release, we're able to recognize and remember our dreams, and use these dreams as guides to our subconscious. In turn, we're able to pray before sleeping and watch the unfoldment of our prayers reveal themselves in our dreams before they become manifest in our lives or in our bodies. All the people in our dreams represent different facets of our nature and conflicts within ourselves. Points eighteen correspond to path eighteen, the fourth stage of spiritual unfoldment, on the Tree of Life and the principles symbolized by The Moon in tarot, and the sign Pisces in astrology.

Once we learn to question and listen (path seventeen), we can use our prayers and our dreams to heal (path eighteen).

When points nineteen are tense, we tend to struggle with our identity of self as the child of our parents and an embodiment of everything we've learned about right and wrong. Our will may be strong but it tends to be expressed as petty willfulness and defiance. When these points release, we become as little children and begin to surrender to the Will of the Divine. We start to experience a rebirth by surrendering all identity of self or purpose for being into the loving, nurturing, protective hands of the Divine Father-Mother. Points nineteen correspond to path nineteen, the fifth stage of spiritual unfoldment, on the Tree of Life and the principles symbolized by The Sun in tarot, and the Sun in astrology.

When we learn to pray and dream for healing, we become changed within the cells of our bodies (path eighteen), and this prepares us for innocence and surrender so we may be baptized in the light (path nineteen).

When points twenty are tense, we tend to be aware of ourselves and others as separate identities because our consciousness is still limited by our physical form, which leads us to relate ourselves within time-space. When these points release, we become aware of our immortality by becoming mentally passive, receptive and responsive to Divine Will. We begin to stop judging ourselves and others, and start to "listen" for which action to take or not take. Points twenty correspond to path twenty, the sixth stage of spiritual unfoldment, on the Tree of Life and the principles symbolized by Judgment in tarot, and the planet Pluto in astrology.

Our innocence and surrender during spiritual rebirth (path nineteen) prepares us to become bodies of light (path twenty).

When points twenty-one are tense, we tend to organize ourselves around duty and obligation to determine what we should or shouldn't do. We tend to govern ourselves by externalizing the origin of our actions, and we build governmental structures to organize and control others. When these points release, we become receptive to the One Organizing Principle and take action according to this Divine Law. When we begin to act in accordance with this Law, we incorporate these Laws within our organization of self and become full participants in Cosmic Government. Points twenty-one correspond to path twenty-one, the seventh stage of spiritual unfoldment, on the Tree of Life and the principles symbolized by The World in tarot, and the planet Saturn in astrology.

When we become bodies of light (path twenty), we become receptive to the Will of the One which organizes us as Divine Beings who consciously participate in God's Work (path twenty-one).

After we release points twenty and twenty-one and fully awaken points twenty-two, twenty-three, twenty-four, twenty-five and twenty-six, we're able to mirror geometric patterns that perfectly reflect Cosmic Law and Divine Probability.

The Tree Of Life As A Love Story

When love and kindness are present, cruelty and abuse are absent. What if you could learn to live your life as the creator and recipient of love and kindness every moment? If someone said, "You can have heaven on earth if you will accept several principles and begin to practice them so you can learn their wisdom," would you do it? Perhaps you'd need to be a Fool to think such things are possible.

Once upon a time just such a Fool set off upon a journey in search of her guiding star. As she stepped into the unknown, she began to feel vital and adventurous. Not knowing what she might discover, she became curious and alert. At first she noticed her surroundings attentively, like a tourist passing through, but as each day passed, the trees all began to look alike and her attention wandered aimlessly until she was aware of only her own breath. Then one day she became aware of how the trees were feeling and she began to develop a fondness for their presence. She began to focus upon her fondness for the trees as she continued along her path until one day an image appeared before her. It was an image of a huge old tree with a gnarly trunk and thousands of branches filled with tiny green leaves, a tree that was nothing at all like the ones she had been passing. This tree seemed to guide her through the woods, until by and by she came upon a meadow and saw to her amazement that the image danced across the grass and merged with itself. There in the center of the meadow stood the huge old tree waiting for her to come and rest among its roots.

She stumbled forward to reach the tree. Her limbs ached and she was feverish from hunger and fatigue. She thought she would sleep the night there and continue on her journey in the morning. But morning came and she awoke unable to lift herself and move about. After many hours had passed and she still could not move, she began to feel desperate. She appealed to the tree to help, but it only stirred with fondness for her. She began to focus on this feeling of fondness and it reminded her of other times when she was well and happy, and could easily run and play. Her reverie deepened and she drifted off to sleep ever so deeply and peacefully. When she awoke, she was amazed to discover that she felt well enough to move about and continue on her journey.

As she stood looking out across the meadow, she felt overwhelmed by its tantalizing beauty that seemed to stretch for miles in all directions. Starting had seemed easy when she first began her journey, but she had soon become accustomed to being guided by the image of the old, gnarly tree. But now the image and the tree were one, and although she could move, she felt reluctant to give up the safety she felt from the tree. Try as she might, she couldn't bring herself to step away from the tree and continue on her journey.

She sank to the ground in despair and once again appealed to the tree to help her, and once again it stirred with fondness toward her. She accepted these feelings of kindness, and then quietly began to listen to the meadow as it moved in rhythm with the wind. Little by little she began to see all the facets of its beauty, even those miles and miles away. As she listened and daydreamed, she imagined little purple flowers just beyond a very tiny hill, and she pretended that she wove them in a wreath about her head. Suddenly she realized that she was standing, and she felt eager to explore the meadow.

She bade the tree farewell and thanked it for its kindness and comfort, and then she set off upon her journey in search of little purple flowers. She walked for days undaunted in her search for the tiny hill she'd seen. For she knew from what she'd seen that the flowers were hidden just beyond that little mound. And then one day she saw the hill and ran as if refreshed to reach the top and look down upon a purple ocean moving softly in the breeze. She moved into the midst of purple and knowing what to do, she picked only the flowers that could be woven into a halo for her head.

After she had gathered enough flowers for her head, she returned to the little hill to sit and weave. At first she thought the flowers must be teaching her fingers how to move, but as she worked, she began to hear a voice instructing her from inside. It directed her to move one stem up, another down, and to twist one flower to the right, another to the left. It spoke to her about shades of dark and light, and when she'd woven almost all the flowers, it told her she was finished and helped her close the circle.

She put the crown upon her head and danced about for hours in delight. Then, feeling safe and comforted by her new guide, she slept peacefully through the night. Eager to get on with her journey, she awakened with the first ray of light. Thinking that the flowers brought the voice, she placed them on her head so she'd be told which way to go. It worked at once. The voice told her to turn to the left to discover the heat of the sun. Off she went in search of the sun's heat, and after several days, she realized that the earth was dry and barren, and her thirst seemed unquenchable. Again she turned to the voice and this time she asked which way to go to become cooler and to satisfy her thirst. The voice told her to go to the right, and she turned obediently on her way. Soon she discovered water and drank until her thirst was quenched. But another day passed, and she began to shiver as the cool air turned to sleet and snow.

She found a cave and huddled under brush for warmth. Feeling betrayed by the flowers, she flung her crown upon the wall and cried. She tried to sleep but longed in loneliness for the kindness of the tree. Her anger and grief soon turned to worry when she realized that she had nothing to eat. Then she felt foolish and ashamed for having crowned herself with such boldness, for believing that she and her crown were invincible. Her sadness left her feeling empty and bereft of trust and friendship, and then she became afraid. In her terror, she cried out for protection from the tree. Finally in exhaustion, she slept and dreamed.

In her dreams, she pleaded with the tree for protection, but the tree just stirred with fondness for her. When she awoke, all she felt was kindness and love. With nothing to do and nowhere to go, she basked in the warmth of kindness and vowed to return to the tree. That night she slept peacefully, and when she awoke in the morning, she knew that nothing could keep her from finding the tree. She jumped up to leave the cave and then realized that her knees trembled with fear, her belly rumbled with hunger, and her whole body shook from the cold. "I will find the tree!" she shouted passionately, and without thinking, she picked up the crown of flowers and, at once, she heard the voice tell her to run very, very fast in the direction of the rising sun.

Without hesitation, she bolted from the cave and ran. Her knees became strong, her hunger disappeared, and soon she was drenched in sweat. Many days and nights passed and still no sight of the tree. Now and then her will faltered but she felt the presence of the tree so unfailingly that her faith became strong. In time, she began to feel much like she had when she first began her journey. At times she felt delirious and fatigued. She had a vision of a cactus and became irritated because it reminded her of the hot, barren soil. The next day she ambled straight into the very cactus she'd seen and felt her body burn with pain from all the prickers embedded in her skin. Furious with the cactus, she cursed the other plants as well and wished them to be as broken and withered as she felt.

Still mumbling to herself about her plight, she plodded onward in search of the tree. Two days passed and on the third day, she awoke to a hot dry wind that seemed to wither everything it touched. In shock at what she saw, she began to plead with the wind. She promised never to curse again. She pledged her love for every living thing. She ran from bush to flower in search of life. In desperation, she searched for water and when she found a small stream, she began to dig a trench so the water could reach the plants. Her work helped some but not nearly enough. Finally, she lay down in tears and thought of the tree. Many other visions passed through her mind and she blessed each one and let it go.

And then a strange thing began to happen. The visions continued of plants great and small, and as each plant passed by, it stirred with fondness for her until she felt so peaceful that she rested and slept through the night. When she awoke in the morning, she felt renewed.

Her will to find the tree now lived in her heart. She knew she'd be reunited soon, she just didn't know exactly how. She stood gracefully and stretched and softly resumed her journey. As visions appeared she watched for each plant to reveal itself along the way, and when the voice spoke, she followed its direction.

Each time she met one of the plants she'd seen, she would stop awhile to chat and listen. Each one guided her a little further by giving her a sign she could expect to find. In time, she learned to trust her visions and the voice. And then one day the path began to widen until it was so wide that there were no plants as far as she could see. Yet the visions continued. In frustration, she was tempted to become angry — but she remembered only too well what had happened before. "I'll think of the tree," she thought, and almost at once, she felt the familiar fondness return to fill her completely. It felt so wonderful and satisfying that she found herself speaking quietly with the tree as if it were there. In return, it seemed as though the tree began laughing at her plight — "But how could this be?" she thought, "I can still feel its fondness for me."

While she was still pondering this dilemma, a vision danced in front of her with a message and then gave her a sign. Now willing to try almost anything, she followed the instructions of the message and continued on her journey, ever watchful for the sign. A little way down the path, she saw a vision of the sign. Within a minute or so a new vision appeared with a new message and a new sign. Almost at once she began laughing and skipped down the path in response to the message she'd been given.

After awhile, her skip lost its bounce and she began to feel shattered and confused. Her delight turned to remorse as she remembered the tree. "Had she imagined its fondness," she wondered. "Did it even exist?!" she questioned with alarm. Distracted by her sadness, she hardly noticed that the path had become narrow once again. Little plants called out to her and trees reached out to comfort her as she passed. By and by she felt their gentle presence and stopped to look upon their forms. "Are you real or just a vision?" she asked in deep despair. And one by one they offered her their seeds and greenery and asked her to take their offerings back to the tree so she would know.

She did as they asked, and when her arms were full, she said farewell and thanked them before she went along her way. Nightfall came soon and she nestled down among the seeds and branches she had carried in her arms. Before she drifted off to sleep, she spoke with fondness to her special nest and recalled the old, gnarly tree with love. Daybreak seemed different than any other she had known. She gathered up her seeds and branches and set off upon the path with confidence. Her step was light, and she felt a peace she'd never known before. Many paths wove in and out and as she turned this way, then that, not once did she falter, never did she fear.

And then one day an image danced before her with delight.
It towered toward the sky, then burst in flames that showered light.

It's trunk was old and gnarly and it beckoned, "Follow me."
It's presence filled the path with love — she knew it was the tree.

She moved like light until she reached the huge expanse of meadow, and then she paused just at the edge to honor the presence in the center. With great humility she softly crossed the grasses and dropped to her knees in gratitude toward this wise, old tree.

She placed her gifts among its roots and asked what she might do,
But the tree just stirred with love for her, and suddenly she knew.

She gathered up the branches and with each one she took its seed.
She walked the meadow end to end to fill an earthly need.

And when she finished with the earth, she turned to look above.
There is a tree, and she is thee and all the world is love.

Appendix

A

Body tension results in body symptoms (the language of the body). When you're giving a flow, focus upon releasing tension and restoring balance rather than relieving "symptoms." I've used acupuncture books as sources for most of this information, and I report it here because people have become accustomed to recognizing body language in the form of symptom identification and classification. I offer it as information for your convenience, but I discourage thinking in this terminology because it's disease related and therefore it may encourage you to form imagery congruent with disease rather than wellness.

Points

Point 1 - Balances ascending and descending energy flows; relieves waist-up tension; and with same side 15 corrects low-grade fever. Digestion (cross hands and hold high 1's); obesity (uncross hands and hold high 1's). **Abdominal:** pain, spasm, inflammation, fluid and swelling. **Genital:** irregular, painful or prolonged menstruation; inflamed or prolapsed uterus; itching, pain, swelling or inflamed outer genitalia; vaginal inflammation or infection; nocturnal emission (wet dreams); impotence; premature ejaculation; inflamed testis; pain in the penis; and diseases of the generative system. **Limbs:** any disorders and pain of the knee joint and surrounding tissue; weak knees; lower leg pain; weak legs; pain in all four limbs; inner thigh muscle pain; muscle spasms of the lower back and hips. **Urinary:** painful or difficult urination; inflammation of the ureter; urine retention; suppression of urine formation by the kidney; inflammation of the kidney; bedwetting; infection in the urinary system; and urine incontinence.

Other: sore throat; chest spasm; colic; dysentary; hernia; itching of the perineum; paralysis of one side of the body; edema; anemia; eczema; hives; insomnia; and beriberi, symptoms which result from a thiamine (vitamin B1) deficiency.

Point 1 **Meridian and Muscle Information** - The Main Meridians that pass through points 1 are: Kidney, Spleen and Liver. The Muscle Meridians that unite at these points are: Kidney, Spleen and Liver. The muscles that have either their origin or insertion at points 1 are: Semitendinosus; semimembranosus; adductor magnus; gracillis; gastrocnemius; and sartorius. These muscles are each connected from points 1 to one of the following areas: points 2, 15 and 25; pubis; and heels.

Point 2 - All leg problems; diarrhea (First Depth Flow); clear if chills in posterior kidney area; can use 5, 6, 7, 8 Release to open. **Genital:** inflammation of the uterus, uterine tubes and ligaments, and ovaries; painful and/or irregular menstruation; leukorrhea; gonorrhea; nocturnal emission; premature ejaculation; impotence; inflammation of the prostate and testis; and pain in the penis. **Intestinal:** spasms; bleeding; acute and chronic inflammation; diarrghea; constipation; dysentary; anal muscle cramp; and hemorrhoids.   **Lower Back:** lumbago; sciatica; stiffness and paralysis of lumbar vertebrae; sprain of lumbar vertebral region; pain in lumbosacral region; and disorder of ilio-sacral joint. **Urinary:** urine incontinence; painful or difficult urination; inflammation of the urinary bladder and urethra; blood in the urine; urine retention; inflammation of the kidney; kidney malfunction; inflammation of the prostate; and bedwetting. **Other:** paralysis of lower limbs; infantile paralysis; hernia; chronic inflammation of the pelvis; abdominal pain and distention; liver dilation; deafness; noise in the ears; hypertension; nosebleed; diabetes melilitus; thirst; insomnia; and neurasthenia (chronic abnormal fatigue, lack of energy, feelings of inadequacy, moderate depression, inability to concentrate, loss of appetite and insomnia).

Between points 2 **on the spine** - Between the second and third lumbars. Symptoms in addition to above: headache; inflammation of the spinal cord; and assists the brain. Can hold crown of head and between the 2's to assist prolapsed (drooping) states of inner organs. Release whole area along the spine from points 2 to points 25 to create diuretic action and promote urine excretion.

Point 2 **Meridian And Muscle Information** - The Bladder Meridian passes through points 2. There are no Muscle Meridians that unite at points 2. The muscles that have their origin or insertion at points 2 are: latissimus dorsi; quadratus lumborum; iliopsoas; erector spinae; gluteus medius; sartorius; and the deltoid of the hip. These muscles are each connected from points 2 to one or more of the following areas: points 1, 4, 8, 9, 15, 23, and 26; the entire spine; base of the skull; and hip joint.

Point 3 - Fever; infections; colds; phlegm; coughing; shoulder tension; fatigue; lymph; bladder; relaxes arms and back; stuttering (left 3). Hold with same side point 19 to release fatigue and toxins from the joints. **Arm and Shoulder:** pain, paralysis, spasm and numbness of scapula, shoulder joint, arm and elbow; and ulnar nerve pain. **Respiratory:** labored or difficult breathing; pleurisy; pneumonia; bronchitis; common cold; flu; whooping cough; pulmonary tuberculosis; asthma; lack of tone or normal strength in the lungs; inflammation of the trachea (windpipe); and pain and spasms along the nerves between the ribs. **Other:** headache; pain in the back of the head and neck; neck muscle spasm; hives; itching; fever; vomiting; inflammation of the mouth; cancer; mental disorder; excessive sleeping; fatigue; lymph system; low back pain; paralysis of one side of the body; and paralysis of all four limbs.

Between points 3 **on the spine** - Between the third and fourth thoracics. Symptoms in addition to above: chest and back pain; stiff back; insanity; cerbral and medullary afflictions; infantile epilepsy; convulsions in children after high fever; fever; night fever; and this point lowers the blood pressure; and dilates the lungs.

Point 3 **Meridian And Muscle Information** - The Main Meridians that pass through points 3 are: Bladder and Small Intestine. None of the Muscle Meridians unite at points 3, but the following Muscle Meridians unite in the shoulder: Lung, Large Intestine and Bladder. The muscles have either their origin or insertion at points 3 are: serratus anterior; levator scapulae; trapezius; rhomboideus minor; supraspinatus; and omohyoideus. Each of these muscles connects from points 3 to one or more of the following areas: points 4, 9, 10, 12, 13 and 22; outer ribs one through nine; spinal cervicals one through four and seven; thoracics one through twelve; and the hyoid bone in the throat.

Point 4 - tonsils; sinus; throat; heart; knees; legs that feel heavy; unconsciousness; opposite eye. Release of points 4 acts like a powerful tonic for all internal organs. **Head and Neck:** all eye, nose and and cerebral problems; brain disorders; headache; pain in the back of the head; migraine; nosebleed; sinusitis; ear infections; deafness; subjective sensation of noise in the ears; dizziness; vertigo; apoplexy (sudden neurologic impairment due to intracranial hemorrhage); facial nerve spasm; tonsillitis; stiff neck; inflammaiton of the larynx and pharynx (throat and voice); and unconsciousness. **Other:** hysteria; depression; insomnia; neurasthenia (a neurosis that includes extreme fatigue, depression, insomnia and feelings of inadequacy); fever; flu; diarrhea; hypertension; heart problems; knee pain; legs that feel heavy; pain in the shoulder and scapula; and paralysis of the body, all four limbs, or one side of the body.

Between points 4 **on the spine** - At the top of the spine called the atlas. Symptoms in addition to above: insanity; mental disorders; schizophrenia; apoplexy (sudden neurologic impairment due to intracranial hemorrhage); stiff or painful neck; common cold; and fever after chilling.

Point 4 **Meridian And Muscle Information** - The Main Meridians that pass through points 4 are Bladder and Gall Bladder. The Muscle Meridians that unite at points 4 are Bladder and Kidney. The muscles that have their origin or insertion at points 4 are: epicranus; levator scapulae; trapezius; digastricus; splenius capitus and cervicis; erector spinae; longissimus thoracis; l. cervicis; l. capitis; and sternocleido mastoid. Each of these muscles is connected from points 4 to one or more of the following areas: points 2, 3, 12, 20, 22 and 23; the entire spine; and the hyoid bone in the throat; and the tongue.

Point 5 - Groin; joints; throat; and acts upon liver, gall bladder and spleen along with points 6, 7, and 8. See 5, 6, 7, 8 Release. **Digestion:** inflammation of or excessive gas in the stomach and/or intestines; indigestion; vomiting; constipation; inflated abdomen; lower belly pain; jaundice; hepatitis; and hemorrhoids. **Genital:** irregular, excessive and/or painful menstruation; prolapse of the uterus (downward displacement); nocturnal emission (wet dreams); and involuntary erection. **Lower Limbs:** pain in the heel, ankle joint or lower limbs; sprained ankle; calf muscle spasm; crooked toes; fatigue in the limbs; and paralysis of the lower limbs. **Mental and Emotional:** psychopathy (any disease of the mind); nightmares; insomnia; fear and restlessness in children; hysteria; and madness. **Mouth and Throat:** tonsillitis; sore throat and pharyngitis. Point 5 has a powerful action on the throat. **Respiratory:** labored or difficult breathing; diaphragm spasm; emphysema; cough; whooping cough; clood-stained sputum; and asthma. **Urinary:** inflammation of the kidney or urinary bladder; painful or difficult urination; urine retention; and bedwetting. **Other:** epilepsy; fever in children; hernia; myopia; and neurasthenia. In acupuncture, this point is used to treat bee or wasp stings, or for emergency concussions or unconsciousness with no convulsions.

Point 5 **Meridian And Muscle Information** - The Main Meridians that pass through points 5 are Spleen and Kidney. No Muscle Meridians unite at points 5, but the Spleen, Kidney and Liver Meridians unite on the ankle bone just above points 5. The muscles that have their origin or insertion at points 5 are: plantaris; flexor hallucis brevis; tibialis posterior; abductor hallucis; flexor digitorum longus; and flexor hallucis longus. Each muscle connects from points 5 to one or more of the following areas: points 6, 7 and 8; and all the toes.

Point 6 - Varicose veins; opens groin and shoulders; works with point 15. See 5, 6, 7, 8 Release. **Digestion:** acute and chronic pain in stomach; spasms of esophagus and stomach; unchecked nausea and vomiting; loss of appetite; indigestion; stomach cancer; intestinal hemorrhage; and diarrhea. **General Incompacitation:** infantile convulsions; hysteria; epilepsy; heatstroke; shock; and spasms of limbs and trunk. **Head and Throat:** pain on the top of the head; nervous headache; coma; cerebral hemorrhage; vertigo; edema of the face and head; temporary loss of consciousness due to deficiency of blood to cerebrum; loss of the power of expression or comprehension of speech or writing; sore throat; pharyngitis; hyoidal paralysis (throat); spasm of esophagus; and acute tonsillitis. **Urogenital:** female sterility; painful menstruatin; prolapsed uterus (dropped down); injury to the testis; painful or difficult urination; urine retention; and for emergency need for urination (point 6 is adjacent to Kidney point 1 which is used in acupuncture to stimulate immediate urination). The release of accumulated toxins and waste from urine retention will assist the skin. **Other:** lower abdominal spasm and pain; fluid in the abdominal cavity; anxiety with palpitations; heart inflammation and other heart afflictions; cough; pleurisy; dizziness; and hot sensation in the sole of the foot.

Point 6 **Meridian And Muscle Information** - The Main Meridians that pass through points 6 are Spleen and Kidney. No Muscle Meridians unite at points 6. The muscles that have their origin or insertion at points 6 are: tibialis posterior; and flexor hallucis brevis. Each of these muscles connects from points 6 to one or more of the following areas: points 7 and8; and all the toes.

Point 7 - Headaches; and hot palms. See 5, 6, 7, 8 Release. **Abdominal and Digestion:** abdominal pain or distention; enlarged or cold abdomen; peritonitis; stomach dilation, inflammation, or spasm; nausea; inability to feed oneself; and constipation. **Head and Face:** headache; facial muscle weakness; redness and swelling of the eyes; sty; conjunctivitis; glaucoma; toothache; and inflammation of the gums. **Mental and Emotional:** insanity; schizophrenia mental disorders; stupidity; fear and restlessness in children; loss of consciousness due to lack of blood to the cerebrum; giddiness; insomnia; excessive dreaming; nervous anxiety with palpitations; convulsions; and epilepsy. **Urogenital:** irregular or excessive menstruation; uterine spasms or pain; prolapsed uterus; inflammation of the testis; pain in the penis; gonorrhea; urine incontinence; inflammation of the urethra; and bedwetting. **Other:** cold sensations or paralysis in lower limbs; pain in the lumbar or intercostal (between the ribs) regions; general fatigue; difficult and labored breathing; night sweats; abnormally diminished secretin of sweat; hot palms; high fever; high blood pressure; excessive mucus discharge; diabetes; and hernia.

Point 7 **Meridian And Muscle Information** - The Main Meridians that pass through points 7 are Liver and Spleen. The Muscle Meridians that unite at points 7 are Liver and Spleen. The muscles that have their origin or insertion at points 7 are: peroneus longus; extensor hallucis longus; flexor hallucis longus; flexor hallucis brevis; and abductor hallucis. Each of these muscles connect from points 7 to one or more of the following areas: points 5, 6, 8 and 24; and the big toe.

Point 8 - Elimination; constipation; reproductive; and rectal. In acupuncture, point 8 is known as a Great Point and may be used for toning the whole body. Hold with points 19 and 25 to assist whole lower body. See 5, 6, 7, 8 Release. **Digestion:** diseases of the gall bladder; bitter taste in the mouth; inflammation of the stomach; indigestion; acid regurgitation; vomiting; diarrhea; constipation; spasms or inflammation of the intestines. **Head and Neck:** headache; eye pain; numbness in throat; giddiness; dizziness; vertigo; nosebleed; facial edema; and loss of hair. **Lower Limbs:** inflammation, pain or swelling of the knee joint; spasms, weakness or paralysis in the legs; gout; sciatica; swollen feet; and lower back pain. **Mental and Emotional:** madness; and epilepsy. **Urinary:** inflammation of the kidney or urinary bladder; suppression of urine formation by the kidney; and difficult or painful urination. **Other:** high blood pressure; heat stroke; pain in the flanks or between the ribs; arthritis; degeneration or metabolic derangement of the connective tissue, especially in the joints; pleurisy; and hemorrhoids.

Point 8 (low front lateral to the shin bone) - **Head, Neck and Mental-Emotional:** epilepsy; schizophrenia; cerebral hyperemia (an excess of blood in the cerebrum); and swelling, pain or inflammation in the pharynx, oropharynx and trachea of the throat.

Point 8 (low back in center of the calf) - **Digestion:** acute inflammation of the stomach; beriberi; and constipation. **Lower Limbs:** Same as for points 8; and pain in the soles of the feet. **Other:** hemorrhoids; and prolapse of the anus.

Point 8 **Meridian And Muscle Information** - The Main Meridians that pass through points 8 are Bladder, Gall Bladder, and Stomach. The Muscle Meridians that unite at points 8 are Bladder, Gall Bladder, and Stomach. The muscles that have their origin or insertion at points 8 are: peroneus longus; peroneus brevis; peroneus tertius; biceps femoris; vastus lateralis; tibialis anterior; extensor hallucis longus; extensor digitorum longus; gastrocnemius; soleus; tibialis posterior; deltoid of the hip; and flexor hallucis longus. Each of these muscles connect from points 8 to one or more of the following areas: points 1, 2, 6, 7, 24 and 25; all of the toes; and the hip joint.

Point 9 - Breathing and digestion; clear if chills in posterior kidney area; dizziness; begining of all problems; fussy baby; opposite back and hip; callouses and corns; and sprained ankle. In acupuncture, this is a special point to assist the diaphragm. **Digestion:** pain, ulcers, or bleeding in the stomcah; stomach cancer; indigestion; vomiting food or blood; nausea; constriction or paralysis of the esophagus; liver diseases; acute and chronic infective hepatitis; enlarged liver; jaundice; inflammation of the gall bladder; bitter taste in the mouth; duodenal ulcers; and diarrhea. **Heart:** palpitations; angina pains; and inflammation of the endocardium or pericardium. **Mental and Emotional:** mental depression; mental disorders; schizophrenia; dream-disturbed sleep; neurasthenia (a neurosis that includes depression, chronic abnormal fatigue, lack of energy, feelings of inadequacy, inability to concentrate, loss of appetite and insomnia); and temporary loss of consciousness due to lack of blood to cerebrum. **Respiratory:** difficult and labored breathing; cough; bronchitis; suffocation; asthma; pleurisy; paralysis or spasm of the diaphragm muscle; and hiccoughs. **Other:** pain in back, vertebral region, shoulder blades, between the ribs, the chest, or hypochondrium (upper lateral abdominal region at the base of the rib cage which affects the spleen, liver and kidney areas); strictures and constrictions of all kinds; rheumatism; fatigue in the limgs; night sweats; chronic hemorrhagic disorders; anemia; hives; edema; chronic eye diseases; watery eyes; and night blindness.

Between points 9 **on the spine** - Between the seventh and eighth thoracics. Symptoms in addition to above: **Digestion:** will empty the gall bladder and stimulate action on liver, spleen, pancreas, stomach and intestines; intestinal rumbling; cold sensation in epigastrium; and lack or loss of appetite. **Other:** stiffness in spine; low back pain; impotence; and peritonitis.

Point 9 **Meridian And Muscle Information** - The Main Meridian that passes through points 9 is Bladder. No Muscle Meridians unite at points 9. The muscles that have their origin or insertion at points 9 are: teres major; latissimus dorsi; serratus anterior; trapezius; and rhomboideus major. Each of these muscles connects from points 9 to one or more of the following areas: points 2, 3, 10, 13, 22, 23, and 26; on the spine from the seventh cervical through all the thoracics and lumbars, and the first two sacral; the outer ribs one through nine; and the anterior upper arm.

Point 10 - Breathing and digestion; dizziness; opposite eye; heart; tuberculosis; bronchopneumonia; high blood pressure; lack of strength in thumb; hoarse voice opposite knee; same side hip; opposite side of neck and shoulder; loss of voice; stuttering; general speech problems; children who aren't speaking; overuse of same side arm; assists ascending energy flows; whiplash; and inability to turn head to opposite side. Points 10 must be free to support all heart and and circulation functions (circulation of both blood and vital energy). Release these points to relieve all chronic maladies. **Heart:** all types of heart disese such as inflammation of the pericardium or endocardium; cariac arrhythmia or pain; rapid heart rate; palpitations; flurry; hypertension (high blood pressure); and angina pectoris. **Mental and Emotional:** schizophrenia; madness; mental disorders; anxiety; hysteria; loss of or poor memory; depression; muteness; stuttering; speech problems; loss of or hoarse voice; throat closes; dizziness; neurasthenia; temporary loss of consciousness due to lack of blood to the cerebrum; and epilepsy. **Respiration and Digestion:** coughing; hiccough; bronchitis; bronchopneumonia; phlegm; asthma; pleurisy; pulmonary tuberculosis; vomiting; heartburn; hemorrhoid or ulcer in stomach region; inflammatin of the stomach or intestines; loss of appetite; peristaltic sounds in the bowel; and pain in the abdomen. **Upper Body:** pain in the chest, shoulders, shoulder blade, upper arm and elbow; top of the head, and back; paralysis, spasm and pain in the shoulder or nape of the neck; inability to lift the arm; fullness and burning in the chest; pain between the ribs; falling hair; baldness; and nosebleed. **Other:** long standing illness with weakened body; itching skin; nocturnal emission; swelling, pain or stiffness in the hip or knee.

Between points 10 **on the spine** - Between the fifth and sixth thoracics. Symptoms in addition to above: headache; cerebral weakness; infantile convulsions; high blood pressure; cowardice; inflammation of the lower jaw; malaria; and stiff back.

Point 10 **Meridian And Muscle Information** - The Main Meridians that pass through points 10 are Bladder and Small Intestine. No Muscle Meridians unite at points 10. The muscles that have their origin or insertion at points 10 are: serratus anterior; trapezius; rhomboideus major; deltoideus; subscapularis; and infraspinatus. Each of these muscles connects from points 10 to one or more of the following areas: points 3, 4, 9, 11, 13, 22, 23 and high back 19; outer ribs one through nine; and the shoulder joint.

Point 11 - Lungs; whiplash; and tense from overuse of opposite arm. See 11, 12 Release. **General Incapacitations:** paralysis of one side of the body, all four limbs, the spine or the whole body; epilepsy; arthrits; bone tuberculosis; coldness and fever; and flu. **Head and Neck:** excessive accumulation of blood in the cerebrum; cerebral anemia; vertigo; weakening vision; blood in the saliva; hyperthyroidism; madness; headache; pain in the back of the head; spasm of the head muscles; and cold sensation in the neck. **Respiratory:** bronchitis; asthma; pleurisy; pneumonia; coughing; and difficult or labored breathing. **Upper Body:** inflammation of the breasts; heartburn; pain, paralysis, stiffness, aching, spasm or motor impaiment of any nature in the shoulder (blade or joint), back, neck, and arms. **Other:** irregular or prolonged bleeding following childbirth.

Between points 11 **on the spine** - This is the area of the first thoracic between the seventh cervical and second thoracic. This is considered a master point for the bony structure of the whole body; a powerful tonic for all internal organs; a revival point in case of asphyxia (use if a person stops breathing); and it will contract the heart, aorta and pericardium, and dilate the pulmonary artery. It's also a hygrometric point along the Triple Warmer to measure moisture in the atmosphere. Hold with points 18 and 19 to augment powers of resistance to illness. Hold alternately with points 19 and 8 to provide a general stimulus and toning to all internal organs, especially the liver, kidneys, intestines and stomach. Symptoms in addition to above: stiff back; acute fever diseases; intermittent fever; general fever; chilling; reactions to weather; malaria; insanity; nervous depression; schizophrenia; heat stroke; pulmonary emphysema; hemorrhoids; inflammation of the gums; and eczema.

Point 11 **Meridian And Muscle Information** - The Main Meridians that pass through points 11 are Small Intestine, Gall Bladder, Triple Warmer, and Bladder.

No Muscle Meridians unite in points 11. The muscles that have their origin or insertion at points 11 are: scalenus medius; scalenus anterior; trapezius; serratus posterior superior; and rhomboideus minor. Each of these muscles connects from points 11 to one or more of the following areas: points 3, 4, 12, 13 and 22; on the spine at all the cervicals and thoracics; and ribs one through five.

Point 12 - Lungs; hip and leg problems; whiplash; tension from overuse of opposite arm; and when 12's release, the 23's open. See 11, 12 Release. There are no acupuncture points at points 12, therefore the following symptoms refer to the point on the spine between points 12 known as Governor Vessel 15 between the first and third cervicals. **Head and Neck:** cerebral paralysis or congestion; meningitis; back of head pain; habitual headache; paralysis of the supra-hyoid muscle (tongue); cystic tumor beneath the tongue; pharyngitis; stiff neck; thyroid; and parathyroid. **Mental and Emotional:** schizophrenia; insanity; epilepsy; neurosis; deaf mutism; and loss of the ability to express or comprehend speech or writing. **Other:** paralysis of one side of the body.

Point 12 **Meridian And Muscle Information** - The Main Meridians that pass through points 12 are Bladder and Gall Bladder. No Muscle Meridians unite at points 12. The muscles that have their origin or insertion at points 12 are: scalenus medius; scalenus posterior; scalenus anterior; trapezius; levator scapula; and splenius capitus and cervicis. Each of these muscles connects from points 12 to one or more of the following areas: points 3, 4, 9, 10, 11, 22 and 23; and on the spine at all the cervicals and thoracics.

Point 13 - Clears intermingling of the descending flows at all three depths and in the center (i.e., Large Intestine - surface flow, Triple Warmer - middle flow, Small Intestine - deep flow and Main Central - central flow); metabolic balance; reproductive; thyroid; chest; abdomen; nausea; head, neck and shoulder tension; appetite; hormonal balance; breathing, digestion and elimination; revitalizes; balances the mind; opens the three belts [13 (surface), 14 (middle), 15 (deep)]; reduces pain before and after surgery; can use self-help Main Central Flow; hold crown and between the 13's for breathing, digestion, reproductive and rejuvenation; and clear if there's fever in the anterior kidney area. **Digestion:** nausea; vomiting food or blood; loss of appetite for food; excessive gas in the stomach or intestines; peristaltic bowel sounds with diarrhea; heartburn; and bitter taste in the mouth. **Respiratory:** cough; lung congestion; difficult and labored breathing; nasal obstruction; asthma; emphysema; pleurisy; and weak sense of smell.

Upper Body: pain and distention between the ribs, and in the chest and rib cage area, especially in the hypochondriac region (lower lateral rib cage area); angina pectoris; tumors or inflammation of the breasts; and pain in the neck, shoulder, scapula or flanks. **Other:** general edema; mental disorder; and fatal paralysis.

Between points 13 **on the center front** - On the sternum between the third intercostal spaces for the third and fourth ribs. Symptoms in addition to above: bronchial asthma; pain in the heart; pulmonary tuberculosis; and all chest diseases. Hold with point one inch below the navel to assist reproductive organs and their functions.

Point 13 **Meridian And Muscle Information** - The Main Meridians that pass through points 13 are Kidney, Stomach, Lung, Large Intestine, Triple Warmer, Heart, and Small Intestine. No Muscle Meridians unite in points 13. The muscles that have their origin or insertion at points 13 are: serratus anterior; pectoralis major; pectoralis minor; and serratus posterior superior. Each of these muscles connects from points 13 to one or more of the following areas: points 3, 9, 10, 11, 14, high 19 and 22; ribs one through nine; on the spine at the seventh cervical and thoracics one through three; and in the shoulder joint.

Point 14 - Epilepsy; opposite side brain problems; unconsciousness; convulsions due to indigestion; valvular heart problems; same side knees; same side arm, lung, thigh and diaphragm; opposite side kidney; low fever; snoring; senility; main breathing and digestion area; hold middle finger to help open 14's; hold first thoracic and thumb if pain in 14's; 12 and opposite 21 also helps snoring; clear if there's fever in the anterior kidney area; hold crown and between the 14's to release mental and emotional problems and bring them up into consciousness; and hold between the 14's and on the spine between the 3's, 9's and 10's to balance the appetite. **Abdominal:** abdominal pain, or distention from gas or air in the intestines or peritoneal cavity; peritonitis; hiatal hernia; and pain or dilation in the region just below the rib cage in the center or on the sides. **Digestion:** all stomach disorders such as dilation, acute or chronic inflammation, ache, pain, spasm, and ulceration; vomiting of all kinds such as food, water, blood, or during pregnancy; indigestion; excessive gas in the stomach or intestines; belching; sudden hyoidal paralysis (throat); constipation or diarrhea; all liver and spleen disorders; and inflammatin of the gall bladder. **Respiratory:** difficult and labored breathing; cough; emphysema; bronchitis; pain between the ribs and in the chest; diaphragm spasm; hiccough; and pleurisy. **Other:** angles of the mouth become slack; eye congestion; spasm or lack of tone in the arm muscles; high blood pressure; and inflammation of the kidney.

Between points 14 **on the center front** - In the pocket at the base of the sternum. This point will assist both the adrenals and pituitary. Because of its action on the pituitary, it affects the whole endocrine system. Symptoms in addition to above: pain in heart; heart problems; mental disorders; insanity; epilepsy; cerebral weakness; chest distention; flank pain; asthma; constrictin of esophagus; nausea; pain in pharynx; and babies vomiting milk.

Point 14 **Meridian And Muscle Information** - The Main Meridians that pass through points 14 are Spleen, Kidney, Liver, Stomach, and Large Intestine. No Muscle Meridians unite at points 14. The muscles that have their origin or insertion at points 14 are: obliquus internus abdominis; transversus abdominis; rectus abdominis; obliquus externus abdominis; and pectoralis major. each of these muscles connects from points 14 to one or more of the following areas: points 2, 13, 15, high 19 and 22; the lower eight ribs; the pubic bone; and the center line and anterior wall of the abdomen.

Point 15 - All heart problems; same side abdomen, leg and foot; clear if there's fever in the anterior kidney area; needs to be released when all the Yin meridians are imbalanced; can use 5, 6, 7, 8 Release to open; and the pubic bone (between the 15's) and coccyx (tailbone) are the major crossroads for all the surface, middle, deep, ascending, descending, left and right flows of energy in the body. **Abdominal:** lower abdominal pain or distention due to gas or air in the intestines or peritoneal cavity; and inflammation or spasm of the stomach. **Genital:** all diseases of the genital system for both males and females such as inflammatin of the uterus, uterine tubes and ligaments, ovaries, testes, spermatic cord, and pelvis in general; prolapsed uterus; itching or pain in the vulva or scrotum; chronic vaginits; leukorrhea; menstruation that may be escessive, irregular, absent, painful or abnormal in some respect; male sterility; nocturnal emissions; sperm insufficiency; scrotal retraction or eczema; and excessive discharge of mucous in males or females. **Lower Back and Limbs:** pain in the lumbar region, medial aspect of the thigh, buttocks, and legs; and paralysis of the lower extremeties. **Urinary:** painful or difficult urination; urine retention; suppression of urine formation by the kidney; bladder paralysis or spasm; bedwetting; and hernia (lower abdomen, pelvis or organs of urogenital system). **Other:** all heart ailments; and inflammation of the kidney.

Between points 15 **on the center front** - At the center top of the pubic bone. This point is called the reunion of the Conception Vessel and the Liver Meridian. Symptoms in addition to above: uterus fails to return to normal size after childbirth; all urogenital problems; urine incontinence; lower belly spasm; and weakness of the internal organs.

Point 15 **Meridian And Muscle Information** - The Main Meridians that pass through points 15 are Spleen, Kidney, Liver, and Stomach. The Muscle Meridians that unite at points 15 are Stomach, Spleen, Kidney, and Liver. The muscles that have their origin or insertion at points 15 are: psoas major; psoas minor; adductor magnus; gracilis; pectineus; adductor longus; adductor brevis; obliquus internus abdominis; and rectus abdominis. Each of these muscles connects from points 15 to one or more of the following areas: points 1, high 1, 2, 14, 23 and 25; on the spine at the twefth thoracic and lumbars one through five; the pubic bone; and the hip joint.

Point 16 - Assists ascending flows of energy. See 16, 17, 18, 19 Release. **Genital:** uterine spasm; swollen and painful vulva; and masturbation. **Head and Neck:** pain in the back of the head; headache; migraine; meningitis; excess blood in the cerebrum; film over the eyes; sty; inflammation of the cornea; nosebleeds; and stiff neck. **Lower Limbs and Back:** pain, paralysis, weakness, spasms or inflammation of the lower limbs; loss of coordination; pain in the lower back or lumbar vertebrae; sciatica; and flank pains. **Mental and Emotional:** epilepsy; schizophrenia; dizziness; vertigo; and insomnia. Respiratory: pulmonary congestion; cessation of breathing; pleurisy; and pain between the ribs. **Shoulders and Upper Limbs:** pain in the shoulder, armpit, and scapula; inflammation of the lymph nodes; and swelling in the armpit. **Other:** multiple sclerosis; beriberi; acute inflammatin of the stomach; gall bladder function; and pain control.

Point 16 **Meridian And Muscle Information** - The Main Meridians that pass through points 16 are Bladder and Gall Bladder. The Muscle Meridians that unite at points 16 are Bladder and Gall Bladder. The muscles that have their origin or insertion at points 16 are: abductor digiti minimi; and peroneus longus. Each of these muscles connects from points 16 to one or more of the following areas: points 8; and the little toe.

Point 17 - Assists ascending flows of energy; and helps open points 26. See 16, 17, 18, 19 Release. **Head and Neck:** headaches; pain in the back of the head, neck, lower jaw, and eyeball; swollen or stiff neck and lower jaw; inflammatin of the maxillary gland and lower jaw; acute paralysis of the suprahyoid muscle (sudden muteness, stiffness, paralysis, or spasm of the tongue); sudden hoarseness of the voice; pharyngitis of the gums; tuberculosis of the cervical lymph nodes; inflammatin of the mucous membrane of the mouth; atrophy of the optic nerve; failing eyesight; eye congestion and pain; inflammatin of the cornea; eye congestion with dizziness and hot face; secretion of tears; subjective sensation of noise in the ears; deafness; nosebleeds; vertigo; and epilepsy. **Mental and Emotional:** hysteria; hysteric aphasia (sudden loss of the ability to express or comprehend speech or written language); psychopathy; mental disorder; schizophrenia; anxiety; phobia; insanity; temporary loss of soncsiousness due to lack of blood to the cerebrum; dizziness; excessive dreaming; insomnia; lack or loss of appetite for food; nervous palpitations; and neurasthenia (a neurosis marked by chronic fatigue, lack of energy, feelings of inadequacy, depression, inability to concentrate, loss of appetite, and insomnia). **Upper Body:** pain, inflammatin or dilation of the heart; inflammatin of the endocardium; angina pectoris; pain in the chest and between the ribs; pleurisy; phlegm; pulmonary tuberculosis; arthritis; and spasm, paralysis or pain in the shoulders and arms. **Urogenital:** leukorrhea; inflammation of the uterus; irregular, prolonged or painful menstruation; post partum hemorrhage; and urine incontinence. **Other:** stomach ulcer; vomiting food, blood, or on an empty stomach; inflammation of the gall bladder; high or low blood pressure; night sweats; fever after chilling; and paralysis of one side of the body.

Point 17 **Meridian And Muscle Information** - the Main Meridians that pass through points 17 are Heart and Small Intestine. The Muscle Meridians that unite at points 17 are Heart and Small Intestine. The muscles that have their origin or insertion at points 17 are: flexor carpi ulnaris; extensor carpi ulnaris; and abductor digiti minimi. Each of these muscles connects from points 17 to one or more of the following areas: points 19; and little finger.

Point 18 - Assists descending flows of energy; restores equilibrium; and helps balance 9's and 10's. In acupuncture, this point is known as "the corpse reviver" because it stimulates lung action. The area in the web of thumb next to points 18 is called "the great eliminator" because it helps eliminate toxins from the body. See 16, 17, 18, 19 Release. **Digestion:** acute or chronic inflammation of the stomach; and indigestion in children and infants. **Mental and Emotional:** mental disorder; anxiety; nervous depression; insomnia; collapse; and neurasthenia (chronic fatigue, lack of energy, feelings of inadequacy, depression, inability to concentrate, loss of appetite, and insomnia). **Respiratory:** difficult, labored or arrested breathing; asthma; bronchitis; emphysema; cough; influenza; common cold with fever; and blood-stained sputum. **Trunk and Limbs:** paralysis or pain of one side of the body, upper limbs, or all four limbs; and pain in upper limb joints, chest, shoulder, back or between the ribs. **Other:** fever; excessive or diminished perspiration; night sweats; high blood pressure; all skin conditions which includes acne or boils; simple thyroid goiter; arrested menstruation; pain control; and assists elimination of mental and physical toxins.

Point 18 Meridian And Muscle Information - The Main Meridians that pass through points 18 are Lung and Large Intestine. The Muscle Meridians that unite at points 18 are Lung and Large Intestine. The muscles that have their origin or insertion at points 18 are: brachioradialis; flexor pollicis longus; and opponens pollicis longus. Each of these muscles connects from points 18 to one or more of the following areas: points 17, 19, and high 19.

Point 19 - Assists descending flows of energy; restores equilibrium; helps balance 9's and 10's; hold with same side 12 to release same side 9; and cross arms and hold high back 19's to release 13's. See 16, 17, 18, 19 Release. **Head and Neck:** facial nerve paralysis or neuralgia; headaches; cerebral congestion; impaired hearing; deafness; vertigo; inflammation of the gums; toothache; swollen cheeks; swollen and painful throat (oropharynx); tonsillitis; goiter; stiff neck; inflamed and tender lymph nodes of the neck; and tuberculosis of the cervical lymph nodes. **Mental and Emotional:** deep depression; psychopathy; schizophrenia; fear and restlessness in children; and epilepsy. **Respiration:** cough; difficult and labored breathing; asthma; bronchitis; pleurisy; pulmonary tuberculosis; and blood-stained sputum. **Skin:** hives; eczema; neurodermatitis (itching skin from an emotional origin rather than inflammation); and skin diseases. **Trunk and Limbs:** pain in the chest, heart, and between the ribs; angina pectoris; inflammation of the heart; palpitation; paralysis of one side of the body or all four limgs; and chorea (ceaseless rapid jerky movements). **Other:** high blood pressure; anemia; lower belly pain; and can be used as a pain control point; to reduce fever; and assist lymphocyte production for immunity; and help enlarged or inflammed glands.

Point 19 Meridian And Muscle Information - The Main Meridians that pass through points 19 are Lung, Large Intestine, Heart, Small Intestine, Pericardium, and Triple Warmer. The Muscle Meridians that unite at points 19 are Lung, Large Intestine, Heart, Small Intestine, Pericardium and Triple Warmer. The muscles that have their origin or insertion at points 19 are: triceps brachii; pectoralis major;

deltoideus; biceps; brachii; brachioradialis; brachialis; flexor pollicis longus; flexor carpi ulnaris; and extensor carpi ulnaris. Each of these muscles connects from points 19 to one or more of the following areas: points 17, 18, 18 (little finger side), 22, and 26; the whole sternum; and the scapula.

Point 20 - Hold crown and between the 20's to enhance memory (deep flow); when points 20 and 21 clear, the 23's open; head; ears; dizziness; anemia; eyes; brain; blood pressure; autism; and respiratory. See 20, 21, 22 Release. **Eyes:** all eye diseases such as glaucoma; inflammation of the cornea; night blindness; eye tremor; itching; pain; watering; redness; swelling; dense white corneal opacity; purulent conjunctivitis; and weak or blurred vision. **Head and Neck:** migraines; headache; cerebral congestion; giddiness; vertigo; neck muscle spasms; and facial problems such as trigeminal neuraligia, nerve paralysis, pain or spasm. **Nose:** nosebleeds; inflamed nostrils and nasal mucous membranes; nose polyps; nasal occlusion; and allergic inflammation of nasal mucous membrane. **Other:** vomiting; paralysis of one side of the body; and epilepsy.

Between points 20 on the center front - At the area between the brows known as "the third eye". Symptoms in addition to above: anxiety; palpitation; dizziness; insomnia; high blood pressure; and accumulation of pus in the head.

Point 20 Meridian And Muscle Information - The Main Meridians that pass through points 20 are Gall Bladder, Stomach, and Bladder. The Muscle Meridians that unite just lateral to points 20 are Small Intestine, Large Intestine, and Triple Warmer (note: all yang arm meridians unite at points 20). The epicranus muscle has its origin at point 20 and its insertion at point 4.

Point 21 - when points 20 and 21 clear, the 23's open; head; ears; dizziness; anemia; eyes; brain; blood pressure; autism; and respiratory. See 20, 21, 22 Release. **Eyes:** acute or chronic conjunctivitis; glaucoma; astigmatism; inflammation of the optic nerve and retina; atrophy of the eye; cataract; night blindness; eye pain or itching; eyelid spasms; eye muscle spasms or loss of tone; paralysis of the eyes; farsightedness; nearsightedness; sty; increased or decreased secretion of tears; and fil over the eyes. **Face and Mouth:** facial nerve paralysis; pain, spasm, abscess, swelling, itching, or inflamed glands; lockjaw; paralysis of the mouth; excessive salivation; fissuring and scaling of the lips and angles of the mouth; pain and swelling of the lips and cheeks; and toothache or pain in all the upper teeth. **Nose:** acute or chronic inflammmation of the mucous membrane of the nose or nasal sinuses with free or profuse discharge; nasal occlusion or polyps; boils on the nose; nosebleed; absent or weak sense of smell; and profuse discharge from mucous membranes with watering eyes (allergic reactions). **Other:** inflammation of the parotid gland; accumulation of pus in the cavities of the head; headache; vertigo; muteness; paralysis of one side of the body; difficult and labored breathing parasites of the bile duct; pain in the stomach region; and thermal burns.

Between points 21 **on the center front** - The tip of the nose. Hold crown of head and tip of nose to restore energy to the reproductive organs. Symptoms in addition to above: rosacea (chronic flushing of the nose, forehead, and cheeks); convulsions in children; vomiting; diarrhea; shock; acute inflammation of the stomach; and may be used for relief from drunkenness.

Point 21 **Meridian And Muscle Information** - The Main Meridians that pass through points 21 are Small Intestine, Stomach, Large Intestine, Heart, Triple Warmer, Liver, and Gall Bladder. The Muscle Meridians that unite at points 21 are Large Intestine, Small Intestine, Stomach, Bladder and Gall Bladder (note: all yang leg meridians unite at points 21). The muscles that have their origin or insertion at points 21 are: levator labii superioris; and levator angular oris. Each muscle connects from points 21 to one or more of the following areas: nose; lips; and sides of the mouth.

Point 22 - Will shut down to prevent toxic overload in the brain; and 144,000 functions pass through these points. See 20, 21, 22 Release. **Neck and Throat:** stiff neck; swollen and sore throat; hoarseness; paralysis of the larynx; inflammation of the trachea, larynx, pharynx, and tonsils; and inflammatin or tuberculosis of the cervical lymph nodes. **Respiration:** asthma; bronchitis; pneumonia; emphysema; pleurisy; pulmonary tuberculosis or congestion; difficult, labored or arrested breathing; cough; whooping cough; diaphragm spasm; and hiccough. **Upper Trunk:** pain in the chest, shoulder, shoulder blade, back, and between the ribs; distention of the chest and hypochondrium; and chest and back spasms. **Other:** insomnia; heart afflictions; headache; vomiting; and lack or loss of appetite for food.

Between points 22 **on the center front** - At the center top of the sternal notch at the base of the throat. Symptoms in addition to above: all throat afflictions; and paralysis of the thorax.

Point 22 **Meridian And Muscle Information** - The Main Meridians that pass through points 22 are Lung, Stomach, Kidney, Triple Warmer, Gall Bladder (lateral), Liver, Large Intestine, Spleen (lateral) and Small Intestine (inner). The Muscle Meridians that unite at points 22 are Lung, Stomach, and Gall Bladder. The muscles that have their origin or insertion at points 22 are: scalenus medius; pectoralis major; serratus anterior; deltoideus; and scalenus posterior. Each of these muscles connects from points 22 to one or more of the following areas: points 3, 9, 10, 11, 12, 13, 14, high 19, and high back 19; cervicals two through seven; the whole sternum; and the outer ribs one through nine.

Point 23 - Energizing; hyperactivity; blood conditions; addictions; points 12, 20, and 21 help open point 23; and hold with same side 15 to release fever due to kidneys. In acupuncture, this is known as a special point to assist chronic afflictions of all internal organs. See 23, 25 Release. **Abdomen:** abdominal distention; accumulatin of serous fluid in the abdominal cavity; upper abdominal pain; and paralysis of the rectus muscle of the abdomen. **Digestion:** stomach ailments such as acute or chronic inflammation; pain; ache; ulcer; cancer; downward displacement; spasm; indigestion; hyperacidity; nausea; and vomiting; all liver diseases such as hepatitis; jaundice; and enlargement; spleen ailments such as diabetes mellitus; and enlargement; intestinal ailments such as inflammatin; constipation; diarrhea; and spasms. **Trunk and Limbs:** pain in the lower back, entire back, vertebral region, shoulder, or scapula; inflammation of the breast; diseases of the female breast; and rheumatism (inflammation and degeneration of the connective tissues and joints). **Urogenital:** inflammation of the kidney; bedwetting; impotence; and blood in the urine. **Other:** weakened body; depression; hives; chronic bleeding disorders; edema; difficult and labored breathing; and neurasthenia (fatigue, lack of energy, depression, feelings of iadequacy, inability to concentrate, loss of appetite, and insomnia).

Between points 23 **on the spine** - The twelfth thoracic between the eleventh thoracic and the first lumbar. This point may be held to stimulate the heart, kidneys, aorta, peritoneum, brain, and adrenals. Symptoms in addition to above: epilepsy; pain and stiffness in loins (the part of the back between the thorax and pelvis); bleeding hemorrhoids; prolapsed anus in children; and adrenal imbalance.

Point 23 **Meridian And Muscle Information** - The Main Meridians that pass through points 23 are Bladder and Kidney. No Muscle Meridians unite at points 23. The muscles that have their origin or insertion at points 23 are: quadratus lumborum; psoas major; psoas minor; latissimus dorsi; trapezius; iliacus; and erector spinae. Each of these muscles connects from points 23 to one or more of the following areas: points 2, 3, 4, 9, 10, 11, 15, and high 19; pubic bone; the spine at cervical seven, thoracics one through twelve, lumbars one through five and the sacrum; and the last rib.

Point 24 - Hold with opposite point 26 to release point 2. This point may be used to bring balance to the six longest meridians, Bladder, Kidney, Gall Bladder, Liver, Stomach and Spleen. Hold with points 18 to assist all pain (especially in the head), neuralgia, and articular (joint) swelling. It will also help all skin diseases, and is good for general exhaustion, weakness, or depletion after a long or serious illness. When points 24 and 18 are combined, they will help rebuild energy resources. See 24, 26 Release. **Head and Neck:** headache; cerebral congestion; giddiness; meningitis; dizziness; vertigo; infantile convulsions; epilepsy; pain in the outer corners of the eys; conjunctivitis; deafness and ringing in the ears. **Trunk and Limbs:** whole body pain or paralysis; muscle spasms, inflammation of or pain in the heart; inflammation of the breast; and pain in the low back, flanks, feet, ankle joints or between the ribs. **Other:** acute inflammation of the stomach; stoppage of milk; chilling; intermittent fever; arested breathing; irregular or painful menstruation; and masturbation.

Point 24 Meridian And Muscle Information - The Main Meridians that pass through points 24 are Gall Bladder, and Bladder. No Muscle Meridians unite at points 24. The muscles that have their origin or insertion at points 24 are: peroneus longus; peroneus brevis; and peroneus tertius. Each of these muscles connects from points 24 to one or more of the following areas: points 7, and 8.

Point 25 - Hemmorrhoids; bleeding ovaries; lower back; and reproductive conditions. See 23, 25 Release. **Trunk and Limbs:** low back pain; sciatica; paralysis of the lower extremeties; hemorrhoids; inflammation of the tissues around the rectum and anus; and boils on the buttocks. **Urogenital:** low back pain during menstruation; leukorrhea; impotence; painful or difficult urination; and suppression of urine formation by the kidney. **Other:** constipation or diarrhea.

Between points 25 on the spine - The coccyx (tailbone). Symptoms in addition to above: prolapsed rectum or anus; painful loins (the part of the back between the thorax and pelvis); intestinal hemorrhage; chronic inflammation of intestines; irregular menstruation; nocturnal emission; arthritic knees; and assists the parathyroid gland.

Point 25 **Meridian And Muscle Information** - The Main Meridian that passes through points 25 is the Bladder. The Muscle Meridians that unite near points 25 at the coccyx and anus are Stomach, Spleen, Bladder, and Gall Bladder. The muscles that have their origin or insertion at points 25 are: biceps femoris; semitendinosus; and semimembranosus. Each of these muscles connects from points 25 to one or more of the following areas: points 1, and 8.

Point 26 - Completion is a point of no beginning and no end; and hold with opposite point 24 to release point 2. See 24, 26 Release. **Head and Neck:** headache; subjective sensation of ringing in the ears; deafness; toothache; eye diseases; and inflammation of the thyroid gland, nape of the neck, and cervical lymph nodes. **Trunk and Limbs:** paralysis of the upper and lower limbs; disorders of the shoulder joint and surrounding tissue; inability to raise the arm freely; and pain, spasm or paralysis of the shoulder, shoulder blade or upper limbs.

Point 26 **Meridian And Muscle Information** - The Main Meridians that pass through points 26 are Small Intestine, and Triple Warmer. The Muscle Meridian that unites at points 26 is Small Intestine. The muscles that have their origin or insertion at points 26 are: triceps brachii, and latissimus dorsi. Each of these muscle connects from points 26 to one or more of the following areas: points 2, 9, and high back 19; on the spine at thoracics seven through twelve, lumbars one through five, and sacrum one and two; and the lower three to four ribs.

Navel (area one to two inches below) - All organs in the body are nourished here. In acupuncture, this is called "the sea of energy" where the body's reserves are opened and rebuilt. It's also the point of reunion for the Conception Vessel, Kidney Meridian, Pericardium Meridian, and the Chong Mo Conception Vessel (Breath of Life). Free this point to raise the energy in the body and assist the thyroid gland. Hold crown and one inch below the navel for deep flow of energy to this area. Symptoms related to points on the Conception Vessel: all intestinal problems; cerebral hemorrhage; all urogenital problems; all lower abdominal problems; mental and nervous depression and debility; neurasthenia (extreme fatigue, depression and sense of worthlessness); stimulates heart, lungs, and abdominal aorta; and assists the thyroid gland.

Toes And Fingers That Have Acupuncture Points

Second Toe - The Stomach Meridian passes through the second toe. **Digestion:** stomach problems such as ache, pain, acute or chronic inflammation, or ulcer; indigestion; excessive gas in stomach or intestines; intestinal problems such as peristaltic sounds, dysentary, diarrhea, and acute or chronic inflammation; liver inflammation or abscess. **Face:** swollen face or eye; facial edema; facial nerve paralysis; parlaysis of mouth or eyes; lack of muscle tone in the lip muscles; sty; eye congestion; inflammtion of the gums; toothache; nosebleed; acute inflammation of the mucous membrane of the nose; and inflamed tonsils. **Groin and Lower Limbs:** inflamed lymph nodes, hernia or pain in the groin; coldness in the lower limbs; and swelling or pain in the dorsal side of the foot. **Mental and Emotional:** headache; epilepsy; madness; dream disturbed sleep; neurasthenia (severe depression, fatigue and sense of worthlessness); cerebral anemia; asthenia (weak, dizzy, fatigued, drowsy and loss of appetite); dementia (organic loss of intellectual function); insomnia; functional disturbances of the peripheral nervous system; and temporary loss of consciousness due to lack of blood to the cerebrum. **Other:** accumulation of serous fluid in the abdominal cavity; general edema; abdominal pain; beriberi (thiamine deficiency); all fever diseases; night sweats; difficult and labored breathing; and coughing.

Fourth Toe - The Gall Bladder Meridian passes through the fourth toe. **Head, Mental and Emotional:** migraine; nervous headache; cerebral congestion; temporary loss of consciousness due to lack of blood to the cerebrum; dizziness; dreaminess; vertigo; noise in the ears; deafness; inflamed corners of the eyes; conjunctivitis; pain or redness in the eyes; dry mouth; inflamed larynx or pharynx; and neurasthenia (severe depression, fatigue, and sense of worthlessness). **Trunk and Limbs:** pain between the ribs, or in the chest; inflamed breast; breast tumor; enlarged heart; pleurisy; obstinate cough; spitting blood; asthma; pulmonary congestion; pain in flanks, lower back ankle joint, or dorsal part of the foot; pain and swelling in the armpit; and rheumatism deformans (inflammation and degeneration of connective tissue and joints).

Little Toe - The Bladder Meridian passes through the little toe. **Head, Mental and Emotional:** headache; cerebral congestion; temporary loss of consciousness due to lack of blood to the cerebrum (fainting); giddiness; dizziness; vertigo; deafness; noise in ears; nosebleed; nasal obstruction; pain in eyeballs; bitter taste in the mouth; mental disorders; madness; frightened feeling; and epilepsy. **Other:** abnormal position of the fetus; difficult labor; disturbed menstruation; difficult and labored breathing; malaria; stiff neck; indigestion; boils; cancerous ulcers; and arthritic ankle joint.

Index Finger - The Large Intestine Meridian passes through the index finger. **Head and Neck:** swelling or pain in throat; hoarseness; inflamed larynx, pharynx, or tonsils; contraction of esophagus; inflamed mouth; lack of muscle tone around the mouth; distorted mouth; dry mouth; swollen tongue; parched lips; teeth ache, especially the lower ones; swollen jaw; facial boils, pain, spasms, or paralysis; eye problems such as itching, distortions, pain, or film over the eyes; noise in the ears; deafness; nosebleed; inflamed nasal mucous membrane; inflamed lymph nodes in the neck; headache; coma; cerebral hemorrhage or congestion; and fainting. **Other:** all fever diseases; vomiting and diarrhea in children; diarrhea or constipation; excessive gas in the stomach or intestines; difficult and labored breathing; asthma; arrested breathing; angina pectoris; pain in shoulders and back; jaundice; absence of perspiration; numbness in fingers; and red, swollen fingers and back of hand.

Middle Finger - The Pericardium Meridian passes through the middle finger. **Head, Mental and Emotional:** headache; coma; cerebral hemorrhage; shock; heat stroke; cerebral congestion; fainting; carotid congestion; noise in the ears; mental disorders; dizziness; insanity; and madness. **Trunk and Limbs:** angina pectoris; inflammation of the heart; heart pain; and palpitations. **Other:** all fever diseases; convulsions in children; epilepsy; and paralysis of the extremties. Hold **center palm** to assist all vascular tissues and circulatory system for ateriosclerosis; inflamed mucous membranes of the mouth; fissuring and dry scaling of the lips and corners of the mouth; bad breath; infantile inflamed gums; hiccough; nosebleed; flank pain; and chronic skin infections of the hand. Hold **hollow at the base of the palm at the wrist** to assist all skin diseases; acute inflammation of the stomach; stomach hemorrhage; vomiting; high blood pressure; tonsillitis; pain between the ribs; arm pain; disorders of the wrist joint and surrounding tissues; inflamed lymph nodes in the neck; neurasthenia (severe depression, fatigue and sense of worthlessness); to promote relaxation and sleep; and when ideas seem to go round and round in the head.

Ring Finger - The Triple Warmer Meridian passes through the ring finger. **Head**

and Neck: headache; fainting; headaches caused by anemia; vertigo; deafness; deafness with sensation of noise in the ears; conjunctivitis; pain and redness in the eyes; film over the eyes; pain and swelling in the throat; inflamed larynx; and paralysis of the suprahyoid muscle (throat and tongue). **Other:** all fever diseases; inability to raise arm with pain in arm and elbow; pain, spasms or paralysis of hands, fingers, elbow, and arm (especially forearm); angina pectoris; vomiting; dementia (organic loss of intellectual function); and lack or loss of appetite for food.

Little Finger - The Heart and Small Intestine Meridians pass through the little finger. **Head and Neck:** all eye diseases; film over the eyes; opacity and inflammation of the cornea; inflamed and swollen tonsils, larynx, and pharynx; paralysis of the larynx; dry throat; deaf mutes; deafness; ringing in the ears; nasal occlusion; nosebleed; torticollis (contracted cervical muscles and twisted neck); pain, spasm or stiffness in the neck; swollen or puffy cheeks; inflamed mucous membrane of the mouth; headache; fainting; cerebral hemorrhage; back of head pain; coma; and pain at the vertex. **Mental and Emotional:** mental disorders; madness; mental deression; melancholy; anxiety; restlessness; nervous palpitations; schizophrenia; and shock. **Trunk and Limbs:** pain, spasm, numbness or paralysis in upper limbs; inflamed breast; shortage of breast milk; enlarged heart; pain in heart, chest, shoulder, upper and lower back, and between the ribs; pleurisy; hot palms; acute inflammation of the stomach. **Urogenital:** itching vulva; excessive menstration; impotence; bedwetting; painful, difficult, or suppressed urination; and urine incontinence. **Other:** epilepsy; convulsions; obstinate cough; all fever diseases; night sweats; itchiness; high blood pressure; and vomiting blood.

Appendix

B

Codes for This Index

For Meridians: Lung = LU; Large Intestine = LI; Stomach = ST; Spleen = SP; Heart = HE; Small Intestine = SI; Bladder = BL; Kidney = KI; Pericardium = PE; Triple Warmer = TW; Gall Bladder = GB; Liver = LV; Conception Vessel = CV; Governing Vessel = GV.

For Fundamental Flows: Main Central = MC; Major Vertical = MV; Minor Diagonal = MD; Elimination of Fatigue = EF.

For Special Flows: Depth Flows = DF; Lung Flows I, II, & II = LF1; LF2; LF3; Breathing and Digestion = B&D; Dizziness = DI; Back of Leg Pain = LP; Hip Pain = HP; Eyes = EY; Vertical Harmony = VH;

For Quick Flows: Fatigue = FA; Thumb Flow = TF; Little Finger Flow = LFF; Chest-Back Flow = CB; Diagonal Muscle Flow = DM; Skin Surface Flow = SS; Deep Skin Flow = DS; Quick Flows 1-5 = QF1; QF2; QF3; QF4; QF5

For Release Flows: The numbers will be used such as 1; (20, 21, 22); 9; or (5, 6, 7, 8). In some cases, it will just say points 7, 23, 22, 4 to let you know the critical point involved so you can refer to Appendix A or the appropriate release flow.

Then check alphabetical listing for codes and numerical listing for points to find the page numbers for these flow patterns. For pulses, see pp. 96, 97, 100, 101.

Alphabetical Listing for Codes:

B&D = Breathing and Digestion, pp. 269, 271, 272
BL = Bladder, pp. 144 - 149 (right flow shown in figure 15)
CB = Chest-Back Flow, pp. 265
CV = Conception Vessel, pp. 104, 105
DF = Depth Flows, pp. 251 - 253
DI = Dizziness, pp. 269, 273, 274
DM = Diagonal Muscle Flow, pp. 266
DS = Deep Skin Flow, pp. 267
EF = Elimination of Fatigue, pp. 96, 98, 99
EY = Eyes, pp. 270, 279, 280
FA = Fatigue Flows, pp. 249 - 251
GB = Gall Bladder, pp. 168 - 173 (right flow shown in figure 19)
GV = Governing Vessel, pp. 106, 107
HE = Heart, pp. 132 - 137 (right flow shown in figure 13)
HP = Hip Pain, pp. 270, 277, 278
KI = Kidney, pp. 150 - 155 (right flow shown in figure 16)
LF1 = Lung Flow I, pp. 254 - 256
LF2 = Lung Flow II, pp. 254, 257, 258
LF3 = Lung Flow III, pp. 254, 259
LFF = Little Finger Flow, pp. 262
LI = Large Intestine, pp. 114 - 119 (right flow shown in figure 10)
LP = Back of Leg Pain, pp. 269, 275, 276
LU = Lung, pp. 108 - 113 (right flow shown in figure 9)
LV = Liver, pp. 174 - 179 (left flow shown in figure 20)
MC = Main Central, pp. 86, 87, 90, 91
MD = Minor Diagonal, pp. 86, 89, 94, 95 (left flow shown in figure 5)
MV = Major Vertical, pp. 86, 88, 92, 93
PE = Pericardium, pp. 156 - 161 (right flow shown in figure 17)
QF1 = Quick Flow 1, pp. 267
QF2 = Quick Flow 2, pp. 267, 268
QF3 = Quick Flow 3, pp. 268
QF4 = Quick Flow 4, pp. 268
QF5 = Quick Flow 5, pp. 268
SI = Small Intestine, pp. 138 - 143 (left flow shown in figure 14)
SP = Spleen, pp. 126 - 131 (left flow shown in figure 12)
SS = Skin Surface Flow, pp. 266
ST = Stomach, pp. 120 - 125 (right flow shown in figure 11)
TF = Thumb Flow, pp. 260

TW = Triple Warmer, pp. 162 - 167 (left flow shown in figure 18)
VH = Vertical Harmony, pp. 260, 261

Numerical Listing for Points:

Alphabitized Index

Abdomen: in general, TW, LF3, B & D, KI, (5, 6, 7, 8); to clear, hold tailbone and between 23's, then between 12's; pain, points 1, 2, 6 (lower), 19 (lower), 7, low front 8, 9 (upper lateral), 10, 14, low 15, 23 (upper); pain and distention (bloated), ST,LI, LV, KI, BL, QF1, points 2, 5, 7, 14, low 15, 23; pain in appendix area, ST, LFF, QF1; spontaneous pain in lower, SI; ascites (accumulation of fluid), KI, LV, points 6, 23; pain in navel, KI, LV; hard and swollen, KI, LV; hard lumps in, KI; soreness in, PE, 13, same side 15; feels like a small animal running around, LV; sensation of heat in, LV; obese in waist and abdomen, KI, BL; pain in solar plexus, LFF; all deep flows meet in the umbilicus (one inch below navel); inflammation, point 1; paralysis of rectus muscle, point 23; spasms, points 1, 6 (lower), between 15's (lower); enlarged and cold, point 7; peritonitis, points 7, 14

Acid-Alkaline Balance: hold middle finger

Acne: DF, KI, LI

Addictions: (23, 25), KI, BL, B & D

Allergies: thumb over ring finger, LU, LI, ST, DF, B & D, BL, GB, LF (1, 2, 3)

Anemia: see also blood conditions; (20, 21, 22), GB, SP, KI, BL, ST, points 1, 9, 19

Ankles: see also legs; 2, LP, 15, (5, 6, 7, 8), 9

Anus: prolapsed in children, between 23's; prolapse of, between 25's (tailbone), point low back 8; anal muscle cramp, point 2; inflammation of tissues around, point 25

Anxiety: see also mental, emotional; ST, SP, points 6, 7, 10, 17, 18, between 20's

Apoplexy (sudden neurological impairment due to intracranial hemorrhage): see also brain; GB, HE, BL, points 4, between 4's

Appendicitis: see also abdomen; QF1

Appetite: to balance, 14, on spine (between 3's, 9's, 10's, 14's), crown, tailbone, MC, 13, LF (1, 2, 3); feeling hungry but no appetite, KI; no appetite, TW; loss of, points 2, 5, 6, 9, 10, 13, 17, 18, 22, 23, between 9's

Arms (overall): in general, B & D, 26, 3; ache, PE, point 11; paralysis, PE, GB, first thoracic, points 3, 4, 11, 17, 18, 19, 26; icy cold, TW, LV; pain under, GB; swollen armpits, GB, point 16; knots in armpits, TF, LFF, HE, SI, LU, LI, point 16; pain in armpits, HE, point 16; stiff, DF; pain, LFF, points 1, 3, lateral 10, 11, 17, 18, 26; bent or stiff, QF3, (16, 17, 18, 19); joints, QF5; and opposite leg, LP; useless arm (can't raise), 14, lateral 10, 26; numb, point 3; spasms, points 3, 6, 11, 14, 17, 24, 26; fatigue, points 5, 9; overuse, points 10, 12; pain in joints, point 18; pain, paralysis, spasm and numbness in elbows, points 3, lateral 10, 14

Arms (upper): aches, LI; pain, HE, TW, TF, LFF; red color, HE; stiff and painful, SI; underarm swells, PE; swollen armpits, GB; pain in armpits, HE

Arteriosclerosis: point 8

Arthritis: TW, QF3, 26, (16, 17, 18, 19), KI, BL, points 8, 11, 17; rheumatism, points 8, low point 8, 9, 23; of knees, tailbone

Ascending Flows: to strengthen, hold middle finger; to balance, 10, MV, MD, B&D; regulated by TW; to assist flow, coccyx (tailbone); to balance with descending, 1; needs to be open, 15

Asphyxia: revival point if someone stops breathing, between 11's (first thoracic)

Asthma: see also lungs; thumb over ring finger; LU, SI, GB, DF, B&D, QF2, LF (1,2,3), 9, 10, (11, 12), 13, 14, points 3, 5, 9, 10, 11, 13, 18, 19, 22, between 14's; bronchial asthma, points 10, between 13's

Autism: see also Appendix A; (20, 21, 22), 14, 4, HE, BL

Baby: MC, 9, 10, LU, LI, B&D

Back: in general, MD, B & D, CB, opposite (5, 6, 7, 8), opposite 9, (11, 12), opposite (16, 17, 18, 19), LF (1,2,3), VH, 3; aches, BL, point 3, 11, and coughing, PE; pain, KI, in backbone in heart region, TW; stiffness and paralysis, opposite (16, 17, 18, 19); muscle spasms of lower, points 1, 11; lower back pain, points 3, 8, 16, 24, 25, between 9's, between 23's; upper back tension, point 6; pain in back, points 9, 10, lateral 10, 11, 18, 22, 23, between 3's; back spasm, points 11, 22; stiff, points 3, 11, between 3's, 10's 11's

Bedwetting: see also urogenital; points 1, 2, 5, 7, 15, 23

Belching: point 14

Beriberi (symptoms which result from a thiamine, vitamin B1, deficiency): points 1, 8, low back 8, 16

Bladder: see also kidney, urogenital, reproductive; in general, BL, KI, 9, 10, 15, 2, 3, (11, 12), 4, 16, (23, 25), 8, DF, MC, MV, MD; chronic problems, 3; inflammation, points 2, 5, 8, low 8; spasm, point 15; paralysis, point 15

Blood Conditions: in general, hold thumb, index & middle fingers, 23, HE, SI; blood in expectoration, KI; anemia, GB, (20, 21, 22), (23, 25), point 11; black blood discharge after childbirth, LV; prolonged after childbirth, point 11; vomiting blood, LV, KI, BL, EF, 3, (11, 12), 15; pus and blood in stools, LV, pubic & tail bones, 15, 25, 2, MD, MC, KI, BL; nosebleeds, KI, BL, 4; menstruation, 2, 15, 8, 16, 5, pubic bone, tailbone; ovary bleeding, 25, 13; blood in urine, KI; blood congested in lungs, MV, BL, 3, 10, 9, (23, 25), 2; blood pressure, EY, 4, (20, 21, 22), (23, 25), 10; circulation, HE, PE, B&D; blood sugar level, SP, LV, 9, 14, (23, 25); leukemia, (23, 25); chronic hemorrhagic disorders, points, 9, 23, (intestinal), point 6, tailbone

Blood Pressure: see also blood conditions; EY, 4, (20, 21, 22), (23, 25), 10, points 14, 17, 18, 19, between 3's, 10's, 20's

Body: feels heavy, SP, heavy sensation throughout, KI; weak, SP; low vitality, SP; debility, SP; many areas troubled at once and can't pinpoint the focus of the problem, HE; swelling of parts of the body, KI; burns, PE; can't turn or twist upper part, PE; unable to turn to side when lying down, GB; alignment, QF4; to augment powers of resistance and tone all internal organs, hold first thoracic and points 18, then 19 — then alternate with first thoracic and points 19 and 8; after long-standing illness with weakened body, points 10, 23; whole body pain and/or paralysis, point 24; prolapsed (drooping) states of inner organs, hold crown of head and between 2's; to tone whole body, point 8; to assist whole lower body, hold point 8 with point 19, then 25; to tone all internal organs, and is a master point for bony structure of whole body, between 11's (first thoracic); pain on one side of body, point 18; muscle spasms, DM, points 6, 24

Bones: become weak, KI; all bone problems, KI, BL, DF; development of bones, nails and teeth, KI, BL;

Brain: in general, 14, (20, 21, 22), 4, toes, fingers, MC, VH, BL, HE; inability to recognize anyone, TW; fag (exhaustion), SP; loss of alertness, SP; excessive imagination, SP; congestion, GB, points 12, 19, 20, 24; hemiplegia, GB; tumor, GB, (20, 21, 22); senility, 14, (20, 21, 22); cerebral disorders, points, 4, 11, 14, 6, 7, 16, 9, 17, low front 8, and between 3's; assists overall functioning, between 2's and 23's; paralysis, point 12; meningitis, point 12; weakness, between 10's, between 14's; coma, points 4, 6

Breast: see also chest; in general, B & D, QF1, LP, same side (16, 17, 18, 19); pain above, ST; pain under, GB; pain in, TF; lumps in, or after mastectomy, (16, 17, 18, 19); inflammation, points 11, 13, 23, 24; tumors, point 13; diseases of female breast, points 13, 23; stoppage of milk, point 24

Breathing: hold crown and between 13's; hold middle fingers; thumb over ring fingernails; TF, LU, LI, LF (1,2,3), B&D, 10, 9, 13, 14, (11, 12), first thoracic, CB, DS, QF1; hardness and fullness in chest, GB; shallow breathing (fear), KI, BL; labored and difficult, points 3, 5, 7, 9, 11, 13, 14, 18, 19, 21, 22, 23; arrested (cessation), points 16, 18, 22, 24, first thoracic

Bronchitis: LU, SP, SI, BL, GB, QF2, 10, 3, MV, MD, MC, EF, points 3, 9, 10, 11, 14, 18, 19, 22

Buttocks: boil on, 25

Cancer: point 3; of stomach, points 6, 9; note - vitalize whole system and release points related to disrupted areas

Chest: fullness, PE, TF; aches with coughing, PE; inability or painful to turn chest, TW; pain, GB; feels full and tight, LV; unbearable warmth in, LV; congestion, B & D, 13; to expand or contract, CB; if problems (enlarged & swollen), use opposite side (5, 6, 7, 8), 9; if problems (protruding ribs, fullness & swelling), use same side, (16, 17, 18, 19); opens, 4; releases and pulls it down, (5, 6, 7, 8); spasm, points 1, 22; tension, point 6; fullness and burning, point 10; pain, points 9, 10, 14, 17, 18, 19, 22, between 3's; distention of points 22, between 14's; all diseases of, between 13's

Chills: and fever, GB, 3; in shoulders and back, LU; (23, 25); points 24, first thoracic

Cholera: TW

Chorea (ceaseless rapid jerky movements): point 19

Circulation: of life force, PE

Colic: DF, LV, LI, LU, B&D, points 1, 9, 10

Common Cold: see also lungs, respiration; points 3, 18, between 4's

Coma: see also brain; MC, points 4, 6

Complexion: SS, DS, LI, KI, LU

Concentration: see also mental, emotional; inability to concentrate, points 2, 5, 9, 10, 17, 18, 23

Consciousness: loss of, points 4, 10, 17

Constipation: LU, LI, 2, EY, (5, 6, 7, 8), LF1, (23, 25), MC, 13, points 2, 5, 7, 8, low back 8, 14

Constrictions: of all kinds, point 9

Consumption (TB): B&D, 10

Convulsions: TW, points 7, 14; due to indigestion, 14; infantile, points 6, 24, between 10's; in children, tip of nose, between 3's (high fever)

Coordination: loss of, point 16

Coughing: LU, BL, PE, DF, (20, 21, 22), 9, 10, (11, 12), points 5, 6, low front 8, 9, 10, 11, 13, 14, 18, 19, 22; whooping, points 3, 5, 22

Cowardice: points 10, between 10's

Crossroads in the Body: for surface, middle, deep, ascending, descending, right and left flows - pubic bone and tailbone

Deafness: see also ears and speech; points, 2, 4, 17, 19, 24, 26; deaf mutism, point 12

Depression: LU, ST, B&D, 9, 10, 14, MC; points 2 (moderate), 4, 5, 9, 10, 17, 18 (nervous), 19 (deep), 23, between 11's (nervous)

Descending Flows: to strengthen, hold middle finger with thumb on palmside; regulated by, PE; to balance ascending and descending, 1

Diabetes: SP, KI, LV, points 2, 7, 23

Diagonals: mediate communication between right and left sides of the body; MD, EF, MV, MC, LF (1,2,3), DI

Diaphragm: see also, chest, upper trunk, and abdomen; seventh thoracic; opposite side (5, 6, 7, 8); same side 14; spasm, points 5, 9, 14, 22, 25; paralysis of diaphragm muscle, point 9

Diarrhea: left 2, right LF1, DF, LV, LI, points 2, 4, 6, 8, 9, 13, 14, 23, 25, tip of nose; dysentary, points 1, 2

Digestion: in general, GB, LV, ST, SP, LF (1,2,3), between 14's, 9, 14, seventh thoracic, B&D, DS, 13, cross hands and hold high 1's, hold crown and between 13's; hold middle fingers; see fingers; food doesn't descend, SP, BL; energy regulated by, TW; dyspepsia, LV; eat a lot but doesn't digest, LV; convulsions from indigestion, 14; inability to eat (feed oneself), point 7; indigestion, points 5, 8, 9, 14, 18; indigestion in infants and children, point 18

Discipline: MC, MV, MD, PE, TW

Diverticulitis: QF1, LI, 13

Dizziness: HE, SI, TW, GB, DF, DI, 9, 10, (18, 19), (20, 21, 22); felt upon standing, KI; points 4, 6, 8, 10, 16, 17, 24, between 20's; giddiness, points 7, low 8, 20, 24

Dreams: fantastic dreams, TW; excessive, points 7, 17; dream disturbed sleep, point 9

Drugs: abuse, B&D, (23, 25), KI, BL; to relieve drunkeness, tip of nose; unconscious, point 4

Ears: to assist ears overall, KI, BL, DF, DI; deafness, SI, points 2, 17, 19, 24, 26 sudden deafness, TW, GB; ringing, SI, TW, DF, point 24, 26; inflammation, SI; buzzing and pain, TW, GB; unclear hearing, TW, DF, point 19; mastoiditis, TW; infections, TW, GB, point 4; dizziness, DF; ache, (20, 21, 22); noise in ears, points 2, 4, 17

Eczema: see also skin; points 1, 19, first thoracic

Edema: points 1, 6, 8, 9, 13, 23

Elbows: ventral pain, HE; tension, PE; spasms, PE; pain, TW, TF, LFF; inability to fold or stretch, TW; pain, paralysis, spasm and numbness, points 3, lateral 10, 14

Elimination: see fingers; LF (1,2,3), DS, B&D, 13, (5, 6, 7, 8)

Emotional: see also Appendix A; hold crown and between 14's; hold middle
fingers; thumb over ring finger; fear and anxiety, HE; crying and hysteria, HE, KI,
LV; irritation, HE; melanchololy, SI; crying spells, BL; nervous breakdown, KI;
ceaseless and excessive laughter, PE; sudden madness, PE; angry and upset for
little or no reason, PE; dazed and dazzled feeling, PE; shyness, PE; afraid of cold
and wind, PE, GB; fear of all persons, PE; cries or moans, PE; continuous anger,
PE, LV; constant sadness, GB; grief, B&D; emotional problems, DS, B&D, DI,
LF (1,2,3), EY; collapse, point 18; neurosis, point 12

Emphysema: B&D, (5, 6, 7, 8), LU, 9, 10, points 5, 13, 14, 18, 22, first thoracic

Energizing: (23, 25), SP; lack of energy, points 2, 5, 10, 17, 18, 23

Epilepsy: SI, BL, PE, GB, LV. EY, 14, TW, points 5, 6, 7, low 8, 10, 11, 12, 14, 16,
17, 19, 20, 24, between 14's, 20's, 23's; infantile, between 3's

Eyes: to assist eyes overall, MD, SI, BL, DF, EY, LU, (LF1, 2, 3), 9 10, 4, (20, 21,
22), 26 MC, hold tailbone and between the 4's; yellowish, LI, HE, BL; red lines,
HE; red below the eyes, HE; congestion, HE, KI, points 14, 17; constantly
jumping about, SI; ache, BL; myopia, BL, point 5; blurred vision, BL, point 20;
itching, BL, GB, points 20, 21; watery, BL, points 9, 20, 21; puffiness below, KI;
weak eyesight, PE, GB, points 17, 11, 20; blurry vision, PE; bloody & inflamed,
PE, TW, points 7, 20; eyelashes curled inward, TW; white veil (film) over eyes,
TW, points 16, 21; upturned eyes (Sanpaku), TW; infections, TW, GB; outer
canthus aches or festers, TW, GB; dazzled by bright light, GB; nearsightedness,
LV, QF5, EY, point 21; irritation, TF; bulging eyeballs, LFF; cataracts, EY, point
21; spots before the eyes, EY; astigmatism, EY, point 21; eye shape correction,
(20, 21, 22); night blindness, points 9, 20, 21; swollen, points 7, 20; sty, points 7,
16, 21; tremor, point 20; conjunctivitis, points 7, 20, 21, 24; inflamed cornea,
points 17, 17, 20; glaucoma, points 7, 20, 21; pain, points low 8, 17, 20, 21, 24;
increase or decrease secretion of tears, points 17, 21; atrophy of optic nerve, point
17; dense white corneal opacity, point 20; farsightedness, point 21; loss of tone,
point 21; inflamed optic nerve and retina, point 21; paralysis, point 21; atrophy
of eye, point 21; eyelid and eye muscle spasms, point 21

Face: cheeks swell, LI, SI, TW, GB, TF, LFF, points 19, 21; cheek pain, TW, point
21; chin pain, SI, GB; chin feels tight, GB; double chin, SI; facial spasms LU,

points 4, 20, 21; trigeminal neuralgia, point 20; facial nerve paralysis, points 19, 20, 21; facial nerve pain, points 20, 21; forehead red, HE; overall color is black especially on forehead and below eyes, KI; upper jaw pain, BL; flushed, PE; hot, point 17; red, PE; congested, PE; perpetual frown, PE; gooseflesh, GB; dusty, wan or livid color, GB; weak & dirty color, LV; yellow-green or greenish complexion, LV; to assist complexion, SS, DS; facial abscess, point 21; chronic flushing of nose, forehead, and cheeks, tip of nose; facial edema, points 6, 8, 21; loss of muscle tone, point 7; itching, point 21

Fatigue: MD, EF, 3, FA, LF (1,2,3), DF, points 3, 4, 7, 10, 23; chronic abnormal lack of energy, points 2, 5, 9, 17, 18

Fear: KI, BL, TW; of all persons, PE; shy, PE; of cold and wind, GB, BL, PE; in children, points 5, 7, 19; phobia, point 17

Fever: points 3, 4, 7, 11, 18, 19, between 4's, (23, 25); in children, point 5; without perspiration, PE, TW; and chills, GB, LV; high, steps 1-4 of LF1; high or low, LF2; from colds and viruses, step 1 of 3 Release; low fever, 14; intermittent, point 24; night fever, between 3's; acute febrile diseases, first thoracic

Feet: in general, QF2, 26; to warm, hold tailbone and pube, steps 1-3 of 15 Release; pain in instep, ST; pain, BL, point 24, in heel, point 5, in soles, low back 8; fever in soles, KI, point 6; icy cold up to knees, KI; development of nails, KI; soles hot without perspiration, GB; to aid circulation to, between the 23's; cold, LFF, same side 15; callouses on bottom, QF2; crooked toes, (5, 6, 7, 8), point 5; hammertoes, BL, MV; callouses, corns, and bunions, same side 9; to assist back and chest, CB; to assist skin, SS; swollen, point 8; paralysis, point 25

Fingers: in general, MD, 26; related to opposite side, 2, 15, 23; backside to opposite side 3, 9, 10, 11; palmside to opposite side 13; for breathing, digestion, elimination and fatigue, FA; hold ring and little fingers simultaneously to calm nerves, FA; development of nails, KI

Thumb: in general, TF; lack of strength, 10; backside related to first & seventh thoracic, and palmside to first rib; backside related to soleside little toe, and palmside to backside big toe - all on same side; thumb over ring finger clears thoracic cavity;

Index: stiffens, LI; good for elimination; backside related to second & eighth thoracic, and palmside to second rib; backside related to soleside fourth toe, and palmside to backside second toe - all on same side

Middle: stiffens, ST; backside related to third & ninth thoracic, and palmside to third rib; backside related to soleside middle toe, and palmside to backside middle toe - all on same side; hold middle finger for - breathing; clears eyes; acid-alkaline balance; with backside thumb to strengthen ascending flows, and with palmside thumb to strengthen descending flows; to open lungs; see FA

Ring: stiffens and cannot bend, TW; bends and cannot straighten, GB; backside related to fourth and tenth thoracic, and palmside to fourth rib; backside related to soleside second toe, and palmside to backside fourth toe - all on same side; thumb over ring clears thoracic cavity

Little: in general, LFF; bends and cannot straighten, BL; backside related to fifth and eleventh thoracic, and palmside to fifth rib; backside related to soleside big toe, and palmside to backside little toe - all on same side

Flu: BL, TW, 3, 9, 10, points 3, 4, 11, 18

Fountain of Youth: TW, VH

Gall Bladder: in general, GB, DF, left 9, right 14, between the 9's; bile problems, SP, GB; circulation of energy, PE; acute bile duct inflammation, GB; stones, QF1; hardened area, opposite (5, 6, 7, 8); has action on, point 5; diseases of, point 8; inflamed, point 9, 14, 17; to assist function, point 16

Gas: excess, ST, GB, KI, LV; foul, LI

Glands: thyroid, KI, (23, 25), 13; parathyroid, between 12's, tailbone; adrenals, KI, between 14's, 23's; all glands, 13, MC, VH; assists enlarged and inflamed glands, points 19, 21; inflamed parotid gland, point 21; pituitary, between 14's

Glaucoma: see also eyes; points 7, 20, 21

Goiter: simple thyroid, points 18, 19

Gout: LV, KI, BL, 2, LP, HP, point 8

Hair: all conditions, LU, LI, SI, LF (1,2,3); falls out, SP, HE, points 8, 10; dandruff, HE; extreme hairiness, SS; baldness, point 10

Hands: in general, 26; no feeling in, PE; palms feverish, LFF, HE, PE, point 7; palms ache, HE; hot palms without perspiration, GB, 7

Head: congestion, SI; inability to turn from side to side, SI, 10; migraines, BL, TW,

GB, DS, QF3; chronic pain and tension, BL, GB, (20, 21, 22), in back, 13, 3, (11, 12), points, 3, 16, 17, in front, 20, on top, points 10, 6; pressure, BL; tight bound feeling, GB; intracranial hemorrhage, 4; muscle spasms, point 11; edema, point 6; accumulation of pus in, points 20 and 21; chronic flushing of nose, forehead and cheeks, tip of nose

Headaches: TW, KI, PE, GB, DS, 1; points 3, 4, 6, 7, low 8, 12 (habitual), 16, 17, 19, 20, 21, 22, 24, 26; between 2's, and 10's

Heart: in general, HE, PE, TW, 10, 15, B & D, left (16, 17, 18, 19), 1, points 4, 6, 10, 15, 22, between 14's; enlarged, HE, GB; inflamed, HE, PE, points 6, 17, 19, 24; endocardium or pericardium inflamed, points 9, 10, 17; hyperactive (palpitations), HE, TF, LFF, EY, 10, points 6, 7, 9, 10, 17 (nervous), 19, between 20's; increased pulsation, KI, PE, TF, LFF; pricking pains in, especially after a big meal, PE; feels heavy and laborious, PE; feels like it's hanging in the chest, PE; pain in backbone in heart region, TW; sudden acute pain, TW; pain, GB, LFF; pain in heart that prevents twisting around, GB; acute pain in heart and liver areas that prevents moving forward or backward, LV; pressure (may cause insanity overnight), GB; mitral valve, 4, 10, 14; angina pectoris, points 17, 19, pains, points 9, 10, 13; to contract aorta, first thoracic; to stimulate aorta, between 23's; arrythmia, point 10; pain, points 10, 17, 19, 24, between 13's, between 14's; dilation, point 17; to contract, first thoracic; stimulates action of, between 23's; associated point for, between 10's

Heartburn: see also digestion, stomach; points 9, 10, 11, 13

Heatstroke: points 6, 8, first thoracic

Hemorrhoids: LI; points 2, 5, 8, low 8, low back 8, 10, 25, between 11's, between 23's

Hepatitis: LV, GB, (5, 6, 7, 8), 9, 14, point 5

Hernia: points 1, 2, 5, 7; hiatal, point 14; lower abdomen, groin, urogenital, point 15

Hiccoughs: LU, 14, 9, points 9, 10, 14, 22

Hips: LU (2,3); pain in buttocks, KI, point 15; pain when straightening, BL; pain and stiffness, GB, same side 10, 15; ache, LV; imbalance, QF4; loosens, QF4;

opposite (5,6,7,8), 9; muscle spasms, point 1; swelling, point 10; problems, point 12

Hives: DS, BL, points 1, 3, 9

Hormones: 13

Hot Flashes: DS, 13

Hyperkinesis: DF, (23, 25), KI, BL, HE, SI, TW, 13

Hypertension: GB, KI, BL, HE, 9, 10, (23, 25), points 2, 7, 8, 10

Hypochondrium: see also stomach, digestion; pain, points 9, 14, 22

Hysteria: see also mental, emotional; points 4, 5, 6, 10, 17; hysteric aphasia (sudden loss of ability to express or comprehend speech or written language, point 17

Ilio-Sacral: joint disorder, point 2

Impatience: KI

Immunity: assists lymphocyte production, point 19; in general, point 3

Inadequacy: feelings of, points 2, 4, 5, 10, 17, 18, 23

Indecisiveness: KI

Infections: 3, (23, 25), PE, TW

Inner Organs: connected and united by PE; energized and nourished by TW; see Body for stimulation and toning of

Insanity: intermingling of, ST, BL, points 7, 12, 17, between 3's, 4's, 11's, 14's

Insomnia: BL, KI, DF, points 1, 2, 4, 5, 7, 9, 10, 16, 17, 18, 22, 23, between 20's; or sleepiness, LV; concentrate on third eye (between brows) to bring one-pointedness

Intermingling: GB with other twelve meridians, release 3, 8, 16, seventh thoracic;

KI and BL, release seventh thoracic and second lumbar, 9, 14, 15 1; LI, SI, TW and spine, release 13; LU and LI, use TF, 3; HE and SI, use LFF, 3, 10 first, third, and seventh thoracics

Itching: point 3; neurodermatitis (itching skin of an emotional origin rather than inflammation), point 19

Jaundice: KI, GB, LV, SP, points 5, 9

Jaw: see also mouth; stiff or swollen, point 17; pain and inflammation in lower jaw, point 17, between 10's; lockjaw, point 21

Joints: stiffness and pain, TW, GB, QF3, KI, BL, 26, (16, 17, 18, 19), MD, EF, QF5; inflammation of connective tissue, point low 8

Kidneys: see also bladder, urogenital, reproductive; in general, KI, BL, TW, DF, 15, 1, (11, 12), (5, 6, 7, 8), opposite side 14, same side 9, 23, point 2; blocked, HE; violent pain in kdney area, BL; congested, BL; works in close cooperation with, TW; infections, GB; chills in kidney region, GB; fever in anterior region, GB, 13, 14, 15; inflammation, points 1, 2, 5, 8, low 8, 14, 23; suppression of urine, points 1, 8; stimulates action of, between 23's, center sole of foot lateral to point 6

Knees: pain and swelling, 4, steps 1-3 of 15 release, 10, 14, LP, KI, BL, points 1, 4, 8, 10, tailbone, (and stiffness, 4, 10); all disorders, point 1;

Large Intestine: in general, LI, GB, DF, LF (1, 2, 3), QF1, LU, B & D, point 23, between 9's; foul smelling stools, LI; pain, LI; constipation or diarrhea, LI, SP, KI, GB, LV, QF1, EY, (5, 6, 7, 8), point 23, constipation, right 2, diarrhea, left 2; bleeding, LI, SP, points 2, 6, tailbone; parasites, LI, SP, TW; pains in anus, BL; hemorrhoids, BL, DF; intestinal walls swell, LI, KI; gas, LI, LV, GB, points 2, 5, 10, 13, 14, between 2's, 9's; pus and blood in stools, LI, LV; inflamed, LI, LV, 13, points 2, 5, 8, 10, 23, tailbone; rectal, BL, DF, (5, 6, 7, 8); diverticulitis, LI, 13, QF1; colitis, LI, 13; spasms, points 2, 8, 23

Laughter: ceaseless and excessive, PE; cackles, PE; excess jolliness, HE, SI; just before crying, 14

Legs: in general, 2, 26, 12; feel heavy, point 4; breaks and sprains, 15; swelling, 15; paralysis, PE; icy cold, TW, LV, point 7; hot, GB; stiff, DF; varicose veins, B & D; bent or stiff, QF3; joints, QF5; pain with tension in opposite arm and shoulder,

LP, HP; relaxes legs, 3; heals breaks and sprains and decrease swelling, 15; pain, points 1, 15, 16, 18; weakness, points 1, 8, 16; spasms, points 5, 6, 8, 16, 24; paralysis, points 4, 5, 7, 8, 15, 16, 18, 19, 25, 26; fatigue, points 5, 9; inflamed, 16

Thighs: tense and feel as though they'll rip open, BL; ache inside, LV; tension, same side 14; pain, points 14, 15

Knees: see also knees; cap swells and pain, ST, GB, LV, 4, opposite 10, same side 14, same side 15; stiff, BL; pain due to leg sprain, same side 14

Lower Leg: icy cold knees to feet, KI; pain in shins, GB; pain from knees down, QF2; swollen, same side 15 (especially steps 1-3)

Calves: tense and feel as though they'll rip open, BL; hold to assist metabolism, DS;

Ankle: violent pain in achilles tendon, BL; pain, GB; sprain, same side 9; pain in dorsal side, ST, GB; pain in ankle joint, or sprained, points 5, 9, 24

Leucorrhea: 13, points 2, 13, 15, 17, 25

Leukemia: see blood conditions; (23, 25), 9, 2, KI, BL

Limbs: fatigue, point 9;

Lips: see also mouth; fissuring, scaling, pain, or swelling, point 21

Liver: in general, SP, GB, LV, left 9, right 14, DF, QF1, QF5, 1, point 14; jaundice, SP, GB, KI, point 23; circulation of energy to, PE, LU, LF (1, 2, 3); pain under, GB; acute pain in liver and can't bend forward or backward, LV; all diseases of, LV, points 9, 23; hepatitis, QF1, opposite (5, 6, 7, 8), points 9, 23; hardened area, opposite (5, 6, 7, 8); stimulates action of, between 9's; dilation, point 2; action on, point 5; abscess, point low front 8; enlarged, points 9, 23

Loins: pain, between 23's, 25's (tailbone); stiff, between 23's

Lumbago: see also back; point 2; lumbar stiff, sprain, paralysis of, point 2; lumbar pain, points 7, 15, 16

Lungs: in general, DF, LF (1, 2, 3), TF, B & D, EY, 10, 9, 14, TW, GB, QF1, opposite side (5, 6, 7, 8), 13, points 3, 12; to open, hold middle finger; congestion, SP, HE, PE, TW, TF, points 13, 16; bronchial, SP, 10, GB, SI, BL; pneumonia, SP, 10, BL; yawning, SP, HE; pain in pleura, GB, pleurisy, LV; asthma, GB, BL, SI; hard to breathe, GB, 10, opposite (5, 6, 7, 8), same side, 14; fit of coughing, LV; coughing, TF, BL; phlegm, TF; colds, SI; fullness in chest, SI, GB; flu, BL;

coughing and phlegm from colds, (20, 21, 22); asthma, lack of tone, or normal strength, point 3; dilates, between 3's; dilates pulmonary artery, first thoracic

Lymph: EF, 3, DS; glands and nodes inflamed, TW; assists lymphocyte production, point 19

Madness: see also mental, emotional, insanity; points 5, low 8, 10, 11

Malaria: between 10's and 11's

Masturbation: points 16, 24

Meat: too much, KI, (23, 25); can't digest, LV, GB, right 14, left 9

Melancholy: LU, LI, SI, EF, LF (1,2,3), B&D

Memory: LI, SP; hold crown of head and third eye (between the brows); loss of or poor, point 10

Meningitis: see also brain; points 16, 24

Menstruation: see also reproductive, urogenital; irregular, points 1, 2, 5, 7, 13, 15, 17, 24, between 25's (tailbone); painful, points 1, 2, 5, 6, 7, 15, 17, 24, 25 (pain in low back); excessive, points 5, 7, 15; prolonged, points 1, 15, 17; absent, 15; arrested, point 18

Mental: hold crown of head and between 14's; hold middle fingers; disorders, points 3, 5, 6, 9, 10, 13, 17, 18, between 4's, 14's; loss of alertness and understanding, SP; brain fag (cerebral exhaustion), SP, HE; excessive imagination, SP; lack of keenness and understanding, HE; phobias, HE; oppression (feeling weighed down), HE; nervous breakdown, SI, KI; insanity, BL and ST intermingle; unbalance, BL; sudden madness, PE; dazed and dazzled, PE; angry and upset for little or no reason, PE; continuous anger, PE, LV; rambling thoughts, TW; constant sadness, GB; madness (person runs constantly), GB; fear of cold and wind (even cold food and water), GB; mental problems, DS, LF (1,2,3), DI, B&D, 13; neurosis, point 12; psychopathy (diseases of the mind), points 5, 17, 19

Metabolism: see also breathing, lungs, digestion, fingers; to balance, CB, DM, DS, 13, MC

Migraines: see also headaches; BL, GB, TW, DS, QF3, (20, 21, 22), 4, (11, 12), (5, 6, 7, 8), 9, 10, (16, 17, 18, 19), points 16, 20

Mouth: conditions, point 3; gums inflamed, LU, points 7, 19, between 11's; teeth ache, LI, DF, TF, points 7, 19, 21, 26; bad breath, LI, PE; dry mouth, ST, TW; lips chap, ST, point 21; root of tongue hardens & pains, SP; difficulty tasting, HE; inability to taste, SI; abscesses in mouth, SI, PE; inflamed mouth, points 3, 17; cold sores on upper lip, SI; pain in upper jaws, BL; pain or inflammation in lower jaw, point 17, between 10's; stiff or swollen jaw, point 17; feels feverish, KI; dry tongue, KI; root of tongue coated, KI; development of teeth, KI; pain in gums, TW; teeth feel tight, TW; bitter taste in, GB, points 8, 9, 13; bad gums, GB; loose teeth, GB; contracted jaws, GB; lockjaw, point 21; foamy mouth, GB; stiff tongue with dry mouth, GB; crooked, LV; angles become slack, point 14; swollen lips, LV, point 21; maxillary gland inflamed, point 17; paralysis, point 21; fissuring and scaling of angles of mouth, point 21

Mucous: see also lungs and respiration: excessive discharge, point 7

Multiple Sclerosis: SI, point 16

Muscles: all problems, GB, MC, VH, DM; cramps, BL; muscular dystrophy, GB; tone, LV, GB

Muteness: in general, 3, 10, 14, 9, point 21, HE; in children, 10; sudden, point 17

Nails: KI, BL, DF

Nausea: KI, PE, ST, LV, GB, QF2, 13, points 6, 9, 13, 23, between 14's

Neck: aids in general, B & D, (11, 12), 10, 13; swells, ST, point 17; pain, SI, point 17, between 4's, in nape, BL, point 26; pain and muscle spasm, points 3, lateral 10, 11, 13, 20, QF2; congestion, SI, KI, PE; stiff, SI, 13, 10, points 4, lateral 10, 11, 12, 16, 17, 19, 22, between 4's; cervical problems, TW; bumps like gravel, peas or marbles at top of neck, GB; tuberculosis of cervical lymph nodes, points 17, 19, 22; inflammation of cervical lymph nodes, points 19, 22, 26; paralysis, point 11;

Nerves: press ring and little fingers together (palmside); LF (1,2,3), MC; ulnar nerve pain, point 3; neuralgia, QF3, point 19; sudden neurological impairment due to intracranial hemorrhage, point 4; neuropathy, point low front 8

Neuralgia: QF3, point 19

Neurasthenia (chronic abnormal fatigue, lack of energy, feelings of inadequacy, moderate depression, inability to concentrate, loss of appetite and insomnia): points 2, 4, 5, 9, 10, 17, 18, 23

Nightmares: see also dreams; point 5

Nocturnal Emission (wet dreams): between 25's (tailbone), point 25

Nose: in general, MD, DF, BL, point 4; nosebleeds, LI, ST, BL, TW, TF, KI, 4, points 2, 4, 8, 10, 16, 17, 20, 21, between 20's; stuffy (occluded), ST, TF, points 13, 20, 21; blemishes, HE; enlarged pores, HE; red, HE; enlarged, HE; runny, BL, point 21; nasal drip, BL; infections, GB; sinus, LI, 4, (20, 21, 22); weak sense of smell, points 13, 21, absent, point 21; inflamed nostrils, point 20; inflamed nasal mucous membrane, points 20, 21, between 20's; chronic flushing of nose, forehead, and cheeks, tip of nose; nose polyps, points 20, 21; boils on, point 21;

Oppression (feeling weighed down): HE

Ovaries: see urogenital, reproductive; bleeding, 13

Overweight: hold high 1's (hands uncrossed); right DM, B&D, 1, (5, 6, 7, 8)

Oxygen: brain requires three times more than other organs; needed for complete metabolism, to purify blood, and to remove waste; helps slow down aging process

Pain: before or after surgery, 13 release; control, points 16, 18, 19

Pancreas: see also spleen, stomach; in general, SP, right 9, between 9's, EY; stimulates action of, between 9's

Paralysis: in general, QF4 & 5, LU; infantile, QF3, point 2, between 20's; point 11; of diaphragm muscle, point 9; of esophagus, point 9; of larynx, point 22; of mouth, point 21; of spine, point 11; of eyes, point 21, of suprahyoid muscle, point 17; of rectus muscle of abdomen, point 23, of upper limbs, points 18, 26; of facial nerve, point 19; of thorax, between 22's on sternal notch; of one side of body, GB, points 1, 3, 4, 8, 11, 12, 17, 18, 19, 20, 21; of lower limbs, PE, points 2, 5, 25, 26; of whole body, points 4, 11, 24; of all four limbs, points 3, 4, 11, 18; fatal, point 13

Parasites: of bile duct, point 21

Parkinson's: HE, SI

Pelvis: see also reproductive, urogenital; to assist, hold crown and tip of nose, then between 13's, then top of pube; if pain in pube, 2; to open, (5, 6, 7, 8), 15; pain in groin, ST, KI; tension, SP; air collects in, KI; hernias in groin, ST, KI; swelling (females), LV; to aid pelvic girdle, B & D, (11, 12), 15, 2, (23, 25), (5, 6, 7, 8); chronic inflammation, points 2, 15

Penis: see also reproductive, urogenital; pain, points 1, 2, 7; impotence, points 1, 2; premature ejaculation, points 1, 2; involuntary erection, point 5

Pericardium: see also heart; inflammation of, points 9, 10; to contract, between 11's (first thoracic)

Perineum: itching, point 1; MC, VH, KI, points 1, 2, 15, 25

Peritoneum: stimulates action of, between 23's; peritonitis, points 7, between 9's

Perspiring: when sleeping, LU, KI, TW, TF, points 7, 9, 17, 18; imbalance, HE, SI, LV, SS; diminished, points 7, 18; excessive, point 18; after eating, KI; fever without perspiration, PE, TW; yet cold, GB; profusely (whole body), GB

Phlegm: see also lungs, respiration; points 10, 17

Physical: fatigue, hold thumb, index, & middle fingers, MD, EF; person works strenuously and fast, HE; bursts of activity with intense output of energy, KI; most tranquil and inactive before sundown, KI; fidgets (inability to remain seated), KI; unable to turn to side when lying down, GB; low level of acitivity (low basal metabolism), GB; skinny look, LV; strenuous use of body, KI; to stimulate whole body, B&D, LF (1,2,3)

Pleurisy: see lungs, breathing; HE, points 3, 6, low 8, low front 8, 9, 10, 11, 13, 14, 16, 17, 19, 22

Pneumonia: see lungs, breathing; SP, LU, BL, 10, points 3, 10, 11, 22

Pockmarks: DS

Prostate: see urogenital, reproductive; 13 release; inflamed, point 2

Psoriasis: DS

Rectum: prolapse, between 25's (tailbone); inflamed, point 25

Rejuvenation: hold crown of head and between 13's, CB, DM, VH, TW, 13

Reproductive Organs: in general, 13, LI, SP, SI, TW, KI, BL, LV, GB, MC, (23, 25), 15, 2, (5, 6, 7, 8), 1, DF, QF4, LF (1, 2, 3); inflammation of sexual organs, SP, KI; all sexual functions disrupted, KI, 13, points 1, 15, between 13's, one inch below the navel; absence of sex drive, KI; drooping sexual organs, KI, points 1, 5, 6, 7, 15; crooked uterus, KI; itching of the vulva, KI, LV; ovarian infection, KI, LV; ovary inflamed, points 2, 15; ovary bleeding, 13; circulation of energy for sexual function and reproductive is regulated by, TW; infection in genitals, GB, 13; heavy discharge, GB, 13, point 15; gonorrhea, GB, points 2, 7; tumors or growths, SP, (23, 25), (11, 12), QF1; hormones, 13; tense groin, point 6; outer genitalia itching, pain, swelling or inflamed, point 1; masturbation, points 16, 24
Female: uterine tumors, SP, (23, 25), (11, 12); inflamed uterus, SP, GB, points 2, 15, 17, and tubes & ligaments, points 2, 15; uterine spasm, points 7, 16; uterine pain, point 7; vaginal infection or inflammation, point 1; chronic vaginitis, point 15; vulva, itching, point 15, pain, points 15, 16, swollen, point 16; frigid or sterile, SP, KI, point 6; menstrual irregularities, SP, KI, 13, points 1, 2, 5, 7, 13, 15, 17, 24, tailbone; heavy menstrual bleeding, SP, points 5, 7, 15; prolonged menstruation, points 1, 15, 17; menstrual pain, SP, QF2, points 1, 2, 5, 6, 7, 15, 17, 24, 25; menstruation absent, point 15, arrested, point 18; pelvic and abdominal swelling in females, LV; uterine hemorrhage, LV, point 17 (post partum); post partum infections, LV; black blood discharge after childbirth, LV; to assist childbirth delivery, LV; uterus fails to return to normal size following childbirth, top of pubic bone;
Male: impotence, SP, SI, 13, KI, points 1, 2, 23, 25, between 9's; early ejaculation, SI, points 1, 2; involuntary erection, KI, point 5; inflamed testicles, GB; small hernias in male genitals, LV; infection in penis, LV; absence of sperm, LV, KI; prostate, 13, point 13, inflamed, point 2; nocturnal emission (wet dreams), points 1, 2, 5, 10, 15; penis, pain, points 1, 2, 7; scrotum, itching, pain, retraction, eczema, point 15; spermatic cord, inflamed, point 14; sperm insufficiency, point 15; sterility, point 15; testis, inflamed, points 1, 2, 7, 15, injury to, point 6;

Respiration: see also lungs; LU, LI, SI, GB, BL, 3, LF (1,2,3), B&D; regulates energy for, TW; phlegm, coughing, DF; pulmonary congestion, point 22

Restlessness: in children, points 5, 7, 19; fidgets, KI; hyperactive, points 23

Rheumatism: see also arthritis; TW, DF, QF3, points 8, low point 8, 9, 23

Ribs: see also upper trunk, chest; pain and spasms between, points 3, 7, 8, 9, 10, 13, 14, 16, 18, 19, 22, 24

Salivation: see also mouth; excessive, point 21

Scapula: see also back, arms, shoulder; spasm and numbness, point 3; pain, points 3, 4, 6, 16, 23; paralysis, point 3

Scars: DS

Sciatica: HP, 3, (16, 17, 18, 19), LP, BL; points 12 and 15 must be released before pain will leave; points 2, 8, 16, 25

Schizophrenia: see also mental, emotional; points 7, low front 8, 9, 10, 12, 16, 17, 19, between 4's, 11's

Scrotum: see also reproductive, urogenital; itching, pain, retraction, eczema, point 15

Senility: point 14

Sexual: circulation of life energy to vitalize, PE; circulation of life energy for function, TW; KI, BL, 13, MC, VH, 1, 15, (23, 25), 2, (11, 12)

Shock: LU, point 6, tip of nose

Shoulders: in general, (5, 6, 7, 8), 10, 13, MD; stiff and painful, SI, TW; full and heavy, TW; sore shoulder blades, TW; pain, LFF, points 3, 4, 6, 9, 10, lateral 10, 11, 13, 16, 17, 18, 22, 23; tension in affects opposite leg, LP, HP; anterior aches, LI; congested and tense, LF1, point 6; too high or low, QF4; tipped forward or back, QF4; paralysis, points 3, lateral 10, 11, 17, 26; aches, stiffness and motor impairment, point 11; spasms, points 3 (joint), 11, lateral 10, 17, 26 (blade); numbness in joint, point 3; arthritis, points 3, 17, 26

Shyness: PE, KI

Sides: fullness in, PE; pain in, GB

Sinus: see also nose; LI, (20, 21, 22), 4, points 4, 21

Skin: all conditions, LI, DF, SS, DS, points 18, 19; pigmentation, LU; surface hot and perspires, ST; complexion dark, ST; body yellowish, ST; goose flesh all over body, ST; white (iron anemia), SP; dry, HE, SI; irritation, SI; itching, point 10; jaundice, SI; no luster, GB; eczema, points 1, 19, first thoracic; neurodermatitis, point 19; releases toxic waste, point 6; acne, KI, LI, point 18; boils, KI, BL, point 18; hives, points 19, 23

Sleep: see also dreams, neurasthenia; tendency to sleep during day, SP; awakens early and sleeplessness in early hours, KI; insomnia or sleepiness, LV; for sound sleep, B&D, LF (1,2,3); excessive, point 3; dream-disturbed sleep, point 9

Small Intestine: in general, TW, QF1, (5, 6, 7, 8); ulcers of, HE, duodenal, TW; swelling of intestinal walls, KI

Snoring: 14, KI, point 14

Sounds: groaning, KI; snoring, KI; cackles, PE, cries or moans, PE; moaning, TW; big sighs, GB; sighing a lot, LV

Speech: stuttering, HE, 3, 10; difficulty speaking, HE; shy about speaking, HE; aversion to speaking, KI; rambling, PE; suddenly dumb and cannot speak, PE TW; talks incessantly, ST; hoarse voice, 10; loss of voice, 10; throat closes, point 10; children who aren't speaking, 10; general speech problems, 10; loss of ability to comprehend speech or writing, between 12's, points 6, 10

Spermatic Cord: see also reproductive, urogenital; inflamed, point 14; sperm insufficiency, point 15

Spine: MC, VH; spinal cord inflammation, between 2's; stiffness, between 9's; pain in vertebral region, points 9, 23

Spleen: see also pancreas, stomach; in general, SP, DF, between 9's, LU, LF (1, 2, 3), right 9, left 14, points 14, 23; hardened area, opposite (5, 6, 7, 8); has action on, point 5, between 9's; diabetes mellitis, point 23; enlargement, point 23

Sputum: see also lungs, respiration; blood-stained, points 5, 11, 18, 19; excessive, point low front 8

Sterility: see also reproductive, urogenital; female, point 6; male, point 15

Stomach: in general, ST, SP, KI, DF, LF3, MC, 9, 10, 14, seventh thoracic; all diseases (heartburn, gastritis, stenosis, ulcers, ptosis, bleeding), ST, points 9, 14, 23; vomiting, nausea, indigestion, pain, ST, SP, between 14's; vomiting after eating, SP; food doesn't seem to descend, SP; inconsistent appetite, SP, between 10's, MC; craving sweets, SP; bleeding, PE, ST; digestive energy regulated by, TW, aids flow of energy to, between 9's, LU, LF (1, 2, 3); bloated, LV; indigestion, LV, ST, SP; inside feels cold and chilly, ST, between 9's; relaxes hard tension in pit of stomach, between 10's, crown of head, between 14's; pain and swelling, KI, BL, points 6, 9, 14, 21, 23; all middle flows meet in the stomach (between 14's); excessive gas, points 5, 13, 14; nausea, point 7; ache, points 14, 23; acid regurgitation, point 8; hyperacidity, point 23; ulcers, points 9, 10, 14, 17, 23; bleeding, point 9; stimulates action of, between 9's; inflammation, points 5, 7, 8, 10, 14, 15, 18, 23; acute inflammation, low back 8, 16, 18, 23, 24 tip of nose; cancer, points 6, 9, 23; dilation, points 7, 14; indigestion, points 5, 6, 23; spasms, points 6, 7, 14, 15, 23; downward displacement, point 23

Stroke: see Appendix A; PE, HE

Stupidity: see also mental, emotional; point 7

Stuttering: see also speech; left point 3, point 10

Suffocation: point 9

Surprise: easily surprised, KI

Suspicion: KI

Swelling: KI, BL, 15, 1

Taste (or cravings): can be a clue to imbalance - bitter, LV, GB; inability to taste, HE, SI; salty, KI, BL; sweets, SP, ST; metallic, LU, LI

Temperature and Weather: poor adjustment to temperature change, TW; sensitivity to cold and wind, BL, GB; regulates body temperature, TW, SS, DS, QF4

Testis: see also reproductive, urogenital; inflamed, points 1, 2, 7, 15; injury to, point 6

Thermal Burns: point 21

Thin: use left DM; if too thin, LV, KI

Thirst: incessant, PE, KI, SP; great, LV; point 2

Thoracic Cavity: to open, thumb over ring finger, 4 release; paralysis of thorax, between 22's (sternal notch)

Throat: in general, QF2, (11, 12), 4, between 22's (sternal notch); pharyngitis, LU, HE, SI, KI, points 4, 5, 6, low front 8 12, 17, 22; pain in pharynx, points low front 8, between 14's; numb, LI, ST, TW, point low 8; lower esophagus, SP, esophagus swells or spasms, KI, point 6, between 14's; tonsilitis, HE, BL, KI, GB, 4, points 4, 5, 6; sore, SI, TF, points 1, 5, 6, 12, 19, 22; spasms and pains, SI, GB; trachea, BL; dry and painful, KI, LV; phlegm, PE; swells, TW, TF, LFF, points 19, 22; infections, TW; inability to swallow, LV; constriction (closes), points 9, 10; paralysis, point 9; larynx inflamed, points 4, 22, or paralysis, point 22; oropharynx swollen, painful, and inflamed, points low front 8, 19; acute paralysis of suprahyoid muscle, points 6, 14, 17; hoarseness, points 10, 12, 19, 22; inflamed and swollen trachea, points 3, low front 8, 22

Thyroid: KI, 13, (23, 25), points 11, 12, 13, 18, 26 between 12's; parathyroid, points 12, between 12's, tailbone; goiter, point 18; inflamed thyroid, point 26

Toes (in general): crooked, (5, 6, 7, 8); 26 release
Big Toe: see thumb and little fingers; corns on, QF2
Second Toe: see index and ring fingers
Middle Toe: see middle fingers; assists breathing and digestion
Fourth Toe: see index and ring fingers
Little Toe: see thumb and little fingers

Tongue: see also mouth, throat; paralysis of supra-hyoid muscle, points 12, 17; spasm, point 17; cystic tumor beneath, point 12

Tonsils: see also mouth, throat; 4, points 4, 5, 19; inflamed, point 22

Tonsilitis: QF2

Toothache: see also mouth; points 7, 19, 21, 26

Toxins: to eliminate, B&D, EF, QF5, SS, DS, (23, 25); controls elimination of mental and physical, point 18

Trunk of body (upper): in general, 1; to open thoracic cavity, thumb over ring finger; can't turn or twist, PE, TW, GB; diaphragm, same side 14; ribs: see relationships to fingers and toes; all surface flows meet at third front rib in center (between 13's); first rib is cross point for DS; if ribs protrude, (16, 17, 18, 19); flank pain, points 16, 24, between 14's

Tuberculosis: B&D, LV, 10; bone, point 11; pulmonary, 3, 10, 17, 19, 22, between 13's

Tumors: see Appendix A; in brain, GB, (20, 21, 22), EY, 4; in reproductive, QF1, 13, SP, (23, 25), (11, 12)

Ulcers: see stomach, digestion; LF3, MC; for stomach or duodenal, point 9

Unconsciousness: 14, DF (do all four in reverse order), 4 release (start with step nine and work backwards), points 4, 6, 7, 9, 14

Urogenital: see also pelvis, reproductive; leucorrhea, SP; kidney and ureter infections, SP, point 1; inflamed ureter, points 1, 2, 7; urine retention or inability to urinate, KI, LV, (5, 6, 7, 8), points 1, 2, 5, 6, 15, 25; bladder spasm, KI; dark brown urine, KI; uremia, KI, GB; bedwetting, LV, KI, BL, 1, 2, (5, 6, 7, 8), points 1, 2, 5, 7; kidney, bladder or urination problems, DF; incontinence, KI, BL, LV, GB, 1, 2, 13, 15, (5, 6, 7, 8), (16, 17, 18, 19) (23, 25), top of pubic bone, points 1, 2, 7, 17; blood in, 2, (23, 25); for all urogenital problems, top of pubic bone; blood in urine, points 2, 23; for emergency urination, point 6; painful or difficult, points 1, 2, 5, 6, 8, 15, 25;

Varicose Veins: LP, (5, 6, 7, 8), 15, 2, point 6

Vascular System: HE, PE

Vertebrae: see also spine; pain in vertebral region, points 9, 23; to straighten, MC, VH

Vertigo: see also dizziness; points 4, 6, 8, 11, 16, 17, 19, 20, 21, 24

Voice: see also speech; 10; sudden hoarseness, point 17

Vomiting: see also stomach, digestion; points 3, 5, 6, 8, 9, 10, 13, 14, 17, 20, 22, 23, tip of nose; babies vomiting milk, points 9, 14, between 14's

Vertical Flows: to assist and balance, MV, EF, MD, DI, B&D, LF (1,2,3), 9, 10, BL, CB

Vitality: SP, TW, DM, (23, 25), 13, MV. VH, CB, hold crown of head and between 13's

Vomiting: see also stomach, digestion; BL, LV, ST, SP; of phlegm, PE; with epilepsy, TW; empty vomiting, TW; of blood, LV, KI, BL; water, KI, BL

Water Retention: KI, GB, 1, 15, (23, 25)

Weather: see also temperature; reactions to, first thoracic

Whiplash: points 11 and 12, and opposite 10; 13 release; see 11, 12 release

Will Power: lack of KI; assisted by TW, PE, MC, VH, LU, LF (1,2,3)

Wrists: swollen and feverish, LI

Yawning: LU, SP, HE, KI

Notes

1. *Jin Shin Jyutsu* is an ancient art of healing. The name means, "The art of the Creator through compassionate man." Jin Shin Jyutsu is incorporated and taught by Mary Burmeister.

2. I've taught and practiced under the name *Psychoenergetics* for fifteen years. Psychoenergetics is to mind-body what psychophysiology is to brain-body. *Touch of Silence* is based on my work in psychoenergetics.

3. The *Twelve-Step* programs mentioned in this book refer to the programs that have emerged as a result of the work done in Alcoholics Anonymous. Check with your local ACA (adult children of alcoholics) group for information about Twelve-Step groups available for survivors of abuse.

4. *The Way of the Female Warrior* is a 16-hour workshop for women who are survivors of abuse. Many women are using what they've learned in the workshop to fulfill their Twelfth-Step (service to others).

5. *Sex, Pleasure and Power: How to Emerge Spiritually Without Going Nuts,* by Jan Kennedy, was published in April, 1988. The material in this book complements the information in *Touch of Silence.* It's available in all major bookstores.

6. Other books I've written:

   Psychoenergetics: A Key to Health, 1980

   Psychoenergetics: A Breath of Life, 1982

   Tales of the Sexy Snake: The Art of Healing Through Touch and Language, 1983

   Self/Not Self: Dreamscapes of Consciousness, 1986

7. For those of you who have some background in acupuncture, Triple Warmer and Pericardium meridians are switched for pulse-reading only. This switch is appropriate for this system.

Bibliography

An Explanatory Book of the Newest Illusrations of Acupuncture Points. Hong Kong: Medicine and Health Publishing Co., 1978.

Austin, Mary. *Acupuncture Therapy.* New York: ASI Publishers Inc., 1975.

Burmeister, Mary. *Jin Shin Jyutsu.* Unpublished manuals, 1971.

Chang, Stephen. *The Complete Book of Acupuncture.* California: Celestial Arts, 1976.

Connelly, Dianne. *Traditional Acupuncture: The Law of the Five Elements.* Maryland: The Centre of Traditional Acupuncture Inc., 1979.

Kapandji, I. A. *The Physiology of the Joints.* Volumes I, II and III. London and New York: Churchill Livingstone, 1977.

Lawson-Wood, D. and J. *Five Elements of Acupuncture and Chinese Massage.* England: Health Science Press, 1975.

Lee, I. J. and T. D. H. Lee. *Guide to Acupuncture: Theory and Practice.* New York: Lycee Trading Corporation, 1974.

Mann, Felix. *Acupuncture: The Ancient Art of Healing and How it Works Scientifically.* New York: Vintage Books, 1973.

Mann, Felix. *The Meridians of Acupuncture.* London: William Heine-Mann Medical Books Ltd., 1974.

Porkert, Manfred. *The Theoretical Foundations of Chinese Medicine.* Cambridge, Massachusetts, and London, England: The MIT Press, 1974.

The Academy of Traditional Chinese Medicine. *An Outline of Chinese Acupuncture.* Peking: Foreign Language Press, 1975.

Warfel, John H. *The Head, Neck and Trunk: Muscles and Motor Points.* London: Henry Kingston Publishers, 1976.

Worsley, J. R. *Acupuncturists' Therapeutic Pocket Book.* Maryland: The Center for Traditional Acupuncture, Inc., 1975.